Prophecies and Prophetic Promises

FROM THE DOCTRINE AND COVENANTS

Prophecies and Prophetic Promises

FROM THE DOCTRINE AND COVENANTS

ROY W. DOXEY

Published By
Deseret Book Company
Salt Lake City, Utah
1969

Library of Congress Number 74-101993

LITHOGRAPHED BY

DESERET NEWS PRESS

IN THE UNITED STATES OF AMERICA

Dedication

To our daughters-in-law, Carol Jean, Karen, Judy, and our son-in-law, Ron. May they always be imbued with the desire to rear our grandchildren in light and truth.

Preface

This book was written primarily for the benefit of members of The Church of Jesus Christ of Latter-day Saints in the hope that it will reaffirm for them the truth that Joseph Smith, the first prophet of the Church, received revelation from God. For those not of this Church, it is sincerely hoped that it will be the means of engendering interest in the teachings of that Church.

The principal function of a prophet of God is to give direction to solving the problems of the day through revelation, past and present. This function is demonstrated in this book. Prophecy is one of the subordinate functions of the prophet, and fulfilled prophecy is one of the supporting evidences to substantiate the divine calling of the prophet. (Deut. 18:21-22). Judged by this criterion, Joseph Smith is a prophet. It is literally true that the books of scripture which have come into existence through his divine calling abound with the prophetic element.

During many years of teaching the Doctrine and Covenants, a standard work of the Church, I have been impressed with the validity of the following verses from the Lord's "Preface" to that volume:

"Search these commandments, for they are true and faithful, and the prophecies and promises which are in them shall all be fulfilled.

"What I the Lord have spoken, I have spoken, and I excuse not myself; and though the heavens and the earth pass away, my word shall not pass away, but shall all be fulfilled, whether by mine own voice or by the voice of my servants, it is the same.

"For behold, and lo, the Lord is God, and the Spirit beareth record, and the record is true, and the truth abideth forever and ever. Amen." (D&C 1:37-39).

Prophecies and promises of the Lord through his servant Joseph Smith are numerous in the Doctrine and Covenants. Elder John A. Widtsoe, an apostle of the dispensation, counted "nearly eleven hundred statements which may be classed as prophecies of the future." (*Joseph Smith*, p. 277).

In this book I have used the following definitions in classifying the prophecies and prophetic promises: (a) a prophecy is a statement, without reservation, about the future, (b) a prophetic promise is conditional; that is, if a certain condition exists, then a given result will follow. The prophetic element in the inspired promise is as certain of fulfillment as is the prophecy. A prophetic promise discussed in this book is: "But learn that he who doeth the works of righteousness shall receive his reward, even peace in this world, and eternal life in the world to come." (D&C 59:23). An example of a prophecy in the Doctrine and Covenants is Section 87, the revelation predicting the American Civil War and other wars.

In this volume, one hundred and five prophecies and prophetic promises make up the fifty subjects discussed. They have been selected at random with no thought of centralizing them into a given period or series of sections. The purpose of this book is to bring to the reader, from one facet—prophecy—the truth that the Doctrine and Covenants is the word of the Lord. There is no attempt to discuss each subject exhaustively, for books could be written on many of them, but to present sufficient facts to give an understanding of the truth expressed by the Lord that "the prophecies and promises which are in them [revelations] shall all be fulfilled."

I plan to publish other volumes on this subject as time allows.

I am indebted to my wife, Alberta, for her inspiration and for the years of devotion shown to me and especially at this time for her helpful suggestions in editing the manuscript.

Appreciation is also expressed to Mary Lynn Hansgen, graduate research assistant, for arranging the footnotes and bibliography, and also to Kay Rice, secretary, for carefully seeing the manuscript to completion.

There is a spirit in the Doctrine and Covenants which one would expect in a book of scripture. The revelations in that book are true, for they were received from God by and through the instrumentality of the Holy Ghost. This knowledge may be received by every person who sincerely desires to obtain that witness. As the devout member of the Church studies these revelations, darkness is dispelled and the light of understanding grows brighter and brighter.

Roy W. Doxey

Brigham Young University
Provo, Utah
July 1969

Contents

xii

Prophecies and Prophetic Promises

Chapter 1

"And The Voice of Warning Shall Be Unto All People . . ."
(D&C 1:2-5)

For verily the voice of the Lord is unto all men, and there is none to escape; and there is no eye that shall not see, neither ear that shall not hear, neither heart that shall not be penetrated.

And the rebellious shall be pierced with much sorrow; for their iniquities shall be spoken upon the housetops, and their secret acts shall be revealed.

And the voice of warning shall be unto all people, by the mouths of my disciples, whom I have chosen in these last days.

And they shall go forth and none shall stay them, for I the Lord have commanded them.[1]

Background of the revelation

After a long period of apostasy from the true gospel and Church, revealed and organized by Jesus Christ in the meridian dispensation, the Lord raised up Joseph Smith to restore the fulness of the gospel and organize his church for the last time. A part of that restoration is included in the revelations received by the Prophet, and recorded in the Doctrine and Covenants. Section 1 of the Doctrine and Covenants is the Lord's "Preface" to the revelations given through the Prophet Joseph Smith. It was received in the conference of The Church of Jesus Christ of Latter-day Saints held on November 1, 1831. It was decided to print the compilation of revelations prepared for publication by the Prophet Joseph Smith under the title "A Book of Commandments."

Background of the prophecy

Inasmuch as the verses comprising this prophecy are introduced by verse 1, that verse follows: "Hearken, O ye

---

[1]D&C 1:2-5.

people of my church, saith the voice of him who dwells on high, and whose eyes are upon all men; yea, verily I say; Hearken ye people from afar; and ye that are upon the islands of the sea, listen together."[2]

Contents of the prophecy

(1) Every person will hear the voice of the Lord. (2) The rebellious shall have their iniquities and secret acts revealed. (3) The Lord's warning will go forth by his disciples, who will deliver their message.

Fulfillment of the prophecy

Because of the importance of the gospel message for the salvation of those who will accept it, the Lord, in this prophecy, says that it is for all men, none excepted. In subsequent revelations it is made known that only those of accountability are responsible for their acts; therefore, little children and the mentally retarded are without sin and under no condemnation.[3] The Book of Mormon is emphatic in denouncing the doctrine of infant baptism, believed by some as necessary for their salvation.[4]

"Every person" in this prophecy means the dead as well as the living. Implicit in the doctrine of salvation of the dead, not fully revealed to the Prophet in 1831, is the fact that men will hear the gospel and have an opportunity to accept it in the spirit world. As the prophecy says, the voice of the Lord is unto *all men* that they might see, hear, and have their hearts be penetrated. The reasonableness of the doctrine and the justice of God in this matter is given by President Wilford Woodruff in these words:

"God is no respecter of persons; he will not give privileges to one generation and withhold them from another; and the whole human family, from father Adam down to our day, have got to have the privilege, somewhere, of hearing the gospel of Christ; and the generations

---

[2]D&C 1:1.
[3]D&C 29:46-50; 74:7.
[4]Moroni 2:8.

that have passed and gone without hearing that gospel in its fulness, power and glory, will never be held responsible by God for not obeying it. Neither will he bring them under condemnation for rejecting a law they never saw or understood; and if they live up to the light they had they are justified so far, and they have to be preached to in the spirit world. But nobody will baptize them there, and somebody has got to administer for them by proxy here in the flesh, that they may be judged according to men in the flesh and have part in the first resurrection."[5]

That the dead are interested in their salvation as they learn of the fulness of the gospel in the spirit world is attested in a revelation received by President Wilford Woodruff. He testifies that the spirits of the signers of the Declaration of Independence gathered around him and requested that the temple ordinances in their behalf be performed. He said that they were baptized for and also most of the presidents of the United States and other eminent people.[6]

Another president of the Church received a vision of the spirit world when the Savior left his body in death and preached the gospel to the righteous in that realm. There, President Joseph F. Smith, saw the prophets gathered together as they were commanded to open the door of the prison house of the spirit world for the preaching of the gospel to those who had not received the opportunity on the earth. This revelation is known as the Vision of the Redemption of the Dead.[7]

The unique missionary system of the Church gives opportunity to the young men and women of the Church who freely spend their time, talents and means (usually that of their parents) for a two-year period of missionary work in eighty-three missions of the Church. The living are hearing the word of the Lord from these approxi-

---

[5] *Journal of Discourses*, 18:190-191.
[6] *Journal of Discourses*, 19:229.
[7] Joseph F. Smith, *Gospel Doctrine*, pp. 473-476.

mately 12,000 missionaries. But other means are employed, such as, radio, television, the printed word in
newspapers, brochures, pamphlets, magazines, and books.
All who do not have the chance of learning of the gospel
in this life, as said, will receive it eventually.

The day will come when those who rebel against the
word of the Lord and continue in their sins will be
pierced with sorrow. The *Doctrine and Covenants Commentary* refers to the "rebellious" in this prophecy as
those who reject the everlasting gospel. Then, the following is given: "When the Church of Jesus Chirst of Latter-
day Saints was established, this position was made clear
to all the world. When the light comes, they can no longer hide their errors, their iniquities, their secret acts. The
light reveals these things. That is the true cause of the
enmity toward the Church. They want the light extinguished. It hurts them."[8]

When a Latter-day Saints missionary teaches someone
the gospel, he is delivering the warning message. It is
unnecessary for the servant of the Lord to say "I warn
you, if you do not accept the gospel," but the rejection of
salvation principles and ordinances brings eventual deep
regret because of the loss of what might have been. This
thought was expressed by President Joseph F. Smith as
follows:

". . . there are many blessings that result from obeying the ordinances of the gospel, and acknowledging the
Priesthood authorized of the Father and restored to the
Church of Jesus Christ of Latter-day Saints, that cannot
be obtained until the person is willing to comply with
the ordinances and keep the commandments revealed in
our day for the salvation of mankind. The true searcher
will see and understand this truth and act upon it, either
in this world or in the world to come, and not until then,
of course, may he claim the blessings, and if he neglects
to accept the laws in this world, knowing them to be

---

[8]Hyrum M. Smith and Janne M. Sjodahl, *Doctrine and Covenants Commentary*, p. 5.

true, it is reasonable to suppose that disadvantages will result that will cause him deep regret."[9]

There is another aspect of the voice of warning. It is the message of frightful and calamitous events which will engulf the wicked in the last days.[10] Prior to and at the second coming of Christ the world will be racked with fire, earthquake, pestilence, flood, war, and desolation. (See "When the Cup of Their Iniquity Is Full"—D&C 101: 10-12). The seriousness of this truth was indicated by President Woodruff when he said: "Can you tell me where the people are who will be shielded and protected from these great calamities and judgments which are even now at our doors? I'll tell you. The priesthood of God who honor their priesthood, and who are worthy of their blessings, are the only ones who shall have this safety and protection. They are the only mortal beings. No other people have the right to be shielded from these judgments."[11]

The record of more than one hundred and thirty-five years since the Church was organized testifies that no obstacle has been too great to keep the servants of the Lord from delivering their message. On the other hand, they have suffered from men and the elements in discharging their duty. There have been some occasions when a door has been closed to them because of enmity, misrepresentation, and prejudice. Also, some countries have excluded their presence for a time. Eventually, the gospel door has been or will be opened to them. Even war has opened opportunities for Latter-day Saint servicemen to plant gospel seeds among their fellow servicemen as well as among the natives where they have served.

Application of the prophecy

With the certainty of sorrow for lost opportunities, even Latter-day Saints have reason for concern when they

[9]Joseph F. Smith, *Gospel Doctrine*, p. 125.
[10]D&C 1:11-16; 29:14-20.
[11]*The Young Women's Journal*, Salt Lake City, Utah, Vol. 5, p. 512.

do not keep the covenants they have made with the Lord. (See "Zion Shall Escape If . . ."—D&C 97:22-28). President Woodruff said: "No other people have a right to be shielded from these judgments. They are at our very doors; not even this people will escape them entirely. They will come down like the judgments of Sodom and Gomorrah. And none but the priesthood will be safe from their fury."[12]

Certainly, those who have the privilege of learning of the restoration of God's kingdom upon the earth and who do not follow its teachings, will find deep regret by their disobedience. No one should feel that because there is a doctrine of salvation of the dead that he can wait until he enters the spirit world to receive the fulness of the gospel. This opportunity is for those who died without a knowledge of the gospel.[13]

To the member of the Church, President Woodruff continued by saying: "Calamities and troubles are increasing in the earth, and there is a meaning to these things. Remember this, and reflect upon these matters. If you do your duty, and I do my duty, we'll have protection, and shall pass through the afflictions in peace and in safety."[14]

---

[12]*Ibid.*, p. 513.
[13]D&C 128:5.
[14]*The Young Women's Journal*, Vol. 5, p. 513.

Chapter 2

"Prepare ye. . . For The Lord Is Nigh . . ."
(D&C 1:12-16)

Prepare ye, prepare ye for that which is to come, for the Lord is nigh;

And the anger of the Lord is kindled, and his sword is bathed in heaven, and it shall fall upon the inhabitants of the earth.

And the arm of the Lord shall be revealed; and the day cometh that they who will not hear the voice of the Lord, neither the voice of his servants, neither give heed to the words of the prophets and apostles, shall be cut off from among the people;

For they have strayed from mine ordinances, and have broken mine everlasting covenant;

They seek not the Lord to establish his righteousness, but every man walketh in his own way, and after the image of his own God, whose image is in the likeness of the world, and whose substance is that of an idol, which waxeth old and shall perish in Babylon, even Babylon the great, which shall fall.[1]

Background of the revelation

By November 1831, the compilation of revelations brought together by the Prophet Joseph Smith was ready for submission to a conference of the Church. Accordingly, the conference authorized that it be printed under the title, "A Book of Commandments". This title of the compilation was given in the revelation known as the Lord's "Preface," the introduction to his revelations.

Background of the prophecy

Section 1 begins with a proclamation to all people that the message of the dispensation is for all men, even the dead who had never heard the fulness of the gospel. The rejection of the Lord's servants will bring sorrow. What is decreed in the revelations will be fulfilled. The day will come when the wrath of God is poured out upon the wicked.

[1]D. & C. 1:12-16.

Contents of the prophecy

(1) Preparation is necessary for the Lord's coming. (2) The arm, or power of the Lord, will be revealed in that those who reject the Lord's servants will be cut off from among the people. (3) The effects of straying away from the gospel in the past is felt in the world, for men do not seek righteousness, but walk after their own gods. (4) The gods or idols which men worship shall perish, as did ancient Babylon.

Fulfillment of the prophecy

A major error in the "Christian" creeds of Joseph Smith's day was the true knowledge of God. God, on the other hand, is personal having a body of flesh and bones, an immortal exalted man, not a spirit which is present throughout the universe. When men flaunt God's laws by ignoring their Creator and Father, his anger is kindled against them. Not only the doctrine of God was changed in the great apostasy, but all the ordinances and teachings of the gospel were reduced to error. Because of this the Savior told Joseph Smith that "all their creeds were an abomination in his sight . . . ."[2] This condition has left men with so much error that the ideas of the creeds have lost their appeal. The loss of the Priesthood, the directing power of the Church, and continuous revelation, the means by which the Church was kept alive, progressive, and able to meet the problems of the day, emasculated the early church.

The consequent loss of faith in God has given the Adversary a hold upon the minds and hearts of men to the extent that they do not seek to establish God's righteousness, but their own pleasures and desires.

Elder James E. Talmage in 1930 evaluated the religious world as follows:

"The great trouble with the world today, as I understand it, is that it has become idolatrous. We read of idol-

---

[2]Joseph Smith 2:19.

atry and think of it as a practice or a series of practices in the past. This is an idolatrous generation, defying the commandment written by the finger of God—'Thou shalt have no other Gods before me',[3] and an idolatrous generation is an adulterous generation. . . . Men are praising the gods of silver and of gold and of all the other valuable commodities that make up wealth, and the God in whose hand their breath is and whose are all their ways they will not recognize. Do you wonder that wickedness and crime have increased to terrifying proportions under those conditions?"[4]

Elder Spencer W. Kimball of the Council of the Twelve, gave some observations on conditions in a world of unrest and a world which had become more carnal:

"Our world is in turmoil. It is aging toward senility. It is very ill. . . .

"What is this illness? Its symptoms are manifest in every corner of the globe. They are found among men in high places, in hut and mansion. Its symptoms are carelessness, casualness, covetousness, slothfulness, selfishness, dishonesty, disobedience, immorality, uncleanness, unfaithfulness, and ungodliness. . . .

"It seems rather than fast and pray, we prefer to gorge ourselves, at the banquet tables and drink cocktails. Instead of disciplining ourselves, we yield to urges and carnal desires. Numerous billions we spend on liquor and tobacco. A Sabbath show or a game or a race replaces solemn worship. Numerous mothers prefer the added luxuries of two incomes to the satisfaction of seeing children grow up in the fear of God. Men golf and boat and hunt and fish rather than to solemnize the Sabbath. Old man rationalization is with us. Because we are not vicious enough to be confined in penitentiaries, we rationalize that we are pretty good people; that we are not doing so badly. The masses of the people are much like those who escaped destruction in the ancient days of this continent.

[3]Exodus 20:3.
[4]*Conference Report*, October 1930, p. 71, 73.

The Lord said to them:

" 'O all ye that are spared because ye were more righteous than they [the slain ones], will ye not now return unto me, and repent of your sins, and be converted, that I may heal you?'⁵"⁶

Each man walks after the image of his own god. Whenever one places *anything,* material wealth, fashion, recreation, education, sports, above the purpose for which he is in this life that thing becomes his god.

Application of the prophecy

Unless there was an apostasy from gospel principles, there would be no reason for the Church of Jesus Christ of Latter-day Saints. Latter-day Saints know that a comparison of the "Christian" creeds with the Bible shows that changes from the Church organized by Jesus Christ have been made. He also knows that with the additional books of scripture in his Church—Book of Mormon, Doctrine and Covenants, and Pearl of Great Price—that the consistency of those books with the Bible, as well as the reasonableness of the doctrines, evidence the truth that a great apostasy made necessary a restoration of the true Gospel.

Latter-day Saints may be assured of this statement from Elder Kimball:

"Our God rules in the heavens. He lives. He loves. He desires the happiness and well being of all his children. He has a prophet on the earth today who receives his revelations. He is a prophet to all the world. He has on numerous occasions outlined the cure for all international as well as local ills. The diagnosis is sure, and the remedy certain. Today's prophet stands in the same position between God and the people as did Isaiah, Samuel, and even Moses who gave to the world the Ten Commandments."⁷

---

⁵3 Nephi 9:13.
⁶*Conference Report,* September 1961, pp. 30-34.
⁷*Ibid.*

Knowing that God lives and his prophet is here, Latter-day Saints may well receive these questions from Elder Talmage:

"Are we worshipping the true and living God, or are we going idolatrously after the gods of gold and silver, of iron and wood, and brass, diamonds and other idols of wealth? Are we worshipping our farms, our cattle and sheep? Who is our God? To whom are we yielding homage, allegiance and worship? Not worship by means of words only, in ritualistic form, but worship in action, devotion, and sacrificial service."[8]

As the days draw nearer to the second coming of the Lord, the need to be prepared should be evermost in the hearts of the covenant people. The parable will be fulfilled concerning the ten virgins:

"For they are wise and have received the truth, and have taken the Holy Spirit for their guide, and have not been deceived—verily I say unto you, they shall not be hewn down and cast into the fire, but shall abide the day."[9]

"And it shall come to pass that he that feareth me shall be looking forth for the great day of the Lord to come, even for the signs of the coming of the Son of Man."[10]

---

[8]*Conference Report*, October 1930, p. 73.
[9]D. & C. 45:57.
[10]*Ibid.*, v. 39.

Chapter 3

". . . From Him Shall Be Taken Even the Light Which He Has Received."

(D&C 1:31-33; 50:23-24; 88:67)

(A) For I the Lord cannot look upon sin with the least degree of allowance;

Nevertheless, he that repents and does the commandments of the Lord shall be forgiven;

And he that repents not, from him shall be taken even the light which he has received; for my Spirit shall not always strive with man, saith the Lord of Hosts.[1]

(B) And that which doth not edify is not of God, and is darkness.

That which is of God is light; and he that receiveth light, and continueth in God, receiveth more light; and that light groweth brighter and brighter until the perfect day.[2]

(C) And if your eye be single to my glory, your whole bodies shall be filled with light, and there shall be no darkness in you; and that body which is filled with light comprehendeth all things.[3](See ". . . You Shall See Me And Know That I Am . . ." —D&C 67:10-14; 88:66-68)

Background of the revelations

(A) With the restoration of the fulness of the gospel through the Prophet Joseph Smith, many revelations were received to restore truths lost through an apostasy from the Church as organized in the meridian dispensation. Section 1 of the Doctrine and Covenants is the Lord's "Preface" to this book of revelation.

(B) Section 50 was received because of some unusual and strange spiritual manifestations in some of the branches of the Church in 1831.

(C) Section 88 is known as the Olive Leaf, a message of peace to the saints. Many theological subjects are found therein which give peace and comfort. The resurrection

---

[1]D&C 1:31-33.
[2]D&C 50:23-24.
[3]D&C 88:67.

of the body, the manner in which God governs his creations, and the reality of universal law, are some of them.

Background of the prophecies

(A) After indicating that the revelations are for all people and that the Lord had appointed Joseph Smith and others to make known these revelations, together with a warning voice against the rebellious and also the effect the revelations had had in the lives of members of the Church by 1831, it is said that there is only one true Church upon the earth. That Church was doing well, but individual members of the Church were in need of repentance.

(B) Because of the possibility of being deceived by false spirits in the world, the Lord reminded his servants that they had a responsibility to become informed about their callings as his servants. They should know that only by the Spirit do men know and communicate convincing knowledge to others.[4]

(C) If one draws unto the Lord he will draw unto them. He should remember, however, that his requests in prayers should be in accordance with the purpose of life and what the Lord has revealed.[5] The Lord's Spirit is truth, and it can abound in one.

Contents of the prophecies

(A) (1) The Lord cannot look upon sin with allowance. (2) If a person repents by keeping the commandments, he may be forgiven. (3) If one does not repent, he loses the light once enjoyed.

(B) (1) Edification, the opposite of darkness, comes from God. (2) By obedience to God's commandments, more light is received.

(C) (1) To realize a fulness of light, it is necessary to have one's eye single to God's glory. (2) The ultimate blessing is to comprehend all things.

---

[4]*Ibid.*, vs. 21-22.
[5]*Ibid.*, vs. 63-65

Analysis and clarification of the prophecies

(A) Sin is abhorrent to the Lord because he is sinless; he knows that for one to come into his presence he must be free of sin.[6] Therefore, the Lord does not condone sin in any degree, for it is God's glory to bring about man's eternal life.[7] Notwithstanding this truth and recognizing that men make mistakes, and therefore sin, through the atonement of Jesus Christ men may repent and become clean by obedience to the gospel of Jesus Christ. This person is placed on the road to eternal perfection.[8] True repentance, the kind that saves in the presence of God and the Son, is keeping the commandments.[9]

If one persists in sin, the Lord declares that he will not have his Spirit with him; for, his Spirit will not always strive with man.

(B) To edify is to enlighten, to instruct in moral and spiritual matters. Ultimately, the purpose of edification is to bring hearers and readers to a condition where they will become subjects of salvation. Darkness is the opposite of light and truth, and therefore, is not edifying. Light is the spiritual knowledge that enlightens men to eventually become saved. The Gospel is known as the true light.[10] The believer in the true gospel is "illuminated by the light of the everlasting word."[11]

(C) To have one's eye single to God's glory is to be fully committed to his word in understanding and practice. Darkness will flee from one so possessed with the Spirit of truth. Eventual fulness of light brings the highest rewards of the gospel.

Fulfillment of the prophecies

Missionaries of the Church of Jesus Christ of Latter-day Saints have learned that some investigators of the gos-

---

[6]Mormon 9:1-5; D&C 67:10-13.
[7]Moses 1:39
[8]2 Nephi 31:17-18.
[9]*Ibid.*, vs. 19-21.
[10]I John 2:8
[11]Alma 5:7.

pel learn truth, but when they fail to act upon this knowledge, the desire to know more, to become one with the saints, is lessened until there is no spark of interest remaining. Repentance of sin is the fundamental require- ment for receiving the Spirit of truth; to know and then to bask in its life-giving power. The key is found in the words of the Savior: "If any man will do his will, he shall know of the doctrine, whether it be of God, or whether I speak of myself."[12] Elder James E. Talmage comments upon this subject as follows:

"Are you unable to realize that baptism is essential to salvation? Perhaps the cause lies in the fact that you have never developed the essential condition of faith in the Lord Jesus Christ; or, perchance, you have never repented of your sins. Faith and repentance, as the Scriptures aver, are prerequisites to effective baptism; and it is as unrea- sonable to expect a faithless unrepentant sinner to compre- hend the essentiality of baptism as to expect one untrained in the rudiments of arithmetic to understand algebra."[13]

Missionaries have learned that even some who have professed a testimony that the gospel and Church are true, have fallen into darkness. The Prophet Joseph Smith in discussing the difference between the Holy Ghost and the gift of the Holy Ghost said that if Cornelius, the devout gentile, who had received the Holy Ghost had not accepted baptism and the laying on of hands for the gift of the Holy Ghost, he would have lost his testimony of the truth.[14]

The second aspect of this subject is that which ap- plies to members of the Church. Although every member has received baptism and the laying on of hands, it does not follow that the blessings of these ordinances remain with one who falls into sin. The Spirit leaves the sinner and he goes into darkness of mind and heart. This condi-

---

[12]John 7:17.

[13]James E. Talmage, *The Vitality of Mormonism*, p. 281.

[14]Acts 10; Joseph Fielding Smith, *Teachings of the Prophet Joseph Smith*, p. 199.

tion does not usually happen at once but gradually the light is diminished by little acts of disobedience, absenting oneself from the sacrament and from meetings where the gospel is taught. What is the result? As President Brigham Young put it: "Those who leave the Church are like a feather blown to and fro in the air. They know not whither they are going; they do not understand anything about their own existence; their faith, judgment and the operation of their minds are as unstable as the movements of the feather floating in the air."[15]

Elder George A. Smith, a Church Historian of the dispensation, related the following example of such a person:

"I have been conversant with early Elders, and I am satisfied that a large number of them fell from their positions in the kingdom of God because they yielded to the spirit of adultery: this was the cause of their destruction. There was an Elder named John Smith who lived in Indiana, who was quite popular in that part of the country as a preacher. He apostatized, but he did not know it. In talking about his faith and how firm it was, he said, I have proven the revelation given to Joseph Smith untrue, which says if a man shall commit adultery he shall lose the spirit of God, and deny the faith. I have proven that not to be true, for I have violated that commandment and have not denied the faith. He was so blind that he could not see through the darkness that the spirit of adultery had placed upon his head, the great apostasy which seemed to shake the Church, and tried men's souls."[16]

Application of the prophecies

The member of the Church who falls into sin is not always, but generally, one who lacks a positive conviction and knowledge of the gospel. He has failed to act upon the privileges of his membership. Where the command-

---

[15]*Journal of Discourses,* 15:136.
[16]*Ibid.,* 11:10-11.

ment is given that he should learn that he be not deceived, he has failed to do this.[17] He has not learned the truth that by succumbing to little temptations, the flaxen cord of the Adversary binds tighter and longer until there is no release.[18] Oft times excuses are made that the Lord will not mind if a little sin is committed, for only minor punishment will come, if at all.[19] It is not long until the Spirit is grieved and the member is one of record only, without the benefit of light and truth.

Elder James E. Talmage gave us this truth:

"Wilful ignorance of Gospel requirements is sin. Man is untrue to his Divine lineage and birthright of reason when he turns away from the truth, or deliberately chooses to walk in darkness while the illumined path is open to his tread. Positive rejection of the truth is even graver than passive inattention or neglect. Yet to every one is given the right of choice and the power of agency, with the certainty of his meeting the natural and inevitable consequence."[20]

The word of the Lord is clear: "Let thy bowels also be full of charity towards all men, and to the household of faith, and let virtue garnish thy thoughts unceasingly; then shall thy confidence wax strong in the presence of God; and the doctrine of the priesthood shall distil upon thy soul as the dews from heaven.

"The Holy Ghost shall be thy constant companion, and thy scepter an unchanging scepter of righteousness and truth; and thy dominion shall be an everlasting dominion, and without compulsory means it shall flow unto thee forever and ever."[21]

---

[17]Joseph Smith 1:37.
[18]2 Nephi 26:22.
[19]2 Nephi 28:8-9.
[20]James E. Talmage, *The Vitality of Mormonism*, p. 281.
[21]D&C 121:45-46.

Chapter 4

". . . Peace Shall Be Taken From The Earth . . ."
(D&C 1:35)

For I am no respecter of persons, and will that all men shall know that the day speedily cometh; the hour is not yet, but is nigh at hand, when peace shall be taken from the earth, and the devil shall have power over his own dominion.

And also the Lord shall have power over his saints, and shall reign in their midst, and shall come down in judgment upon Idumea, or the world.[1]

Background of the revelation

Section 1 of the Doctrine and Covenants is the Lord's preface to his revelations. This revelation indicates the purpose for which the revelations were given, to whom they were directed, and the Lord's counsel to the world, as well as to the members of his Church.

Background of the prophecy

In a context of the need for repentance, the Lord then declared that he is desirous of making known certain conditions that will exist on the earth in the last days.

Contents of the prophecy

(1) All men are entitled to know of coming events. (2) The day is soon at hand when peace will be taken from the earth. (3) When that day comes, the devil will have power over his own. (4) The Lord shall reign in the midst of his people. (5) He shall come in judgment on the world.

Analysis of the prophecy

The peace mentioned in this prophecy is the opposite of civil strife and war. In the chronologies of world events such terms as these are used to report conflicts: revolt, rev-

---

[1]D&C 1:35-36.

olution, uprising, insurrection, riots, civil war, declaration of war, and war.[2] It is evident that the members of the Church at the beginning of the year 1831, the Lord's Preface being received November 1831, were concerned about world conditions. During the summer of 1830, a revolution occurred in France, insurrections in Southern Netherlands, and in Poland and Brazil, political unrest was present. The Belgian revolution threatened all Europe.[3]

Ten months before the prophecy in Section 1 was received, the Lord told his saints that although there were wars in far countries, the saints should know this information: "... ye know not the hearts of men in your own land."[4]

Fulfillment of the prophecy

The prophecy—"peace shall be taken from the earth" —began its fulfillment with the American Civil War although the world was not at complete peace before 1861. The First Presidency in 1853 wrote that "peace is taken from the earth . . ."[5] The Lord revealed that the Civil War should be the beginning war of modern times. (See "The Wars That Will Shortly Come To Pass;" Part I— The American Civil War—D&C 87:1-3; 130:12-13).

Interestingly, I. S. Bloch, in 1899, used the beginning of the Civil War to terminate the period preceding modern wars. He wrote the following in the Preface to his book on war:

"Every change in conditions or disposition is affirmed only after a struggle of elements. An analysis of the history of mankind shows that from the year 1496 B.C. to the year 1861 of our era, that is, in a cycle of 3357 years, there were but 227 years of peace and 3130 years of war:

---

[2]Neville Williams, *Chronology of the Modern World.*

[3]Hyrum M. Smith and Janne M. Sjodahl, *Doctrine and Covenants Commentary,* p. 208.

[4]D&C 38:29.

[5]*Millennial Star* 15:437.

in other words, there were thirteen years of war for every year of peace."[6]

Has peace fled from the earth since the end of the American Civil War? The answer to this question depends upon the definition of peace. If one includes, as indicated above, the conflicts within nations and also between nations, with the preparations for war and the tensions created thereby, the answer is clear. Without reference to conditions of unrest, except actual warfare, history has recorded that from the end of the American Civil War (1865), the beginning of wars of the last days, to 1900, there were only four years in which there was no war.[7] Professor Pitirim A. Sorokin, Harvard University, and Nicholas N. Golovin, formerly a Lieutenant-General in the Imperial Russian army, in an exhaustive study of the frequency of war, learned that, "despite the many glamorous stories of chivalrous conflict that have come down to us, war was comparatively insignificant among man's activities up to the seventeenth century in Europe. Beginning with that century it increased enormously, and did not diminish during the eighteenth century. In the nineteenth century there was a considerable lull in war activities, though they were still more than one hundred times as great as in the medieval centuries."[8]

During the one hundred years since 1861 there have been 20 years in which there were no wars.[9] Wars, since the American Civil War have grown in intensity and universality, especially in World War I and II. The following is said about the impact of the American Civil War on other wars: "In its tactics as well as weapons this struggle [American Civil War] is the first in history which can readily be identified with the warfare of the present day."[10]

---

[6]I. S. Bloch, *The Future of War*, pp. 43-49.
[7]Neville Williams, *Chronology of the Modern World*, pp. 262-388.
[8]*Literary Digest*, January 20, 1934, p. 13.
[9]Neville Williams, *Chronology of the Modern World*, pp. 262-683.
[10]Lynn Montross, *War Through the Ages*, p. 591, quoted in "The Wars That Will Shortly Come to Pass; Part I—The American Civil War.")

Since World War II, peace has not returned. Not only war but turmoil, with accompanying feelings of distrust among the nations and uncertainty of the future welfare of the world, have increased. As one fire is extinguished, another conflagration occurs, leaving no peace. (See "The Wars That Will Shortly Come To Pass; Part II—Conditions After The American Civil War—D&C 87:4, 8).

Peace has been taken from the earth! In 1907, President George Q. Cannon wrote that since the American Civil War, wars and rumors of wars have prevailed throughout the world and that "Peace has fled . . ."[11] President Joseph Fielding Smith, has said on many occasions that peace has fled from the earth in fulfillment of prophecy. This is one of these statements:

"One year after the organization of the Church, peace could not have been taken from the earth, in justice, but the Lord said the time would speedily come. That time has come. Peace has departed from the world. The devil has power today over his own dominion. This is made manifest in the actions of men, in the distress among the nations, in the troubles that we see in all lands, including this land which was dedicated to liberty.

"There is no peace. Men's hearts are failing them. Greed has the uppermost place in the hearts of men. Evil is made manifest on every side, and people are combining for their own selfish interests."[12]

Other predictions in the Doctrine and Covenants give one an understanding of the extent of wars and other troubles in these last days. The Lord has said that when the times of the Gentiles are fulfilled, there "shall be heard of wars and rumors of wars, and the whole earth shall be in commotion, and men's hearts shall fail them, and they shall say that Christ delayeth his coming until the end of the earth."[13] Among the wicked, men shall curse God

[11]George Q. Cannon, *Life of Joseph Smith*, pp. 126-127.
[12]*Conference Reports*, April 1937, pp. 58-59.
[13]D&C 45:26.

and die. Earthquakes and many desolations shall visit the earth, and men shall take up the sword against each other.[14] In fact, these calamities will continue until the second coming of Christ.[15]

Inasmuch as this prophecy is linked directly with the American Civil War and other wars, it is appropriate to use the following counsel from the Lord: ". . . if ye are prepared ye shall not fear . . ."[16] Safety lies in keeping the commandments of the Lord. (See "Prepare Ye . . . For the Lord is Nigh"—D&C 1:12-16). Due to the wickedness of men in the last days, Nephi prophesied that a great division would occur among men.[17] The Lord promised, however, that ". . . he will spare his people, yea, even if it so be that he must destroy the wicked by fire."[18]

Latter-day Saints may be assured that if they are prepared, they may have peace despite the turmoil which exists in the world.[19] (See "Even Peace In This World . . ." —D&C 59:23). The hymn "Who's On the Lord's Side, Who?" has a meaningful lesson for all members of the Church. (See "Zion Shall Escape If . . ." —D&C 97:22-28).

---

[14]*Ibid.*, 25:32-33.
[15]*Ibid.*, 97:22-24.
[16]D&C 38:30.
[17]2 Nephi 30:10
[18]*Ibid.*

Chapter 5

". . . By The Hand Of Elijah the Prophet"
(D&C 2:1-3).

Behold, I will reveal unto you the Priesthood, by the hand of Elijah the prophet, before the coming of the great and dreadful day of the Lord.

And he shall plant in the hearts of the children the promises made to the fathers, and the hearts of the children shall turn to their fathers.

If it were not so, the whole earth would be utterly wasted at his coming.[1]

Background of the revelation

On the night of September 21-22, 1823, Moroni, an ancient Nephite prophet and custodian of the Book of Mormon plates and a resurrected being, instructed Joseph Smith in events which were shortly to come to pass. Among these events was the one found in Section 2 of the Doctrine and Covenants.

Background of the prophecy

The last two verses of the Old Testament are a prophecy given by Malachi about Elijah the Old Testament prophet who lived about 900 B.C.[2] Differences between this prophecy and the one given by Moroni are noted below.

Contents of the prophecy

(1) The Priesthood was to be restored by Elijah before the second coming of Christ. (2) By this restoration, the promises made to the fathers would be planted in the hearts of their children. (3) The children would, therefore, have their hearts turned to their fathers. (4) If this prophecy were not fulfilled, the earth would be wasted at the great and dreadful day of the Lord.

---

[1]D&C 2:1-3.
[2]I Kings 17-19; 21:17-29; 2 Kings 1-2; 2 Chronicles 21:12-15; Malachi 4:5-6.

Analysis of the prophecy

Whereas Malachi referred to the coming of Elijah, Moroni said that Elijah would reveal the Priesthood. This restoration would take place in the last days, for it would be before the great and dreadful day of the Lord when judgments and calamities would visit the earth. (See "The Wars That Will Shortly Come To Pass; Part II—Conditions After the American Civil War—D&C 87:4-8;" "When the Cup Of Their Iniquity Is Full"—D&C 101:10-12).

Malachi recorded that if his prophecy were not fulfilled, the earth would be cursed. Moroni said that this curse would be the utter wasting of the earth at the Savior's coming.

As recorded in Malachi the heart of the fathers would be turned to the children and the heart of the children would be turned to the fathers. The work of salvation of the dead is implied in this statement, if one understands the fathers to be dead and the children to be living. The modern rendition says that the promises made to the fathers would be planted in the hearts of the children who would have their hearts turned to their fathers.

Two significant things would transpire according to the prophets: (1) Elijah would visit the earth in the last days to restore Priesthood. (2) The purpose of this restoration would be to turn the hearts of the living (children) toward their fathers (dead).

Fulfillment of the prophecy

On Sunday, April 3, 1836, in the Kirtland (Ohio) Temple, which had been recently dedicated, four personages appeared to the Prophet Joseph Smith and Oliver Cowdery, one of whom was Elijah the ancient prophet. This is the record of that event:

"After this vision had closed, another great and glorious vision burst upon us; for Elijah the prophet, who was taken to heaven without tasting death, stood before us, and said:

"Behold, the time has fully come, which was spoken of by the mouth of Malachi—testifying that he [Elijah] should be sent, before the great and dreadful day of the Lord comes.

"To turn the hearts of the fathers to the children, and the children to the fathers, lest the whole earth be smitten with a curse—

"Therefore, the keys of this dispensation are committed into your hands; and by this ye may know that the great and dreadful day of the Lord is near, even at the doors."[3]

Although Oliver Cowdery was excommunicated from the Church and later returned, he did not deny his testimony of the visit of angelic beings to him and the Prophet Joseph Smith. The Prophet went to his death as a witness of the restoration of the gospel. In a powerful testimony of his acquaintance with the Prophet, Lorenzo Snow, said:

"I knew him to be a man of God, full of the spirit of his calling—a man whose integrity could not be disputed, and who was honest in all his endeavors. No one that was as intimately acquainted with him as I was could find any fault with him, so far as his moral character was concerned. As to the second individual here that bears this last testimony, Oliver Cowdery, I was partially acquainted with him. I heard him preach, and talked with him; and while he was engaged in promulgating the principles of the religion which he espoused, the same that you and I have espoused, no fault could be found with him. At the time he was a good man, and always bore a faithful testimony to these things which God had plainly manifested to him."[4]

Two events, one on April 3, 1836, and the other has been occurring since that day, evidence the fulfillment of this prophecy. First, the Jewish people have looked forward to the coming of Elijah as promised by Malachi. In fact, each year in the spring, the Paschal Feast is observed in orthodox Jewish homes at which time a door is

---

[3]D&C 110:13-16.
[4]Millennial Star, June 27, 1895, p. 402.

opened that Elijah might come in and sit at that feast. Elder Joseph Fielding Smith said:

"It was, I am informed, on the third day of April, 1836, that the Jews, in their homes at the Paschal Feast, opened their doors for Elijah to enter. On that very day Elijah did enter—not in the home of the Jews to partake of the Passover with them, but he appeared in the House of the Lord, erected to his name and received by the Lord in Kirtland, and there bestowed his keys to bring to pass the very things for which these Jews, assembled in their homes, were seeking.[5]

The second event is the organization of genealogical societies in various parts of the world. Before 1836, there were no organizations gathering records of the dead. But, in 1837, Great Britain made it necessary to preserve the records of the dead. In the United States in 1844, the New England Historical and Genealogical Society was organized, and in 1869 the New York Genealogical and Biographical Society was organized in New York City. Other organizations having a similar purpose came into existence. Also, by 1836, only fewer than 200 family histories were published.[6]

The Priesthood powers restored by Elijah were the sealing powers by which all ordinances might be validated in heaven as they are performed upon the earth.[7] Although in 1829, the Aaronic and Melchizedek priesthoods were restored to perform salvation ordinances, it was necessary that Elijah restore the sealing and binding powers.

The "spirit of Elijah" is permeating the hearts of members and non-members of the Church of Jesus Christ to perform a search for the records of their kindred dead, thus the promises made to the fathers before this earth was formed are being fulfilled in the works of their living children. One of the largest, if not the largest, collections

---

[5]*Conference Report*, April 1936, pp. 74-75.
[6]*Ibid.*
[7]Joseph Smith, *History of the Church of Jesus Christ of Latter-day Saints*, Vol. 4, p. 211. (Hereafter referred to as *DHC*.)

of genealogical data has been gathered for the use of Latter-day Saints by the Genealogical Society of the Church in Salt Lake City, Utah—another evidence of the return of Elijah to the earth. As important as this fact is, more important is the fact that the work of performing ordinances in behalf of the dead is a continuing labor in the temples of the Lord. During 1968 more than six million ordinances were performed in behalf of the dead in 13 temples.

Application of this prophecy

Because Elijah restored the Priesthood and the work thus inaugurated is continuing in the Church of Jesus Christ of Latter-day Saints, the earth will not be utterly wasted at the second coming of Christ. Despite atomic or hydrogen bombs and other destructive weapons, the inhabitants of the earth will not be destroyed, although the calamities of the last days will take a terrible toll.

Premortally, the sons and daughters of God committed themselves to perform a work for their kindred dead which was not possible by their progenitors because they did not have the opportunity to hear the gospel while on the earth.[8] By covenant committment in baptism, the member of the Church is under the responsibility of performing the necessary genealogical research for his kindred dead and then having the salvation ordinances performed in a temple in their behalf. Without the performance of this necessary work neither the dead nor the living can be perfected.[9] The work of salvation of the dead is so vast that in 1844 the Prophet said the following: "The Saints have not too much time to save and redeem their dead, and gather together their living relatives, that they may be saved also, before the earth will be smitten and the consumption decreed falls upon the world."[10] The consumption decreed is apparently the one mentioned in the revelation on wars where many devastating conditions will exist "until the

---

[8]Roy W. Doxey, The Doctrine and Covenants Speaks, Vol. 1, p. 34.
[9]D&C 128:15, 18.
[10]DHC 6:184.

consumption decreed hath made a full end of all nations."[11]
(See "The Wars That Will Shortly Come To Pass—Part
II—Conditions After the American Civil War. D&C 87:4-
8") With moral and political conditions worsening in the
world, the prophecies concerning the last days are being
fulfilled. It, therefore, behooves members of the Church
to look to their responsibility in saving their dead.

---

[11]D&C 87:6.

Chapter 6

" . . . A *Marvelous Work Is About to Come Forth* . . ."
(D&C 4:1; 6:1; 11:1; 12:1; 14:1)

Now behold, a marvelous work is about to come forth among the children of men.[1]

A great and marvelous work is about to come forth unto the children of men.[2]

Background of the revelations

The five revelations in which this prophecy appears were given for the benefit of individuals in this order: Joseph Smith, Sen.; Oliver Cowdery; Hyrum Smith; Joseph Knight, Sen.; and David Whitmer. The period of time involved was from February to June 1829. Of these individuals Joseph Smith, Sen. was the father of Joseph Smith, and Hyrum Smith was his older brother.

Background of the prophecies

In each case the prophecy opens the revelation. The subject matter of these revelations is: Section 4—qualifications of those who labor in the ministry; Section 6—Oliver Cowdery had just met Joseph Smith and received by this revelation knowledge that the work in which Joseph was engaged was of God; Section 11—Hyrum's desire to engage in the ministry was to come later, but he was always to judge righteously by the Holy Spirit, and never reject the principle of revelation; Section 12—Those who have desires to build Zion may enter into the work; Section 14—the important message is given that Zion should be established, and eternal life is the greatest gift God bestows upon his children.

---

[1]D&C 4:1.
[2]Ibid., 6:1; 11:1; 12:1; 14:1.

Contents of the prophecies

A marvelous work is to come forth.

Analysis of the prophecies

The word "marvelous" means that which causes wonder and astonishment; something that is extraordinary; in fact, so extraordinary as to be improbable, incredible, or miraculous.

There are probably two events or matters foretold in these prophecies: (1) the coming forth of the Book of Mormon and, (2) the coming forth of the Church of Jesus Christ of Latter-day Saints, custodian of the Priesthood and the Gospel of Jesus Christ.

Joseph Smith had beheld the Father and the Son, Jesus Christ, received the several visits by the Angel Moroni, and had received the plates from which was to come the Book of Mormon. Also, the Aaronic Priesthood was restored by John the Baptist, and the Melchizedek Priesthood was restored in June 1829, the same month in which the revelation to David Whitmer was received. The Book of Mormon was yet to be printed, and the Church was not organized.

Fulfillment of the prophecies

The Book of Mormon plates were translated between April and July 1829, during the time when four of the five revelations carrying this prophecy were received; consequently, the coming forth of the Book of Mormon is particularly mentioned as the marvelous work which was about to come forth to the children of men. This fact is further suggested by the chapter in the book of Isaiah to the coming forth of the Book of Mormon in the last days because of the religious apostasy then existing. Isaiah prophesied:

"Wherefore the Lord said, Forasmuch as this people draw near me with their mouth, and with their lips do honour me, but have removed their heart far from me, and their fear toward me is taught by the precept of men:

"Therefore, behold, I will proceed to do a marvelous work among this people, even a marvelous work and a wonder: for the wisdom of their wise men shall perish, and the understanding of their prudent men shall be hid."[3]

Isaiah's prophecy was literally fulfilled in the Book of Mormon, for the wise men have sought to account for this ancient record other than its being an ancient history of the forefathers of the American Indian. Their wisdom has failed; each theory of its origin has been successfully controverted. On the other hand, the evidence for its authenticity has mounted since its publication in 1830, particularly during the twentieth century. In Hugh Nibley's *Lehi In The Desert and the World of the Jaredites* one will find almost one hundred examples of Semite and Asiatic customs, unknown when the Book of Mormon was published, that authenticate the first 40 pages in the Book of Mormon and the 32 pages of the Book of Ether, a book in the Book of Mormon.

Joseph Smith or any man could not have written the Book of Mormon; it had to be the product of many historians who witnessed the events they recorded. The following excerpt from a letter addressed to Elder James E. Talmage, an apostle of this dispensation, from Dr. Henry Drinker, past-president of Lehigh University, is on this subject:

"To me, perhaps, the marvel is that an untutored farmer youth should have had the literary ability to express in the language used by Joseph Smith, the record he presented—how at his age, he could have had the knowledge of the scriptures, both Old and New Testament, which enabled him, as a familiar story, to so forcibly use and reuse, and to reaffirm, the scriptural teachings. If you seek for miracles, this was one—a miraculous record whether the 'Mormon' or anti-'Mormon' view be taken; for from the 'Mormon' view it was a divine revelation; if this is denied; it is an instance of phenomenal wisdom and utter-

[3]Isaiah 29:13-14.

ance from one as was Christ, when, as a child, he argued with the elders in the temple."[4]

The complexity of writing the Book of Mormon, the miraculous record, as stated, is pointed up in the following from President Hugh B. Brown:

"I ask anyone to undertake to write a story on the ancient inhabitants of America. Write as he did without any source material. Include in the story fifty-four chapters dealing with wars, twenty-one historical chapters, fifty-five chapters on visions and prophecies, and, remember, when the writer begins to write on visions and prophecies he must have the record agree meticulously with the Bible. He must write seventy-one chapters on doctrine and exhortation, and, here too, he must check every statement with the scriptures or he will be proved to be a fraud. He must write twenty-one chapters on the ministry of Christ and everything the writer claims Jesus said and did and every testimony he writes in the book about him must agree absolutely with the New Testament.

"I ask, would anyone like to undertake such a task? I point out too that he must employ figures of speech, similes, metaphors, narration, exposition, description, oratory, epic, lyric, logic, and parables. I ask the writer to remember that the man who translated the Book of Mormon was a young man and he hadn't had the opportunity of schooling that many today have had and yet he dictated that book in just a little over two months and made very few, if any, corrections."[5]

The real miracle of the Book of Mormon is the power its pages possess, with prayer, to implant a divine witness to its truth by the Holy Ghost.[6] Millions of people have known of its truth by this power. In addition, this fulfilled promise includes the knowledge that Jesus Christ is divine, the Son of God, man's Atoner.[7] Only God can

---

[4]*Juvenile Instructor*, August 1928, p. 431.
[5]Hugh B. Brown, *Eternal Quest*, pp. 132-133.
[6]Moroni 10:3-5.
[7]*Ibid.*, v. 7.

bestow this knowledge upon man! The Book of Mormon is a "marvelous work."

The marvelous work to come forth unto men in the last days is primarily the restored Church with the Gospel and the Priesthood, for the Book of Mormon is a part of that restoration. Wherein has the history of the Church shown it to be a marvelous institution? Probably, in its impact upon the lives of the millions who have accepted its teachings. The Gospel has transformed the lives of bad men into good ones and good men into better men. Elder John A. Widstoe, an apostle of this dispensation, referred to the man who baptized him into the Church as a man, who, before his conversion was,

". . .a rope-walker with a jug of beer two or three times a day, a glass of whiskey a little later, and a cud of tobacco mostly all day long, living a useless, purposeless life, except for three meals a day, and the satisfaction of some of the carnal appetites. He heard the Gospel and accepted it. . . . The man grew in power and stature in the Church. As I recall it, he filled five or six missions and presided over one of the missions of the Church. He was the same man, with the same arms, same feet, same body, same mind, but changed because of the Spirit that comes with the acceptance of eternal truth. Have we not seen this in our families and friends, in the little towns in which we live? Have not we felt our own strength grow mightier in love for our fellow men, in love for our daily tasks, in love for all the good things of life?"[8]

Another part of the marvelous work was the pioneer movement across the plains from Iowa to what is now Utah and to other parts of Western United States. It was the faith of these Latter-day Saint pioneers that opened this great frontier. No other explanation of this great accomplishment can exclude this religious motivation. They had faith in the prophecy of Joseph Smith that they would

---

[8]*Conference Report,* April 1952, p. 34.

settle in the Rocky Mountains, in the leadership of Brigham Young, and the knowledge of the Spirit that they had accepted the only true and living Church upon the face of the earth.[9] (See "Zion Shall Flourish Upon the Mountains. . ."—D&C 49:25) Recognition was given to the power of the Book of Mormon, of the faith of these pioneers, by the Secretary of Agriculture Henry A. Wallace, in a discussion of great books. He said:

"It reached perhaps only one percent of the people of the United States, but it affected this one percent so powerfully and lastingly that all the people of the United States have been affected, expecially by its contribution to opening up one of our great frontiers."[10]

Another influence of the Church indicating it as a marvelous work is the influence its teachings have had upon the world. Elder John A. Widtsoe, said:

"A few days ago I picked up a recent number of a great magazine, and my feelings were roused within me and my testimony increased when I found one of the writers declaring to the readers of the magazine that God cannot look upon sin with the least degree of tolerance, borrowed almost word for word from section one of the Doctrine and Covenants. In such a way have the doctrines taught by the despised Latter-day Saints been appropriated by the nations of the earth; and whether the people of the earth accept the inspiration of Joseph Smith, nevertheless, in fact the whole current of human thought has been changed by the doctrines of this people."[11]

Another factor is the growth of the Church, from fewer than ten members when the Church was organized to 2,700,000 at the end of 1968. Then, of course, the hundreds of thousands who joined the Church and have passed away would constitute a very large number. (See "Triumph of the Kingdom of God"—D&C 103:5-8).

---

[9]D&C 49:25; 1:30.
[10]*New York Times*, November 5, 1937.
[11]*Conference Report*, October 1921, p. 109.

If one considers the miracles performed by the Priesthood, and the gifts of the Holy Ghost, as a part of the marvelously miraculous work then there is a vast evidence to contribute to these prophecies. (See "The Elder of the Church. . .Shall. . .Lay Their Hands Upon Them"—D&C 42:43-44).

Application of the prophecies

To the member of the Church of Jesus Christ of Latter-day Saints there comes a swelling in his bosom when he seriously thinks of the value of his membership. His appreciation is heightened when he remembers that he may make a contribution to the building of that Church. His contribution, though small, perhaps, in the large total, nonetheless is necessary for his own salvation.[12] To be associated with the "marvelous work," the only one like it in the world, is a prize worth everything, especially in the fact that it is the only means whereby one may be saved in the eternal worlds.

---

[12]D&C 38:40; 6:6-7.

Chapter 7

". . . They Have Been Shown Unto Me By The Power Of God. . ."
(D&C 5:25; 17:1-4)

(A) And then he shall say unto the people of this generation: Behold, I have seen the things which the Lord hath shown unto Joseph Smith, Jun., and I know of a surety that they are true, for I have seen them, for they have been shown unto me by the power of God and not of man.[1]

(B) Behold, I say unto you, that you must rely upon my word, which if you do with full purpose of heart, you shall have a view of the plates, and also of the breastplate, the sword of Laban, the Urim and Thummim, which were given to the brother of Jared upon the mount, when he talked with the Lord face to face, and the miraculous directors which were given to Lehi while in the wilderness, on the borders of the Red Sea.

And it is by your faith that you shall obtain a view of them, even by that faith which was had by the prophets of old.

And after that you have obtained faith, and have seen them with your eyes, you shall testify of them, by the power of God;

And this you shall do that my servant Joseph Smith, Jun., may not be destroyed, that I may bring about my righteous purposes unto the children of men in this work.[2]

Background of the revelations

(A) The gold plates received from the Angel Moroni were being translated by Joseph Smith. The plates referred to Three Special Witnesses who would testify to their truth.[3] The Prophet is told that he should not show them to any one except those appointed by the Lord.

(B) The Three Special Witnesses of the Book of Mormon—Oliver Cowdery, David Whitmer and Martin Harris —were appointed. Section 17 informs them of their responsibility in this regard.

---

[1]D&C 5:25.
[2]*Ibid.*, 17:1-4.
[3]Ether 5:2-4; 2 Nephi 11:3; 27:12.

Background of the prophecy and promise

(A) Martin Harris had sought a witness to know of the truth of Joseph Smith's claim that he had the gold plates. The fact that there would be three special witnesses was made known in the revelation, and the importance of their testimony to the world. Joseph Smith is counseled that he should remain firm in keeping the commandments, even if he should be slain.

(B) The opening verses of Section 17 constitute the prophetic promise for examination in this article.

Contents of the prophecy and promise

(1) Martin Harris, who desired a witness of the Book of Mormon plates, is to view them, provided he will humble himself. (2) His testimony must be the truth: that he has seen the things to be shown him, for they are shown by the power of God. (3) The Three Special Witnesses will have a view of the following: the plates, breastplate, sword of Laban, Urim and Thummim, and the miraculous directors. (4) Only by their faith will they see them. (5) They must testify of this knowledge.

Analysis of the prophecy and promise

The Angel Moroni, a resurrected being, appeared to Joseph Smith and instructed him about some Bible prophecies and told him about some gold plates which contained a record of the ancient inhabitants of the American continent. Four years later Joseph received these plates after having been instructed yearly by the Angel at the site of the ancient depository of these records in Manchester township, New York.

Special mention is made of the need for Martin Harris to be humble that he might be one of the witnesses. Before this, he had implored Joseph Smith to permit him to take 116 pages of translated material from the plates to show them to his wife and others that they might be convinced that Joseph was not trying to defraud him. The manuscript was lost, thereby bringing the Lord's condemnation upon Joseph, even the loss of the plates and the Urim and Thummim, all of which were later returned to him.[4]

The ancient artifacts to be shown to the witnesses were: plates made of gold upon which were inscribed ancient engravings; the breastplate was used by the translator to carry the Urim and Thummim; the sword of Laban that was taken by Nephi from Laban, relative of the Prophet Lehi whose family, according to the Book of Mormon, came to the American continent about 600 B.C.; the Urim and Thummim were the divine instruments used in translating the gold plates; the miraculous director called Liahona was "a round ball of curious workmanship" of brass, and within the ball were two spindles to assist the Lehites in the wilderness.[5]

Fulfillment of the prophecy and promise

Not long after Section 17 was given in June, 1829, the three witnesses to be, and Joseph Smith retired to a secluded area on the Peter Whitmer farm near Waterloo, New York, where the prophecy and promise of viewing the plates were fulfilled. Each prayed in turn, but without success. Martin Harris left the other three believing that he was unworthy. Whereupon, the angel with the plates showed them to the three, turned the leaves that they might see the engravings, and a voice from the heavens declared them to have been translated by the power of God.

Joseph Smith left Oliver Cowdery and David Whitmer and found Martin Harris and prayed with him. Again, the same appearance of the angel with the plates, and the voice was heard testifying to their authenticity.

The following testimony of these Three Special Witnesses appears in every copy of the Book of Mormon:

"Be It Known unto all nations, kindreds, tongues, and people, unto whom this work shall come: That we, through

[4]*DHC* 1:20-23.
[5]1 Nephi 16:10.

the grace of God the Father, and our Lord Jesus Christ, have seen the plates which contain this record, which is a record of the people of Nephi, and also of the Lamanites, their brethren, and also of the people of Jared, who came from the tower of which hath been spoken. And we also know that they have been translated by the gift and power of God, for his voice hath declared it unto us; wherefore we know of a surety that the work is true. And we also testify that we have seen the engravings which are upon the plates; and they have been shown unto us by the power of God, and not of man. And we declare with words of soberness, that an angel of God came down from heaven, and he brought and laid before our eyes that we beheld and saw the plates, and the engravings thereon; and we know that it is by the grace of God the Father, and our Lord Jesus Christ, that we beheld and bear record that these things are true. And it is marvelous in our eyes. Nevertheless, the voice of the Lord commanded us that we should bear record of it; wherefore, to be obedient unto the commandments of God, we bear testimony of these things. And we know that if we are faithful in Christ, we shall rid our garments of the blood of all men, and be found spotless before the judgment-seat of Christ, and shall dwell with him eternally in the heavens. And the honor be to the Father, and to the Son, and to the Holy Ghost, which is one God. Amen."

The lives of each one of these three men verify the truth that their testimony is true. Oliver Cowdery, David Whitmer, and Martin Harris were excommunicated from the Church. When the hand of fellowship was withdrawn, the opportunity came for them to deny all of what they said was true regarding the angel, the voice, and the plates. But at no time did they falsify. Some may ask why men who had received such a glorious experience would be subjects of excommunication. The answer lies in the simple truth: they failed to keep the commandments. The Spirit of the Lord will not remain with those who fail to observe his teachings. (See ". . .From Him Shall Be Taken

Even The Light Which He Has Received"—D&C 1:31-33; 50:23-24; 88:67). The spirit of repentance impelled Oliver Cowdery and Martin Harris to seek baptism into the Church, but David Whitmer failed to rejoin the kingdom of God.

The Witnesses, as promised in Section 17, also saw the other artifacts. While out of the Church, David Whitmer was visited by Elders Orson Pratt and Joseph F. Smith, who reported this fact. Part of his testimony follows: "The fact is, it was just as though Joseph, Oliver and I were sitting just here on a log, when we were overshadowed by a light. It was not a light of the sun, nor like that of a fire, but more glorious and beautiful. It extended away round us, I cannot tell how far, but in the midst of this light about as far off as he sits (pointing to John C. Whitmer, sitting a few feet from him), there appeared as it were a table with many records or plates upon it, besides the plates of the Book of Mormon, also the sword of Laban, the directors (i.e., the ball which Lehi had) and the interpreters. I saw them just as plain as I see this bed (striking the bed beside him with his hand), and I heard the voice of the Lord, as distinctly as I ever heard anything in my life, declaring that the records of the plates of the Book of Mormon were translated by the gift and power of God."[6]

A series of ten scholarly articles on the three witnesses, written by Dr. Richard L. Anderson of the College of Religious Instruction of Brigham Young University, appear in the *Improvement Era*, August 1968 to August 1969. These articles present new evidence to support the testimony of these witnesses.

Application of the prophecy and promise

Every Latter-day Saint may take justifiable pride in the fact that the foundations of the Church are secure as indicated in the testimonies of those persons who, under

---

[6]Andrew Jenson (ed.), *Historical Record*, 6:207-208.

divine direction, laid its foundations. The testimony of the Three Special Witnesses is a good example of the strength of those foundations. Every attempt to disprove their testimonies has failed.

With such evidence for belief in the hereafter (the resurrected Moroni) as the Spirit bore witness by the Holy Ghost to the prophets in the Book of Mormon, as well as the personal witness to each member of the Church, motivation is given to live the Lord's commandments.

The Angel singled out David Whitmer when he, Martin Harris, and Joseph Smith were viewing the plates and gave him a warning message which is significant in view of the fact that David Whitmer died outside of the Church. The message given then is applicable to all: "David, blessed is the Lord, and he that keeps His commandments."[7]

---

[7]*DHC* 1:54.

Chapter 8

". . . The Field Is White Already To Harvest . . . Whoso Desireth To Reap . . . Reap While The Day Lasts . . ."
(D&C 6:3; 11:3; 12:3; 14:3; 4:4-5)

(A-D) Behold, the field is white already to harvest; therefore, whoso desireth to reap, let him thrust in his sickle with his might, and reap while the day lasts, that he may treasure up for his soul everlasting salvation in the kingdom of God.

(E) For behold the field is white already to harvest; and lo, he that thrusteth in his sickle with his might, the same layeth up in store that he perisheth not, but bringeth salvation to his soul;

And faith, hope, charity, and love, with an eye single to the glory of God, qualify him for the work.[2]

Background of the revelations

(A-D) Section 6 was given for the benefit of Oliver Cowdery, who had just met the Prophet at Harmony, Pennsylvania; Section 11 was given for Hyrum Smith, the Prophet's brother; Section 12 was given for the benefit of Joseph Knight, Sen., who had given material assistance to the Prophet; and Section 14 was given for David Whitmer, son of Peter Whitmer, who lived at Fayette, Seneca County, New York, where the Church was organized.

(E) Section 4 was given for the benefit of Joseph Smith, Sen., the Prophet's father.

Background of the prophetic promises

(A-D) Each one of these sections (6, 11, 12, and 14), was given because the individuals concerned desired to learn of their part in the work which was about to come forth through the Prophet Joseph Smith. In verse 6 of each revelation, except Section 14, it says: "Now, as you have

---

[1]D&C 6:3; 11:3; 12:3; 14:3.

[2]Ibid., 4:4-5.

asked . . ." In the *History of the Church* by Joseph Smith, it says that David Whitmer inquired of the Prophet regarding his duties.[3]

Contents of the prophetic promises

(1) The field is white ready to harvest. (2) He who desires to reap may do so. (3) Reap while the day lasts. (4) Everlasting salvation will come to the diligent worker in the field. (5) Faith, hope, charity, and an eye single to the glory of God qualify one for the labor.

Analysis of the prophetic promises

All of these prophetic promises were made before the Church was organized on April 6, 1830. Joseph Smith had received the plates from which later came the Book of Mormon. By the time Section 14 was received, the Aaronic Priesthood was restored. The "great and marvelous work," the Book of Mormon and the restored Gospel of Jesus Christ and the Church, were about to come forth. (See ". . . A Marvelous Work Is About To Come Forth . . ."— D&C 4:1; 6:1; 11:1; 12:1; 14:1).

From a revelation explaining the parable of the wheat and the tares given by the Savior, we learn about some expressions found in the prophetic promises.[4] The field is the world, and the apostles (who direct missionary work) are the sowers, while the tares are the work of Satan.

All of these brethren to whom the prophetic promises were made were to wait until the Church was organized before they were to thrust in their sickle in reaping the harvest of souls. Before this dispensation, the "Christian" world had been prepared for this work by the period of the Reformation when men were permitted to exercise their freedom in religious matters. An example of a clergyman who was making preparations among the people for this harvest was Sidney Rigdon.[5]

[3]*DHC* 1:48.
[4]Matthew 13:36-43; D&C 86:1-7.
[5]D&C 35:3-7.

When a missionary is instrumental in harvesting souls into the Kingdom of God, he is laying up blessings in store for the future.

To have one's eye single to the glory of God is to dedicate one's efforts to the work at hand. (See ". . . You Shall See Me And Know That I Am . . ."—D&C 67:10-14; 88:66-68).

Faith in Christ is the assurance that he is the Savior and that his promise of salvation is certain of attainment. It is the principle that makes possible all things.

Hope is that ingredient which spurs men on to success. Paul said: ". . . Tribulation worketh patience; and patience, experience; and experience, hope; and hope maketh not ashamed; because the love of God is shed abroad in our hearts by the Holy Ghost which is given unto us."[6] Mormon said: "Wherefore, if a man have faith he must needs have hope; for without faith there cannot be any hope."[7]

Charity which encompasses all faith and hope is defined as: ". . . the pure love of Christ, and it endureth forever; and whoso is found possessed of it at the last day, it shall be well with him."[8]

Love "suffereth long, and is kind, and envieth not, and is not puffed up, seeketh not her own, is not easily provoked, thinketh no evil, and rejoiceth not in iniquity but rejoiceth in the truth, beareth all things, believeth all things, hopeth all things, endureth all things."[9]

Fulfillment of the prophetic promises

All of the brethren in these revelations were baptized on the day the Church was organized or shortly thereafter. Joseph Knight was told in April 1830, that it "is your duty to unite with the true church," so the following June he obeyed this command from the Lord.[10]

---

[6]Romans 5:3-5.
[7]Moroni 7:42.
[8]*Ibid.*, 7:47.
[9]*Ibid.*, v. 45.
[10]D&C 23:6-7.

That each one of these five elders thrust in their sickle to reap a harvest is attested in the history of the Church. Oliver Cowdery and David Whitmer were two of the Three Special Witnesses of the Book of Mormon. Joseph Smith, Sen., and Hyrum Smith were among the eight witnesses of that record. All of these men except David Whitmer died in full fellowship in the Church. It is to the credit of Brother Whitmer that he affirmed his testimony of the Book of Mormon to the end of his life. Of Joseph Knight, the Prophet wrote that he "is a righteous man . . . and it shall be said of him by the sons of Zion, while there is one of them remaining, that this man was a faithful man in Israel, therefore his name shall never be forgotten."[11]

An example of constancy in the faith and reaping a harvest occurred in the life of Joseph Smith, Sen., as reported by his wife. Brother Smith was sent to prison for inability to pay a debt, which would have been canceled if he would burn the copies of the Book of Mormon in his possession. This conversation with his son William was related about a subsequent experience:

" 'Immediately after I left your mother, the men by whom I was taken commenced using every possible argument to induce me to renounce the Book of Mormon, saying, 'how much better it would be for you to deny that silly thing, than to be disgraced and imprisoned, when you might not only escape this, but also have the note back, as well as the money which you have paid on it.' To this I made no reply. They still went on in the same manner till we arrived at the jail, when they hurried me into this dismal dungeon. I shuddered when I first heard these heavy doors creaking upon their hinges; but then I thought to myself, I was not the first man who had been imprisoned for the truth's sake; and when I should meet Paul in the Paradise of God, I could tell him that I, too, had been in bonds for the Gospel which he had preached. And this has been my only consolation.

---

[11]*DHC* 5:124-125.

"From the time I entered until now, and this is the fourth day, I have had nothing to eat, save a pint basin full of very weak broth; and there (pointing to the opposite side of the cell) lies the basin yet.' "[12]

Mother Smith continued: "He preached during his confinement there every Sabbath, and when he was released he baptized two persons whom he had thus converted."[13]

The early period of the Church was a harvest of souls, for the field was white. In a revelation the Lord declared that what he had said to one he had said to all.[14]

Unto all who labor faithfully in the harvest of souls, the promise is given: "And thus, if ye are faithful ye shall be laden with many sheaves, and crowned with honor, glory, and immortality, and eternal life."[15] The names of these faithful brethren are too numerous to mention. They constitute the presidents of the Church, apostles, seventies, and other faithful, devoted persons. An example of one, not among the general authorities, will illustrate the great work performed in this bounteous harvest.

Dan Jones, born in Wales, a convert to the Church in the days of Joseph Smith, was the subject of a prophecy made by the Prophet. From his life the following extracts are taken:

"The night of June 26, 1844, was spent by Captain Jones with the Prophet and his fellow prisoners in Carthage jail; and when all were apparently fast asleep, save the captain and the Prophet, the latter remarked in a whisper to Brother Jones: 'Are you afraid to die?' The one addressed replied, 'Has that time come, think you? Engaged in such a cause I do not think that death would have many terrors.' And then came that memorable prophecy: 'You will yet see Wales and fulfill a mission appointed you before you die.' "[16]

[12]Lucy Mack Smith, *History of Joseph Smith By His Mother*, p. 185.
[13]*Ibid.*, p. 186.
[14]D&C 93:49.
[15]*Ibid.*, 75:5.
[16]Thomas C. Romney, *The Gospel in Action*, p. 88.

Upon learning from a guard at the jail that Joseph Smith would never leave the jail alive, he reported this remark to the Prophet, who sent him to notify the Governor of the state of Illinois of this threat. Governor Thomas Ford would not believe that this could happen. When Brother Jones returned to the jail at Carthage, the guard would not let him in. Thus, it appears that the Lord made it possible for him to fulfill the Prophet's prediction concerning the mission to Wales.

Dan Jones went to Europe in 1845 where he was appointed president of the Welsh Mission. The devil inspired hundreds to threaten his life. In 1848, however, he reported phenomenal success in establishing 55 branches of the Church, with a total membership of 3,603. "In one year under his presidency there were led into the waters of baptism the almost unbelievable number of 1,939 souls, an average of 1,001 a year since the coming of this great missionary into his native land."[17]

"Returning to America where he continued to labor in the field until 1852, when he served another mission to Wales, he added 2,000 converts to the rolls of the Church in a three and one-half year period."[18]

Not all the elders reaped such a harvest, but the numbers would be legion who made their contribution of souls to the fold of Christ.

Application of the prophetic promises

Although the desire to reap a harvest of souls is paramount for success, not every one who has the desire is formally called to the service. Today, the missionary force is made up of young, unmarried elders and young women, and some older couples.

Hyrum Smith desired to labor in the cause of truth, as did the others to whom these promises were given, but he, and the others learned, that one must be called by authority to preach the Gospel of Jesus Christ.[19]

[17]*Ibid.*, p. 91.
[18]*Ibid.*, p. 92.
[19]D&C 11:15; Article of Faith, No. 5.

"Every member a missionary" is the call of the Prophet David O. McKay today. Each may interest, inform, and lead the way for the non-member to know the fulness of truth from the stake and foreign missionaries, who are called to this service.

There is a time for all men to show their earnest desires and their dedication. That time is now, while the day lasts. There may come a time in each person's life when neither desire nor the opportunity may be present; consequently, when the call comes to service, that is the day of opportunity.

To him whose desires bring action in the day of opportunity comes the rewards of everlasting salvation in the kingdom of God. In Section 6, the Lord tells Oliver Cowdery that the greatest gift to man is salvation.[20] Three months later, David Whitmer is told that eternal life is the greatest gift of God.[21] Eternal life is the greatest measure of salvation available to man. This blessing is exaltation in the celestial kingdom. (See "They Are They. . .Who Have Received Of His Fulness, And Of His Glory. . ."— D&C 76:50-60; 132:4-5; 131:1-4; 132:21-22).

---

[20]D&C 6:13.
[21]*Ibid.*, 14:7.

Chapter 9

"Pray always . . . And Great Shall Be Your Blessing . . ."

(D&C 19:38; 90:24; 112:10; 88:63-65)

(A) Pray always, and I will pour out my Spirit upon you, and great shall be your blessings—yea, even more than if you should obtain treasures of earth and corruptibleness to the extent thereof.[1]

(B) Search diligently, pray always, and be believing, and all things shall work together for your good, if ye walk uprightly and remember the covenant wherewith ye have covenanted one with another.[2]

(C) Be thou humble; and the Lord thy God shall lead thee by the hand, and give thee answer to thy prayers.[3]

(D) Draw near unto me and I will draw near unto you; seek me diligently and ye shall find me; ask, and ye shall receive; knock, and it shall be opened unto you.

Whatsoever ye ask the Father in my name it shall be given unto you, that is expedient for you;

And if ye ask anything that is not expedient for you, it shall turn unto your condemnation.[4]

Background of the revelations

(A) A doctrinal revelation about eternal punishment and the atonement of Christ.

(B) Section 90 clarifies the position of Joseph Smith as President of the Church and appoints Sidney Rigdon and Frederick G. Williams as counselors. Responsibilities of the First Presidency are told.

(C) Section 112 was given for the benefit of Thomas B. Marsh, president of the Twelve Apostles, and for the instruction of the Twelve.

(D) The Olive Leaf (Section 88) was given that members of the Church might have peace through its teachings.

---

[1]D&C 19:38.
[2]D&C 90:24.
[3]D&C 112:10.
[4]D&C 88:63-65.

Background of the prophetic promises

(A) Section 19 was addressed to Martin Harris. It mentions the Lamanites as Jews and that remission of sins comes by water and Spirit baptism. Individual instructions are given to Brother Harris about his property and the need to preach the gospel.

(B) Instructions are given concerning the temporal welfare of Frederick G. Williams, Joseph Smith, Sen., and Sidney Rigdon. The need for an agent to assist in keeping the Lord's storehouse full is admonished.

(C) Elder Marsh is told that he should preach the Gospel at all times, and success would follow his labors among the Jew and the Gentile, even to the ends of the earth. All of his success would be dependent upon the prophetic promise in verse 10. (See "Pray Always Lest You. . .Lose Your Reward"—D&C 31:12; 61:39; 10:5; 93:49).

(D) A Parable about the populating of other worlds than the earth is given. To secure additional information concerning God's work, he should be called upon while he is near.

Contents of the prophetic promises

(1) Pray always, search diligently, be humble, and believing. (2) The Lord's Spirit is promised. (3) Great blessings will be received, even greater than material treasures. (4) By walking uprightly, remembering the covenants, prayers will be answered, and all things shall work for your good.

Analysis of promises

To "pray always" means to have a prayer in one's heart, in addition to praying formally in secret and in public. To think a prayer, or a righteous desire, is a part of this admonitory expression. These ideas are given in the revelations, as follows: "And again, I command thee that thou shalt pray vocally as well as in thy heart; yea, before the world as well as in secret, in public as well as in private."[5] Enos, the Book of Mormon prophet, prayed "all day long. . .yea, and when the night came I did still raise my voice high that it reached the heavens."[6]

As also given in the Book of Mormon, the people prayed with desire when they were in the presence of the resurrected Lord.[7]

The humble person is one who submits his will to the will of God. A synonym is teachableness. He who can be taught is divested of pride of learning, the antithesis of humility.[8] The truly humble person recognizes that there is neither salvation in this world nor in the world to come without faith in Christ as his Savior.[9]

Verses 64 and 65 of Section 88 add an important qualification to the fulfillment of prayers. Prayer is answered, provided it "is expedient for you"; if, however, one asks for that which is not expedient, then condemnation will follow. It appears that the Lord is telling us that we should seek for his guidance to know what is a legitimate request. If we are not too insistent, but leave the matter in his hands, we shall have the proper spirit.

There are other considerations about prayer which should also be given some attention. Prayer is the avenue of communication between the individual and God. If judged by the criterion of the revealed purpose of life, then there is no success without prayer. Satan knows the value and need for prayer; consequently, he teaches that one should not pray.[10] So important is the need to pray that Nephi taught "that ye must not perform anything unto the Lord save in the first place ye shall pray unto the Father in the name of Christ, that he will consecrate thy performance unto thee, that thy performance may be

---

[5]D&C 19:28.
[6]Enos 4.
[7]3 Nephi 19:24.
[8]I Peter 5:5; 2 Nephi 9:28-29.
[9]2 Nephi 9:6-13.
[10]2 Nephi 32:8.

for the welfare of thy soul."[11] This truth gives meaning to the prophetic promise that if we seek diligently to know the best thing for us, always with the thought that the Lord's will be done, success will result. We also must seek diligently with faith in Christ, that we shall receive that which is best for us.[12]

In harmony with the injunction that we seek for blessings that are expedient for us is the instruction that we must have the Spirit with us—"I will pour out my Spirit upon you," if you "pray always".[13] No person can have that Spirit unless he is humble; and therefore, keeps the commandments of the Lord. Ultimately, all blessings from God come by obedience to his laws.[14] The receiving of enlightenment and wisdom is contingent upon one's humility.[15] In other words, prayer alone will not give results, though it is difficult to believe that a prayerful man is evil, but on the other hand, he may not be living essential laws that bring successful prayers.

President Brigham Young reminded the saints of his day that one should not expect to receive answer to prayers for things which the person could supply himself. If, however, the person is placed in a position where it is impossible for him to do for himself, as for example, locked in prison to starve, "it is then time enough for God to interpose, and feed him."[16]

President Joseph F. Smith felt that we should not learn a prayer by heart, nor should we pray: "Give us this day our daily bread," when we have ample food, but rather we should express gratitude for the food we have.[17]

To pray meaningfully requires that one, insofar as possible, knows the true character of God. Prayer leads to sal-

---

[11]*Ibid.*, v. 9.
[12]Hebrews 11:6.
[13]D&C 19:38.
[14]D&C 82:10.
[15]D&C 136:32-33.
[16]*Journal of Discourses* 1:108.
[17]Joseph Fielding Smith, *Gospel Doctrine*, pp. 220-221.

vation, and ignorance is a deterrent to that goal. To know God by the Spirit as one's personal Father is requisite to the true faith which leads to sincere, diligent prayer. Elder John A. Widstoe said: "The extent of a person's faith depends in part on the amount of his knowledge. . . ."[18]

"The degree of faith possessed by any man depends not upon the extent of his knowledge, but upon the certainty of his knowledge, which leads to the proper use of his knowledge."[19]

Fulfillment of the prophetic promises

The examples of fulfilled prayers in the lives of Latter-day Saints are multitudinous. Three specific examples are given in the Doctrine and Covenants as the result of the Prophet Joseph Smith praying on certain subjects: (1) When concerned about world events and particularly those in the United States, the Lord told him that because of his prayers and those of the saints that though there were rumors of wars in far countries "ye know not the hearts of men in your own land." [See "The Wars That Will Shortly Come To Pass" —Part 1 — The American Civil War (D&C 87: 1-3; 130:12-13)]. (2) Another prayer which was answered by a "voice" foretold the probable origin of the American Civil War through the slave question.[20] (3) While in prison the Prophet prayed for the oppressed saints and himself, whereupon the Lord gave him consolation amidst his tribulations.[21] Although the Prophet prayed earnestly to know the time of the coming of Christ, the answer given left him in doubt—"I was left thus, without being about to decide. . . ."[22] By and large, the revelations in the Doctrine and Covenants came as a result of an inquiry by the Prophet.

---

[18]John A. Widtsoe, *Joseph Smith*, p. 163.
[19]*Ibid.*
[20]D&C 130:12-13.
[21]D&C 121:1-6.
[22]D&C 130:14-17.

The young as well as the old are beneficiaries of praying. President David O. McKay related the time when he, as a young child was frightened at night, but upon praying he heard a voice speaking clearly: "Don't be afraid; nothing will hurt you."[23]

In addressing his counsel to the young people of the Church, President McKay said that sincere faith and prayer will bring forth at least the four following great blessings: (1) Gratitude, (2) Guidance, (3) Confidence, and (4) Inspiration.

(1) *Gratitude.* "Their souls will be filled with thanksgiving for what God has done for them. They will find themselves rich in favors bestowed. . . ."

(2) *Guidance.* "I cannot conceive of a young man's [or young girl] going astray who will kneel down by his bedside in the morning and pray to God to keep himself unspotted from the sins of the world. . . . Guidance: Yes, God will be there to guide and direct him who will seek him in faith with all his might and with all his soul. . . ."

(3) **Confidence.** "In the Church, let us teach these students that if they want to succeed in their lessons they would seek their God; that the greatest Teacher known to the world stands near to guide them. . . . Confidence comes through sincere prayer."

(4) *Inspiration.* "It is not imagination, if we approach God sincerely seeking light and guidance from him, our minds will be enlightened and our souls thrilled by his Spirit."[24]

The guidance and inspiration that can come to a prayerful man is given in the following account related by Elder John A. Widstoe:

"I could tell you a number of experiences, but the one that impressed me most happened a few years ago when I accompanied Brother Reed Smoot to Europe. We came to Stockholm; he had his work to do; I decided to see

---

[23]David O. McKay, *Gospel Ideals*, p. 524.
[24]*Conference Report*, April 1961, pp. 7-8.

what I could do in the way of finding books on Swedish genealogy. I knew the names of two big bookstores in Stockholm. I went to the one, made my selections, and then started across the city to the other bookstore in the hope that I might find some more suitable books. As I hurried along the street filled with people, I was stopped suddenly by some voice which said to me: 'Go across the street and down that narrow side street.' I looked across the street and saw a little narrow street. I had not been in Stockholm before. I thought: This is all nonsense, I have little time to spend here. I am not going down that street, I have to do my work, and I walked on. Almost at once the voice came again, as distinctly as any voice I have ever heard. Then I asked myself: What is your business in this city? Are you not on the Lord's errand? And I crossed over; went down the little narrow street, and there, half-way down, found a little bookstore that I had known nothing about. When I asked for books on genealogy the lady said: 'No, we do not carry books on genealogy. When we get such books we send them to the bookstore'—naming the store for which I was headed. Then, just as I was leaving in disappointment, she said: 'Stop a minute. A leading book collector, a genealogist, died about a month ago, and we bought his library. Many of his genealogical books are in the back room ready to be sent to the bookstore, but if you want to buy them you may have them.' Thus we secured the foundation of Swedish genealogy in our library. I could relate many such experiences."[25]

Application of the prophetic promises

When viewed from the purpose of life as known in the revelations, the principle of prayer becomes an absolute need. That the covenant member of Christ's Church may not be deceived, he is admonished to pray.[26] The commandment to pray has been given many times, but

---

[25]*The Utah Genealogical and Historical Magazine,* July 1931, p. 101.
[26]D&C 46:7.

this one from a modern revelation is pertinent: "And a commandment I give unto them—that he that observeth not his prayers before the Lord in the season thereof, let him be had in remembrance before the judge of my people."[27] The season of prayer is morning, noon, and night, during the day; yes, "always," "without ceasing." The prayerful man is likely to be striving to keep the commandments, but prayer without this action is futile, except as it may lead the person to repent.

A blessing of prayer is to enjoy the Lord's Spirit. President Brigham Young said: "Let us be humble, fervent, submissive, yielding ourselves to the will of the Lord, and there is no danger but that we shall have His Spirit to guide us."[28] This is the reason why Satan persuades people not to pray.[29]

President Young said on prayer:

"If we draw near to him, he will draw near to us; if we seek him early, we shall find him; if we apply our minds faithfully and diligently day by day, to know and understand the mind and will of God, it is as easy as, yes, I will say easier than, it is to know the minds of each other. . ."[30]

Should we expect an immediate answer to our prayers? There are no doubt occasions when this is true, saving a sick person from death by administration, if it be the Lord's will; the protection of a loved one, as in the following case when President George A. Smith prayed for his son whose boat capsized in the Provo river:

"John Henry became entangled in some driftwood and was kept under water for some time. People who were standing on the shore had given him up for lost, when suddenly an unseen power seemed to lift him bodily on the bank. It was afterwards learned that at that very

---

[27]D&C 68:33.
[28]*Journal of Discourses* 13:155.
[29]2 Nephi 32:8.
[30]*Journal of Discourses* 13:312.

time his father had become forcibly impressed with the feeling that his son was in extreme danger, and he went and robed himself in his Priesthood apparel and prayed the Lord to save his son, which was done in the manner named."[31]

On the other hand, there are prayers which may take a long time to be fulfilled, as the return of a loved one who has drifted from the road of righteousness, or the parents or other relatives who have not yet joined the Church. We must also remember that it is necessary for us to work for the fulfillment of our prayers, but by our righteous desires being known to the Lord through prayer, we gain necessary assistance. Important is the fact that prayers should not be set aside because it appears that their fulfillment is not answered. The case of the importunate widow carries a lesson for all of us.[32] We are to seek the Lord's will for that which will be of most benefit for us.

So important is the commandment to pray that parents are under condemnation if they do not teach their children to pray and prepare them for righteous conduct throughout life.[33] In addition, the Church is to strengthen those who preside over them by praying for them.[34]

The saints who were driven from Jackson County, Missouri, by a mob were, in part, responsible, because they failed to keep the commandments.[35] The lesson for us today as well as then is:

"They were slow to hearken unto the voice of the Lord their God; therefore, the Lord their God is slow to hearken unto their prayers, to answer them in the day of their trouble.

"In the day of their peace they esteemed lightly my

[31]Andrew Jenson, *LDS Biographical Encyclopedia* 1:142.
[32]D&C 101:81-94; Luke 18:1-9.
[33]D&C 68:25-28.
[34]D&C 108:7.
[35]D&C 101:1-6.

counsel; but, in the day of their trouble, of necessity they feel after me."[36]

---

[36]*Ibid.*, 7-8.

Chapter 10

"For His Word Ye Shall Receive, As If From Mine Own Mouth . . ."
(D&C 21:4-6).

Wherefore, meaning the church, thou shalt give heed unto all his words and commandments which he shall give unto you as he receiveth them, walking in all holiness before me;

For his word ye shall receive, as if from mine own mouth, in all patience and faith.

For by doing these things the gates of hell shall not prevail against you; yea, and the Lord God will disperse the powers of darkness from before you, and cause the heavens to shake for your good, and his name's glory.[1]

Background of the revelation

On the day the Church of Jesus Christ was organized, April 6, 1830, the Lord gave this revelation. Under the law of common consent, Joseph Smith and Oliver Cowdery were sustained as the First and the Second Elders, respectively. These brethren were then ordained elders, the Melchizedek Priesthood having been conferred upon them about one year before by Peter, James and John.

Background of the prophetic promise

A record of the Church was commanded to be maintained. In this record Joseph Smith was to be known as "a seer, a translator, a prophet, an apostle of Jesus Christ, an elder of the church . . ."[2] Mention is made of the organization of the church on that day.

Contents of the prophetic promise

(1) The Church should give heed to the words and commandments as they are received from God through Joseph Smith. (2) The Church should walk in all holiness.

---

[1]D&C 21:4-6.
[2]*Ibid.*, v.1.

(3) The Prophet's words are to be received as if the Lord spoke them. (4) These words are to be received in patience and faith. (5) If these commandments are followed, the gates of hell shall not prevail against the Church and the members. (6) If faithful to these commandments, the powers of darkness will be dispersed.

Analysis of the prophetic promise

Joseph Smith was the first Prophet of the restored Church of Jesus Christ in this dispensation. Inasmuch as he had received the duties of seer, apostle, and so forth, he, as he had done already on numerous occasions, was to continue to receive the mind and will of the Lord for the people of his Church.

In a subsequent revelation, the Lord reminds his people of the need to accept his servants, as follows: "And also all they who receive this priesthood receive me, saith the Lord;

"For he that receiveth my servants receiveth me;

"And he that receiveth me receiveth my Father;

"And he that receiveth my Father receiveth my Father's kingdom; therefore all that my Father hath shall be given unto him."[3]

The expression the "gates of hell" is found in the New Testament,[4] and in at least six other places in the Doctrine and Covenants. In all places where it appears the protection promised against the gates of hell is contingent upon the keeping of the commandments. What is the penalty of disobedience to the Lord's will? It is to succumb to the evil forces or powers of the unseen world. For the evil forces of Satan to overcome a member of the Church brings the disappointment mentioned in the following statement from the Prophet Joseph Smith: "The great misery of departed spirits in the world of spirits, where they go after death, is to know that they come

---

[3]D&C 84:35-38.
[4]Matthew 16:18; D&C 128:10.

short of the glory that others enjoy and that they might have enjoyed themselves, and they are their own accusers."[5]

If one attains salvation by obedience to the teachings of the Gospel, he will triumph over evil forces in this world and in the world to come. The following from the Prophet is pertinent to this point: "Salvation is nothing more nor less than to triumph over all our enemies and put our enemies under our feet in this world, and a knowledge to triumph over all evil spirits in the world to come, then we are saved, as in the case of Jesus, who was to reign until He had put all enemies under His feet, and the last enemy was death."[6]

Fulfillment of the prophetic promise

The prophetic promise under consideration indicates that it pertains to the Church and also to the individual Church member. As to the Church, it is true that despite persecutions, hardships and the malignity of men, it has survived for 139 years, as of this writing. The prophetic continuance of the Church is assured. (See "Triumph of the Kindgom of God"—D&C 103:5-8; and "The Keys of The Kingdom of God"—D&C 65:2; 109:72).

As to the individual members of the Church, time has proven that the keeping of the commandments in all patience and faith disperses the powers of darkness. The converse of this truth is also a fact. When men weaken their faith by disobedience or rebellion, the Adversary darkens their minds and the "gates of hell" claim them.

John C. Bennett, a man of unusual ability as a physician, and one who became a university professor, and a brigadier-general, offered his services to the Church in 1840. The Prophet informed him that he should not expect worldly riches or acclaim but only the approval of God. Within two years he was excommunicated from the

---

[5]*DHC* 5:425.
[6]Joseph Fielding Smith, *Teachings of the Prophet Joseph Smith*, p. 297.

Church because of adultery. From the *Doctrine and Covenants Commentary* the following information is given about him:

"Then he became one of the most bitter enemies of the Church. His slanders, his falsehoods and unscrupulous attacks, which included perjury and attempted assassination were the means of inflaming public opinion to such an extent that the tragedy at Carthage became possible. . . ."

"Bennett lived to be despised by all who knew him. 'For some years before his death he suffered from violent fits; he also partly lost the use of his limbs and of his tongue; and it was difficult for him to make himself understood. He dragged out a miserable existence, without a person scarcely to take the best interest in his fate, and died without a soul to mourn his departure.' (Andrew Jenson, *Historical Record*, p. 496.)"[7]

In John C. Bennett's life we have an example of one who was given opportunities for service in the Kingdom of God, but the spirit of evil overcame him, and his bitterness toward the Church was not unusual for one cut off because of sexual immorality. His fate is an example of the prediction about such apostates as found in Section 121, verses 13 through 25. He failed to heed the words of the Lord through his Prophet, which blessings were contingent upon the word "if."[8]

Men may be faithful and true for a long period of time, but when evil forces bear against them, if they do not resist with all their hearts in following the Lord's counsel through his Prophet, they fall away into oblivion. Such an one was Elder John E. Page, member of the Council of the Twelve from 1836 to 1846, who was excommunicated from the Church, June 26, 1846. Elder Page failed to follow the prophetic promise concerning the

---

[7]Hyrum M. Smith and Janne M. Sjodahl, *Doctrine and Covenants Commentary*, pp. 770-771.

[8]D&C 124:16-17.

Prophet Joseph Smith: "For his word ye shall receive, as if from mine own mouth, in all patience and faith."

In April, 1840, he was appointed to accompany Elder Orson Hyde to Jerusalem where in 1841, Elder Hyde dedicated that land for the return of the Jewish people, but Brother Page did not leave the shores of America. (See "The Children of Judah"—D&C 109:61-64). In June, 1841, he was offered the means by which to join Brother Hyde, but he did not go. Other incidents occurred where he failed to accept authority. He was disfellowshipped in February, 1846, and became bitter toward his former associates and advised the saints to join James J. Strang, apostate claimant to the presidency of the Church following the martyrdom of the Prophet Joseph Smith. Not long after this he was excommunicated, and he dwindled into obscurity and died in 1867.

The names and faithful records of thousands, on the other hand, who remained true to the counsel of the Lord through his Prophet are held in honor by the saints, but the following statement concerning the members of the Twelve, five of whom were excommunicated from the Church, describes the lot of the faithful and the unfaithful:

"To the Twelve it was not only a call to the ministry; for some of them it was a call to martyrdom.

"Of the disciples chosen then and of those since selected to keep the quorum complete, not one has escaped the afflictions of time.

"With some the pains were too intense to be endured, the burdens too heavy to be borne; and they dropped aside from the on-marching ranks to find, as they hoped, repose and safety amidst the cooling shadows of that world from which they had been chosen to be special witnesses of the Son of God. Such are no longer His Apostles.

"But the others, with unshaken resoluteness, have gone forward in fulfillment of their high mission, under the scorching heat of fiery persecution. Joseph is their captain and their fellow soldier in the cause of Christ. With him and after him many of them have, with continuous and unyielding zeal, toiled steadily on until worn out in the performance of the duty assigned them by their Master Jesus; they have passed to the enjoyment of His promised rest. With Him they and the other faithful Apostles will stand triumphant when human time shall be no more, and when the voice of the Eternal shall fill the universe with the thunder of his judgments. They shall not then be only twelve; for they who have been called of God to this holy calling and who endure faithful, though they may lay down their mortality, yet shall they not lose their Apostleship; for it abideth with them in this world and in the worlds to come."[9]

Newell Knight was the subject of the first miracle performed in the Church. The Prophet persuaded him to pray in public, whereupon he said, "he would try and take up his cross, and pray vocally during meeting."[10] He failed, but retired to the woods the next morning and was overcome by an evil power. Upon reaching home, he summoned the Prophet, who, when he arrived, found "his visage and limbs distorted and twisted in every shape and appearance." The Prophet commanded the evil spirit to come out of him, and Brother Knight said "he saw the devil leave him and vanish from his sight." Brother Knight remained a faithful, devoted member of the Church until his death January, 1847, on the plains of Nebraska, leaving his wife, Lydia, and their seven children. When she and her family were confronted with the trek across the plains alone, she cried out in her loneliness: "Oh Newel, why hast thou left me?" As she spoke, he stood by her side, and said: "Be calm, let not sorrow overcome you. It was necessary that I should go. I was needed behind the veil to represent the true condition of

---

[9]George Q. Cannon, *Life of Joseph Smith*, pp. 178-179.
[10]*DHC* 1:82.

this camp and people. You cannot fully comprehend it now; but the time will come when you shall know why I left you and our little ones. Therefore, dry up your tears. Be patient. I will go before you and protect you in your journeyings. And you and your little ones shall never perish for lack of food. Although the ravens of the valley should feed you and your little ones, you shall not perish for the want of bread."[11]

Again, when her eighth child was born amid very difficult conditions, she cried out: "Oh Newel, why could you not have stayed with and protected me through our journeyings?" A voice answered her and said: "Lydia, be patient and fear not. I will still watch over you, and protect you in your present situation. You shall receive no harm. It was needful that I should go, and you will undertand why in due time."[12]

Yes, this good man, proven and true through many persecutions had walked in all holiness before the Lord. Obedient to the words of the Lord through his Prophet, the blessing of a happy, meaningful, spirit existence awaited him. The "powers of darkness" dispersed from before his wife, and the "heavens shook for your [her] good."

Application of the prophetic promise

The Lord has revealed that there is only one at a time on the earth who has the power to speak for him.[13] The Prophet Joseph Smith received from angelic beings keys, powers, authorities, everything necessary to direct the Kingdom of God upon the earth. So important was his calling, and those who have succeeded him, that the Lord said: "And thou shalt not command him who is at thy head, and at the head of the church.

"For I have given him the keys of the mysteries, and

---

[11]Susan (Young) Gates, *"Lydia Knight's History,"* pp. 71-72.

[12]*Ibid.*, pp. 74-75.

[13]D&C 28:2; 43:3.

the revelations which are sealed, until I shall appoint unto them another in his stead."[14]

When one rebels against God's authority, he is traveling on the road to damnation. Betrayal of the brethren, the revelations of God in the standard works of the Church "or any other that ever was or ever will be given and revealed unto man in this world or that which is to come," will cause one to "go down to hell."[15]

The Prophet also said: "That man who rises up to condemn others, finding fault with the Church, saying that they are out of the way, while he himself is righteous, then know assuredly, that that man is in the high road to apostasy; and if he does not repent, will apostatize, as God lives."[16]

Those who feel that they may reject the revelations and the words of the brethren should remember the last words of the first apostolic martyr of the dispensation, David W. Patten: "Whatever you do else, Oh, do not deny the faith."

---

[14]D&C 28:6-7.
[15]Joseph Fielding Smith, *Teachings of the Prophet Joseph Smith*, p. 156.
[16]*Ibid.*, pp. 156-157.

Chapter 11

"... Leave A Cursing Instead Of A Blessing ..."
(D&C 24:15; 75:19-20; 60:15; 84:92; 99:3-4).

(A) And inwhatsoever place ye shall enter, and they receive you not in my name, ye shall leave a cursing instead of a blessing, by casting off the dust of your feet against them as a testimony, and cleansing your feet by the wayside.[1]

(B) And in whatsoever house ye enter, and they receive you, leave your blessing upon that house.

And in whatsoever house ye enter, and they receive you not, ye shall depart speedily from that house, and shake off the dust of your feet as a testimony against them.[2]

(C) And shake off the dust of thy feet against those who receive thee not, not in their presence, lest thou provoke them, but in secret; and wash thy feet, as a testimony against them in the day of judgment.[3]

(D) He that receiveth you not, go away from him alone by yourselves, and cleanse your feet even with water, pure water, whether in heat or in cold, and bear testimony of it unto your Father which is in heaven, and return not again unto that man.[4]

(E) And who receiveth you as a little child, receiveth my kingdom; and blessed are they, for they shall obtain mercy.

And whoso rejecteth you shall be rejected of my Father and his house; and you shall cleanse your feet in the secret places by the way for a testimony against them.[5]

Background of the revelations

(A) Although less than four months had passed since the organization of the Church, persecution was intense.

(B) Section 75 is a missionary revelation in which the duties of the missionary are given.

(C) Several elders and the Prophet Joseph Smith were

---

[1]D&C 24:15.
[2]D&C 75:19-20.
[3]D&C 60:15.
[4]D&C 84:92.
[5]D&C 99:3-4.

returning from the State of Missouri, on the Missouri river, to their homes in Ohio.

(D) The importance of the Priesthood in the salvation and exaltation of men is found in Section 84.

(E) Elder John Murdock is given instructions regarding his ministry.

Background of the prophetic promises

(A) Instructions are given to Oliver Cowdery concerning his responsibility to declare the Gospel. Miracles are not to be performed, except when inspired, unless they are requested.

(B) The names of elders who are paired together to perform missionary service are given, including their areas of activity.

(C) The Prophet and some elders were to travel to Cincinnati, while the others were to go to St. Louis and then to their churches. They were instructed to preach the Gospel enroute, and not idle away their time.

(D) Missionaries for the Church are counseled to take neither purse nor scrip, for the Lord will raise up friends to them. Preparation should be made for their ministry by study that, when necessary, the Spirit will draw it forth. Blessings will acrue to those who befriend the Lord's servants, while cursings will follow those who do not help them. (See". . . The Laborer Is Worthy Of His Hire."— D&C 84:79-91).

(E) Elder Murdock is told that he should travel from city to city to proclaim the Gospel.

Contents of the prophetic promises

(1) Those people who receive the missionary as a servant of Christ should be blessed by the missionary. (2) If they receive you not, then a curse should be pronounced against them. (3) The cursing is accomplished in secret by "casting off the dust of your feet," "cleansing the feet even with water," and "bear testimony of it unto your

Father which is in heaven." (4) The testimony against them is for the day of judgment.

Analysis of the prophetic promises

These prophetic promises made to missionaries are conditioned upon the receptivity of the people to caring for their wants (food, etc.) as servants of the Lord. Also, the promise, whether positive or negative, pertains to the treatment accorded the missionaries when they deliver their message. The penalty—cursing—may have dire physical effects in this life, or it may be reserved for the after-death judgment. It is apparent for many reasons that the elder should not curse someone because he indicates no interest in the Gospel message; also, if a woman at the door is busy preparing dinner or bathing her baby does not have the time to listen. In other words, the elder should be directed by the Spirit in what he should do. All judgments should be made in righteousness. The following counsel given to Hyrum Smith is applicable to this point:

"And now, verily, verily, I say unto thee, put your trust in that Spirit which leadeth to do good—yea, to do justly, to walk humbly, to judge righteously; and this is my Spirit.

"Verily, verily, I say unto you, I will impart unto you of my Spirit, which shall enlighten your mind, which shall fill your soul with joy;

"And then shall ye know, or by this shall you know, all things whatsoever you desire of me, which are pertaining unto things of righteousness, in faith believing in me that you shall receive."[6]

In harmony with the foregoing instruction President Wilford Woodruff said to missionaries:

"I want to give you a word of exhortation and counsel, brethren: that is, whenever you are in doubt about any duty or work which you have to perform, never proceed to do anything until you go and labor in prayer and

---

[6]D&C 11:12-14.

get the Holy Spirit. Wherever the Spirit dictates you to go or to do, that will be right; and, by following the dictates you will come out right.

"We shall be brought to many places during our career in the ministry among the nations of the earth, where we may consider a certain course of procedure to be right; but, if we do not know, it will be better for us to go before the Lord and ask in faith that we may be instructed in the way of life."[7]

Whether the testimony against a person is visited upon him in this life, is something that the missionary may not be able to determine at the time, but, if the Spirit has inspired the action, it is certain that the judgment will follow, either in this life or the life to come.

Fulfillment of the promises

The first time in this dispensation that judgment was pronounced against one who failed to assist a missionary occurred when Samuel H. Smith, brother of the Prophet, undertook the first missionary journey of the Church. His mother relates the following account:

"When evening came on, he was faint and almost discouraged, but coming to an inn, which was surrounded with every appearance of plenty, he called to see if the landlord would buy one of his books. On going in, Samuel enquired of him, if he did not wish to purchase a history of the origin of the Indians.

" 'I do not know,' replied the host; 'how did you get hold of it?'

" 'It was translated,' rejoined Samuel, 'by my brother, from some gold plates that he found buried in the earth.'

" 'You liar!' cried the landlord, 'get out of my house —you shan't stay one minute with your books.' "

Samuel was sick at heart, for this was the fifth time he had been turned out of doors that day. He left the house, traveled a short distance, and washed his feet in a

---

[7]*Journal of Discourses*, 5:85.

small brook, as a testimony against the man. He then proceeded five miles farther on his journey, and seeing an apple tree a short distance from the road, he concluded to pass the night under it; and here he lay all night upon the cold, damp ground. . . ." [Samuel continued on the next day and was successful in receiving food, for which he gave the party a copy of the Book of Mormon. What happened two weeks later is related by his mother.]

"This time, Mr. Smith, and myself accompanied him, and it was our intention to have passed near the tavern, where Samuel was so abusively treated a fortnight previous, but just before we came to the house, a sign of small-pox intercepted us. We turned aside, and meeting a citizen of the place, we enquired of him, to what extent this disease prevailed. He answered, that the tavern keeper and two of his family had died with it not long since, but he did not know that any one else had caught the disease, and that it was brought into the neighborhood by a traveler, who stopped at the tavern over night."[8]

In the foregoing account Samuel left a copy of the Book of Mormon with the Rev. John P. Greene, brother-in-law of Brigham Young. These brethren subsequently joined the Church and reaped the blessings as predicted.

To several elders the Lord said this in 1831: "Nevertheless, ye are blessed, for the testimony which ye have borne is recorded in heaven for the angels to look upon; and they rejoice over you, and your sins are forgiven you." (D&C 62:3). A commentary on this scripture confirms the message of the prophetic promises under consideration:

"In this Revelation we are told that angels are scrutinizing the records kept of the testimonies of the Elders, and that they rejoice over the witnesses. It appears from this that the ministry on earth has its effects beyond the veil as well as on this side. An Elder who bears his faithful testimony to the truth does not know how far-reaching

---

[8]Lucy Mack Smith, *History of Joseph Smith By His Mother*, pp. 169-170.

the result may be, though his visible audience may consist of but few."[9]

Application of the prophetic promise

Patience and humility should characterize the ministry of Latter-day Saint missionaries. The rule stated by President Brigham Young in the following example is correct: He sent an elder to a city in England to perform missionary work, but by the end of the day he had returned having sealed the people up to damnation. President Young believed that this good man lacked knowledge, but if President Young had had this assignment he would have patiently labored with the people until released.[10]

They must seek for the Spirit to guide and direct them in their activities.[11] The Lord recognized the administrations of his faithful servants; therefore, caution should always be exercised in the discharge of any missionary responsibility. The Lord has said that "in the day of judgment you shall be judges of that house, and condemn them. . ."[12] "And as ye shall lift up your voices by the Comforter, ye shall speak and prophesy as seemeth me good;

"For, behold, the Comforter knoweth all things, and beareth record of the Father and of the Son."[13]

Faithful and devoted service in the missionary call will bring forth the following promise: "And thus, if ye are faithful ye shall be laden with many sheaves, and crowned with honor, and glory, and immortality, and eternal life."[14]

---

[9]Hyrum M. Smith and Janne M. Sjodahl, *Doctrine and Covenants Commentary,* p. 371.

[10]*Journal of Discourses,* 3:91.

[11]D&C 42:14.

[12]D&C 75:21.

[13]D&C 42:16-17.

[14]D&C 75:5.

Chapter 12

". . . They Shall Be Gathered in Unto One Place . . ."
(D&C 29:7-8; 45:65-71)

And ye are called to bring to pass the gathering of mine elect; for mine elect hear my voice and harden not their hearts;

Wherefore the decree hath gone forth from the Father that they shall be gathered in unto one place upon the face of this land, to prepare their hearts and be prepared in all things against the day when tribulation and desolation are sent forth upon the wicked.[1]

And with one heart and with one mind, gather up your riches that ye may purchase an inheritance which shall hereafter be appointed unto you.

And it shall be called the New Jerusalem, a land of peace, a city of refuge, a place of safety for the saints of the Most High God;

And the glory of the Lord shall be there, and the terror of the Lord also shall be there, insomuch that the wicked will not come unto it, and it shall be called Zion.

And it shall come to pass among the wicked, that every man that will not take his sword against his neighbor must needs flee unto Zion for safety.

And there shall be gathered unto it out of every nation under heaven; and it shall be the only people that shall not be at war one with another.

And it shall be said among the wicked: Let us not go up to battle against Zion, for the inhabitants of Zion are terrible; wherefore we cannot stand.

And it shall come to pass that the righteous shall be gathered out from among all nations, and shall come to Zion, singing with songs of everlasting joy.[2]

Background of the revelations

Both of these revelations are similar in that their emphasis is given to the signs of the last days which herald the second coming of Christ. Section 29 was received before some of the elders were to undertake a mission; consequently, the Lord wanted them and his Church to know

[1]D&C 29:7-8.
[2]D&C 45:65-71.

some fundamental doctrines relative to the times and also of salvation so essential for all to understand. Because of some foolish ideas extant about the Church, the Lord gave Section 45 that all might know the truth.

Background of the prophecies

Missionaries are reminded in Section 29 that a purpose of the Church is to gather together those who will not harden their hearts against the Savior. The Lord will be with the missionaries as they declare the gospel. Faith and prayer are necessary ingredients to receive success in their labors.

On March 7, 1831, Section 45 was received for the purpose of clarifying some important concepts concerning the second coming of Christ and events to precede it. The following subjects are given: teachings of the Savior to his disciples during his mortal ministry and the predicted judgments in the last dispensation. The gathering of the Jewish people to their homeland; calamities in the form of pestilence, plague, earthquake, and war, are a part of the conditions to precede the second coming of Christ. Throughout the revelation the saints are informed of the need to stand in holy places, to watch for the signs of the times prophesied for the period when the times of the gentiles are fulfilled. Immediately preceeding the prophecy the saints are told that they are the ten virgins mentioned in the parable, and it is necessary to always have oil in their lamps for the coming of their Lord. The imminence of war in America is indicated also. (See "The Wars That Will Shortly Come to Pass," Part I—The American Civil War."—D&C 87:1-3; 130:12-13; DHC 1:301)

Contents of the Prophecies

Section 29: (1) The Lord's servants are called to gather the elect. (2) Those gathered out of the world are to assemble in one place upon the land. (3) This gathering is to prepare the saints for the desolations to come upon the wicked. *Section 45:* (1) The members of the Church are to contribute to the purchase of an inheritance in the New Jerusalem, a land of peace, refuge, and safety. (2) The New Jerusalem is known also as Zion where the Lord's power and glory will be present. (3) The saints will be gathered from all nations unto this place when the world is at war. (4) The wicked will not come against Zion because of the power of God there.

Fulfillment of the Prophecies

From the time when the Church was organized missionaries have preached the gospel of salvation by divine appointment. That there would be a center-place of gathering known as the New Jerusalem in the last days was known anciently.[3] Some members of the Church assembled in Jackson County, Missouri, designated as the place where the New Jerusalem would be built, beginning in 1831 until they were driven from the area in 1834.[4] It is evident from the revelations that their sojourn there was to be short-lived. (See "After Much Tribulation"—D&C 58:3-5). While there the people did not build the promised temple, although the site was dedicated August 1831 by the Prophet Joseph Smith.[5]

The Lord promised that his saints would return to build the city of Zion, as indicated in Section 45 and other revelations.[6] The land of Zion, whenever occupied, will be secured by purchase, not by blood.[7] The Church will one day return to Jackson County, Missouri, as prophesied. President Brigham Young said: "If that is back to Jackson County, do not be scared, for as the Lord lives this people will go back and build a great temple there. . . . This people will surely go back to Jackson County. How soon that may be, or when it may be, I do not care; but that is not now the gathering place for this people."[8]

---

[3]Ether 13:4, 6-10.
[4]D&C 57:1-5.
[5]D&C 84:1-5; Roy W. Doxey, *Zion in the Last Days*, pp. 11-12.
[6]D&C 101:17-19; 105:13, 34.
[7]D&C 63:24-31.
[8]*Journal of Discourses*, 3:278-279.

When the Lord revealed that his people would go westward from the centerplace, other places of gathering than the West were to arise.[9] These stakes of Zion are holy places of gathering where the saints are to prepare for the second coming of Christ.[10] As a result, these holy places are today found in many parts of the world where there is instruction in how to live, how to act, how to come closer to the ideal of perfection in preparation for any eventuality. At the end of 1968 there were 2,144,766 members living in 448 stakes.

In the beginning of the dispensation the call went forth for the saints to assemble in certain places—Ohio, Missouri, Illinois, and then in the Far West. It was intended that in today's period the saints should be found among the nations and not settled in any one locality.[11] Eventually, in the due time of the Lord, there was to be a headquarters, a center-place of Zion, in Missouri. But there will be calamitous events in this world before that day comes. Wickedness will increase, men's hearts will fail them, diseases will be rampant, there will be unrest among the nations, fear will strike men's hearts, and wars will continue, until as the prophecy asserts: Zion's inhabitants will be the only ones who will not be at war one with another.[12] President Wilford Woodruff declared:

"It is the decree of the Almighty God that the Kingdom of Heaven shall be established and shall never again be overthrown, that judgments shall lay waste the nations, enough at least to give that kingdom room to grow and spread and prosper. This is the truth and you will find it so. Those judgments have begun that will never leave the earth until it is swept as with the besom of destruction, until thrones are cast down and kingdoms overthrown, until each man draws his sword against his neighbor, and every nation and kingdom that exists will be at war with each

[9]D&C 101:20-21.
[10]*Ibid.*, vs. 22-23.
[11]I Nephi 14:14.
[12]D&C 29:14-21; 45:30-33, 65-71.

other, except the inhabitants of Zion. The Lord has spoken it and it will come to pass."[13]

The Prophet Joseph Smith said: "It is . . . the concurrent testimony of all the Prophets, that this gathering together of all the Saints, must take place before the Lord comes to 'take vengeance upon the ungodly,' and 'to be glorified and admired by all those who obey the Gospel.' The fiftieth Psalm, from the first to the fifth verse inclusive, describes the glory and majesty of that event."[14]

Application of the prophecies

From Section 29 we learn that the elect are those who hearken unto the voice of the Lord, and furthermore, they do not harden their hearts against him.[15] This truth emphasizes the need for constancy in one's life. The dedication to gospel truth should be constant and unwavering. He that endures to the end will be saved.[16]

In commenting upon several passages from the scriptures on enduring to the end, Elder Mark E. Petersen of the Council of the Twelve, wrote:

"Why endure to the end? Why is it important to our salvation? Can we not be faithful part of the time and stray a bit, and yet get our salvation? Why does he limit the application to 'whosoever is of my church, and endureth of my church to the end?' (D&C 10:69)

"To answer these questions we must ask and answer one more: What is the purpose of our existence?

"We are the children of God, actually his offspring. . . . We are in this life to prove ourselves, and develop within us Godlike traits of character. We must become Christlike in our souls in order to come into his presence. No unclean thing may go there.

"Inasmuch as we are the children of God, it is within

---

[13]*Testimonies of the Divinity of The Church of Jesus Christ of Latter-day Saints by Its Leaders*, p. 54.
[14]*DHC* 4:272.
[15]D&C 29:7.
[16]D&C 53:7.

our power to become like him. It is only natural for a
child to become like his parents.

"To impress this great fact upon us, and to direct us
more definitely in the right way, he commanded in the
Sermon on the Mount that we become perfect even as our
Father which is in heaven.

"Perfection does not come suddenly, or overnight.
We must have a plan to follow: we must have instructions
by which we may build Christlike characters.

"The gospel is the plan. The commandments are the
detailed instructions. By living them, we achieve our goal.
But where does 'enduring to the end' come in?

"Steadfastness is part of good character. If we are not
steadfast, we are not strong. If we are not steadfast, we
waver, we are undecided, unpredictable; we stumble and
fall; we lack the 'backbone' to achieve; we are weaklings;
we cannot make up our minds; we never overcome.

"There is nothing Christlike in weakness, neither in
disobedience. We are commanded to 'overcome.' What is
it that we are to overcome? Weakness, indecision, turning
back, failure, sin. We are to fight a battle and win. The
victory and all the effort leading up to it build character.
Do we build character in being wishy-washy? Do we
build character in only partial performance?

"To become like him we must be strong. We must not
bow to temptation. We must not be idle. Only in labor is
there true excellence. But we must follow the right road to
perfection. We must adopt the correct instructions. That
is why he emphasized that he is the door to the sheepfold,
that the way to life is straight and narrow. There is only
one way."[17]

---

[17]Mark E. Petersen, *Your Faith and You*, pp. 288-289.

Chapter 13

"Pray Always Lest You . . . Lose Your Reward."
(D&C 31:12; 61:39; 10:5; 93:49)

(A) Pray always, lest you enter into temptation and lose your reward.[1]

(B) Pray always that you enter not into temptation, that you may abide the day of his coming, whether in life or in death. Even so. Amen.[2]

(C) Pray always, that you may come off conqueror; yes, that you may conquer Satan, and that you may escape the hands of the servants of Satan that do uphold his work.[3]

(D) What I say unto one I say unto all; pray always lest that wicked one have power in you, and remove you out of your place.[4]

Background of the revelations

(A) Instructions were given to Thomas B. Marsh, who later became president of the Twelve Apostles. (B) The Prophet Joseph Smith and some elders were traveling from Missouri to Ohio on the Missouri River when W. W. Phelps saw the destroyer riding on the face of the waters. (C) Joseph Smith is instructed concerning the translation of the Book of Mormon plates and also of the power of the devil.

Background of the prophetic promises

(A) Thomas B. Marsh is promised success in his labors, even to be a "physician unto the church." He is warned, however, to govern his house in meekness.

(B) Directions are given to the elders in preaching the gospel enroute to their homes in Ohio. They are counseled to be sober and watchful, for the day the Savior will come will be when they think not.

(C) Although Joseph Smith had lost the means to

[1]D&C 31:12.
[2]*Ibid.*, 61:39.
[3]*Ibid.*, 10:5.
[4]*Ibid.*, 93:49.

translate the gold plates because of the loss of the 116 pages of translated material from the plates, his gift to translate is restored. He is admonished to be diligent.

(D) Members of the First Presidency, especially Frederick G. Williams and Sidney Rigdon, are criticized for being lax in bringing up their children in light and truth. The family of the Prophet is to listen more diligently to him or lose their reward.

Contents of the prophetic promises

(1) In every verse, the Lord uses the expression "pray always." (2) Without prayer, the chance of entering into temptation is sure, with the resulting loss of reward. (3) To pray always brings victory over the wicked one and endurance in life or in death.

Analysis of the prophetic promises

"Pray always" is the important admonitory statement that brings success to prayer. It is probable that one cannot be thinking or expressing in words a prayer "always," but one can have a prayer in one's heart "always;" that is, prayer is such an integral part of one's life that he prays many times a day in thought for blessings received and those he needs. The Lord's words give us an understanding of this expression: "And again, I command thee that thou shalt pray vocally as well as in thy heart; yes, before the world as well as in secret, in public as well as in private."[5] The Apostle Paul wrote: "Pray without ceasing. In every thing give thanks; for this is the will of God in Christ Jesus concerning you."[6] To pray vocally for a long period of time may be necessary to bring forth the desired blessing. Enos, the Book of Mormon prophet, prayed in this manner.[7] The people prayed continually for their desires while the Lord ministered to them on this continent, but they did

---

[5]*Ibid.*, 19:28.
[6]I Thessalonians 5:17-18.
[7]Enos 1:4.

not multiply words in doing so, for "it was given unto them what they should pray, and they were filled with desire."[8]

The word of the Lord is definite: "Search diligently, pray always, and be believing and all things shall work together for your good, if ye walk uprightly and remember the covenant wherewith ye have covenanted one with another."[9] Obedience to the commandment to pray always, receiving the spirit of humility, and keeping the commandments brings blessings greater than the material wealth of this world: "Pray always, and I will pour out my Spirit upon you, and great shall be your blessing—yea, even more than if you should obtain treasures of earth and corruptibleness to the extent thereof."[10] (See "Pray Always . . . And Great Shall Be Your Blessing . . ."—D&C 19:38; 90:24; 112:10; 88:63-65). The blessing of knowing the "mysteries of God," even all things, and to be effective in building God's kingdom are promised.[11]

Satan may have power over a member of the Church "to remove you [him] out of your [his] place." This expression has several applications or meanings: in Section 93, the words were addressed to the Prophet Joseph Smith; therefore, there is no one who may not be reached by Satan through his temptations to bring about that person's fall from grace and consequently from office or place. To the member of the Church, without office, there is a warning that he too may lose his place as a member in God's kingdom. In this day when the Lord has instituted the Home Evening Program, his words to Bishop Newel K. Whitney which follow are significant: ". . . set in order his family, and see that they are more diligent and concerned at home, and pray always, or they shall be removed out of their place."[12]

---

[8]3 Nephi 19:24.
[9]D&C 90:24.
[10]*Ibid.*, 19:38.
[11]Alma 26:22.
[12]D&C 93:50.

Fulfillment of the prophetic promises

The promises under consideration in this article are truly prophetic. The revelation to Brother Marsh promised him that if he would, "Govern your [his] house in meekness, and be steadfast," as well as pray always to avoid entering into temptation, he would not lose his reward.[13]

Four years after this revelation was received, Brother Marsh was one of the first to receive the apostleship in this dispensation. Subsequently, he became the president of the Twelve Apostles, and while in this office the following occurred as reported by President George A. Smith at a conference of the Church:

". . . while the Saints were living in Far West, there were two sisters wishing to make cheese, and, neither of them possessing the requisite number of cows, they agreed to exchange milk.

"The wife of Thomas B. Marsh, who was then the President of the Twelve Apostles, and Sister Harris concluded they would exchange milk, in order to make a little larger cheese than they otherwise could. To be sure to have justice done, it was agreed that they should not save the strippings, but that the milk and strippings should all go together. . . .

"Mrs. Harris, it appeared, was faithful to the agreement and carried to Mrs. Marsh the milk and strippings, but Mrs. Marsh, wishing to make some extra good cheese, saved a pint of strippings from each cow and sent Mrs. Harris the milk without the strippings.

"Finally it leaked out that Mrs. Marsh had saved strippings, and it became a matter to be settled by the Teachers. They began to examine the matter, and it was proved that Mrs. Marsh had saved the strippings, and consequently had wronged Mrs. Harris out of that amount.

"An appeal was taken from the Teachers to the Bishop, and a regular Church trial was had. President Marsh did not consider that the Bishop had done him and his lady

---

[13]*Ibid.*, 31:9, 12.

justice, for they decided that the strippings were wrongfully saved, and that the woman had violated her covenant."

"Marsh immediately took an appeal to the High Council . . . but the High Council finally confirmed the Bishop's decision.

"Marsh, not being satisfied, took an appeal to the First Presidency of the Church, and Joseph and his Counselors had to sit upon the case, and they approved the decision of the High Council.

"This little affair, you will observe, kicked up a considerable breeze, and Thomas B. Marsh then declared that he would sustain the character of his wife, even if he had to go to hell for it."

Brother Marsh failed to accept the Lord's counsel in governing his house in meekness, succumbed to the temptation to sustain his wife despite her guilt, failed to pray always that he might sustain the truth and,

"The then President of the Twelve Apostles, the man who should have been the first to do justice and cause reparation to be made for wrong, committed by any member of his family, took that position, and what next? He went before a magistrate and swore that the 'Mormons' were hostile towards the State of Missouri.

"That affidavit brought from the government of Missouri an exterminating order, which drove some 15,000 Saints from their homes and habitations, and some thousands perished through suffering the exposure consequent on this state of affairs."[14]

Application of the prophetic promises

To pray always will bring down the blessings of heaven upon the members of the Church. If one has a prayer in one's heart always, it is probable that the rich quality of humility will also be his possession. As President Heber J. Grant said:

---

[14]*Journal of Discourses,* 3:283-284.

"The prayerful and humble man will always realize and feel that he is dependent upon the Lord for every blessing that he enjoys, and in praying to God he will not only pray for the light and the inspiration of His Holy Spirit to guide him, but he will feel to thank Him for the blessings that he receives, realizing that life, that health, that strength, and that all the intelligence which he possesses comes from God, who is the Author of his existence."[15]

It should be understood that prayer only will not bring forth the blessings of heaven. As President Joseph F. Smith said:

"Our first enemy we will find within ourselves. It is a good thing to overcome that enemy first and bring ourselves into subjection to the will of the Father, and into strict obedience to the principles of life and salvation which he has given to the world for the salvation of men."[16] If, as is apparent, Brother Marsh had been sufficiently humble and prayerful; if he had conquered himself, and then governed his house in meekness, his fall from his apostolic office would not have happened. But, to the credit of Brother Marsh he later returned to the Church by baptism, some years after his excommunication, confessing his fault when he left the kingdom in following his wife, who later left him. Broken in health and penniless, he was an example of what happens when a person loses the light of truth and enters darkness by his apostasy. (See ". . . From Him Shall Be Taken Even The Light Which He Has Received"—D&C 1:31-33).

---

[15]*Improvement Era*, December 1942, p. 779.
[16]*Conference Report*, October 1914, p. 128.

Chapter 14

"For They Will Hear My Voice, And Shall See Me . . ."
(D&C 35:20-21; 38:7-8; 50:44-46; 88:47-50; 93:1-4).

(A)   And a commandment I give unto thee—that thou shalt write for him; and the scriptures shall be given, even as they are in mine own bosom, to the salvation of mine own elect;

For they will hear my voice, and shall see me, and shall not be asleep, and shall abide the day of my coming; for they shall be purified, even as I am pure.[1]

(B)   But behold, verily, verily, I say unto you that mine eyes are upon you. I am in your midst and ye cannot see me;

But the day soon cometh that ye shall see me, and know that I am; for the veil of darkness shall soon be rent, and he that is not purified shall not abide the day.[2]

(C)   Wherefore, I am in your midst, and I am the good shepherd, and the stone of Israel. He that buildeth upon this rock shall never fall.

And the day cometh that you shall hear my voice and see me, and know that I am;

Watch, therefore, that ye may be ready. Even so. Amen.

(D)   Behold, all these are kingdoms, and any man who hath seen any or the least of these hath seen God moving in his majesty and power.

I say unto you, he hath seen him; nevertheless, he who came unto his own was not comprehended.

The light shineth in darkness, and the darkness comprehendeth it not; nevertheless, the day shall come when you shall comprehend even God, being quickened in him and by him.

Then shall ye know that ye have seen me, that I am, and that I am the true light that is in you, and that you are in me; otherwise ye could not abound.[4]

(E)   Verily, thus saith the Lord: It shall come to pass that every soul who forsaketh his sins and cometh unto me, and calleth on my name, and obeyeth my voice, and keepeth my commandments, shall see my face and know that I am;

---

[1]D&C 35:20-21.
[2]D&C 38:7-8.
[3]*Ibid.*, 50:44-46.
[4]*Ibid.*, 88:47-50.

And that I am the true light that lighteth every man that cometh into the world;

And that I am in the Father, and the Father in me, and the Father and I are one—

The Father because he gave me of his fulness, and the Son because I was in the world and made flesh my tabernacle, and dwelt among the sons of men.[5]

Background of the revelation

(A) This revelation was given for the benefit of Sidney Rigdon, a recent convert from the Cambellite religion. Great blessings are promised him.

(B) Section 38 was received on January 2, 1831. It tells of the doom of the wicked, and of the promise of the "Law" (Section 42) to be received by the Prophet when he arrived at the Ohio.

(C) Section 50 was received as a result of certain spiritual manifestations present in some branches of the Church which were not understood by some of the elders, including Parley P. Pratt. Criteria are given to detect evil spirits.

(D) The Olive Leaf (Section 88) is a doctrinal revelation, the purpose of which is to speak peace to the saints.

(E) Section 93 is one of the wonderful revelations containing marvelous insights into the divinity of Jesus Christ, man's relationship to God, and his eternal nature.

Background of the prophetic promises

(A) The prophecy in Section 35 is preceded by Sidney Rigdon being told that Joseph Smith is the restorer of the Gospel, holding the keys of the mysteries of sealed knowledge.

(B) The prophetic promise in Section 38 begins with the truth that the Lord Jesus Christ is omniscient, the creator of worlds. He received the city of Enoch into his bosom. He is the mediator between God and man and the wicked are kept in chains of darkness until the day of judgment.

---

[5]*Ibid.*, 93:1-4.

(C) The prophecy in Section 50 closes the revelation. Just preceding this promise instructions are given to several elders, all of whom are designated "little children" who are to grow in the knowledge of the truth.

(D) Immediately preceding the prophecy in Section 88 is a discussion of law throughout the universe—"All kingdoms have a law given; And there are many kingdoms . . ." The earth and all the worlds move in their times and seasons. Then, "Unto what shall I liken these kingdoms, that ye may understand?"[6]

(E) The prophetic promise of Section 93 opens the revelation.

Contents of the prophecies and promises

(1) The elect will hear the Lord's voice and see him. (2) They shall abide the coming of Christ. (3) The Lord is in our midst though not seen. (4) To abide the day of the Lord's coming requires purification. (5) To see God's creations is to see him. (6) Jesus is the true light that is in man. (7) By coming unto Christ, forsaking one's sins, keeping his commandments, one shall see him and know him.

Analysis of the prophecies and prophetic promises

In an earlier revelation it is said that the "elect" are those who hear the Lord's voice "and harden not their hearts."[7] To purify one's heart is to so live that the Spirit of the Lord may be one's companion. Missionaries are commanded to "purify your hearts before me" when they go forth to preach. They should so seek for the Spirit in preparation for their missions.[8]

The light which comes from Christ is known as the "light of Christ" which is received by every person in the world.[9]

Although the Lord says that he is in our midst and

---

[6]*Ibid.*, 88:46.
[7]*Ibid.*, 29:7.
[8]*Ibid.*, 112:28; 42:14.
[9]John 1:9; D&C 84:45-48.

his presence is near at all times, it is not essential for salvation for one in this life literally to see him. The Prophet Joseph Smith saw in vision the Twelve Apostles of his day fatigued, feet swollen, eyes downcast, "and Jesus standing in their midst, and they did not behold him. The Savior looked upon them and wept."[10] As the Doctrine and Covenants Commentary says: "He came in like manner as He ascended when He first appeared to the Prophet Joseph, and He has remained with the Church ever since, though invisible except on a few occasions, as, for instance, at the time of the manifestations in the Kirtland Temple"[11]

Fulfillment of the prophecies and prophetic promises

To hear the voice of the Lord is not only actually to hear his voice in an audible revelation, as did the Prophet Joseph Smith concerning the American Civil War. "It may probably arise through the slave question. This a voice declared to me, while I was praying earnestly on the subject, December 25th 1832."[12] A "still small voice" may be felt, as explained by the Prophet: "Yea, thus saith the still small voice, which whispereth through and pierceth all things, and often times it maketh my bones to quake while it maketh manifest, saying:"[13]

Here is still another way in which the voice of the Lord is known: "Verily, verily, I say unto you who now hear my words, which are my voice, blessed are ye inasmuch as you receive these things . . ."[14] Through the Lord's revelations we hear his voice! To the Twelve the Lord said:

"And now I speak unto you, the Twelve . . .

"These words are not of men nor of man, but of me; wherefore, you shall testify they are of me and not of man;

"For it is my voice whch speaketh them unto you; for they are given by my Spirit unto you, and by my power

---

[10]*DHC* 2:381.
[11]Hyrum M. Smith and Janne M. Sjodahl, *Doctrine and Covenants Commentary*, p. 201.
[12]D&C 130:13.
[13]D&C 85:6.
[14]D&C 84:60.

you can read them one to another; and save it were by my power you could not have them;

"Wherefore, you can testify that you have heard my voice, and know my words."[15]

Every member of the Church may testify that he has heard the voice of the Lord if he has a divine testimony of the scriptures!

The promise is given that the day will come when the saints who have kept their covenants will see the Lord. In the prophecies and prophetic promises under consideration one will find these expressions which indicate this thought: (A) ". . . and shall see me, and shall not be asleep, and shall abide the day of my coming . . ." (B) "But the day soon cometh that ye shall see me . . . he that is not purified shall not abide the day." (C) ". . . the day cometh that you shall hear my voice and see me, and know that I am." (D) ". . . the day shall come when you shall comprehend even God . . . Then shall ye know that ye have seen me, that I am . . ." (E) ". . . and keepeth my commandments, shall see my face . . ." "While the Lord made the promise that those who are faithful and true to every covenant may receive the presence of the 'second Comforter,' while still in mortal life, yet this passage implies that those who call upon Him and obey His voice and keep His commandments, shall eventually see Him when their reward for their faithfulness shall come, and they shall dwell in His presence."[16]

To comprehend God, or to know him in the fullest sense, is to be like him as an immortal, exalted Being: "But if ye receive me in the world, then shall ye know me, and shall receive your exaltation; that where I am ye shall be also.

"This is eternal lives—to know the only wise and true God, and Jesus Christ, whom he hath sent. I am he. Receive ye, therefore, my law."[17]

---

[15]D&C 18:31-36.

[16]Hyrum M. Smith and Janne M. Sjodahl, *Doctrine and Covenants Commentary,* p. 588.

[17]D&C 132:23-24.

The prophecy or prophetic promise made in some passages in the Doctrine and Covenants make just such a prediction. At sometime the faithful will see him, but generally, with some exceptions, after the resurrection, and then, they shall know him, for they will be like him. It should be borne in mind also that everyone will not see God or Christ in the spirit world. There are some scriptures which say that the spirits of men go back to God who gave them life. (Alma 40:11; Eccl. 12:7). These passages, however, are interpreted to mean that men and women in the spirit world are in God's presence by his Spirit, but not in his literal presence.[18] It is conceivable that some will see the Lord in the spirit world, but only on the basis of their being prepared, but, to know him in the ultimate sense is to be like him, after the resurrection.[19]

Application of the prophecies and prophetic promises

The faithful saint may see God in mortal life! (See ". . . You Shall See Me And Know That I Am . . ."—D&C 67:10-14; 88:66-68) The true saint may hear the voice of God in this life by "feasting upon the word of Christ" as revealed in the Standard Works of the Church! Enos, the Book of Mormon prophet, had such an experience through prayer: "And while I was thus struggling in the spirit, behold, the voice of the Lord came into my mind again, saying: I will visit thy brethren according to their diligence in keeping my commandments."[20]

The faithful saint will see God and know him and be like him forever and ever! Salvation is an individual matter. The door is open, one need only knock and enter therein. The following personal experience related by Elder Orson F. Whitney was received before he became an apostle of this dispensation:

---

[18]Brigham Young, *Journal of Discourses* 3:368; 4:133; George Q. Cannon, *Gospel Truth*, p. 73.

[19]D&C 76:54-62.

[20]Enos 1:10.

"I seemed to be in the Garden of Gethsemane, a witness of the Savior's agony. I saw Him as plainly as ever I have seen anyone. Standing behind a tree in the foreground, I beheld Jesus, with Peter, James and John, as they came through a little wicket gate at my right. Leaving the three apostles there, after telling them to kneel and pray the Son of God passed over to the other side, where He also knelt and prayed. It was the same prayer with which all Bible readers are familiar; 'Oh my Father, if it be possible let this cup pass from me; nevertheless not as I will, but as thou wilt.'

"As He prayed the tears streamed down His face, which was toward me. I was so moved at the sight that I also wept, out of pure sympathy. My whole heart went out to Him; I loved Him with all my soul, and longed to be with Him as I longed for nothing else.

"Presently He arose and walked to where those apostles were kneeling—fast asleep! He shook them gently, awakened them, and in a tone of tender reproach, untinctured by the least show of anger or impatience, asked them plaintively if they could not watch with Him one hour. There He was, with the awful weight of the world's sin upon His shoulders, with the pangs of every man, woman and child shooting through His sensitive soul— and they could not watch with Him one poor hour!

"Returning to His place, He offered up the same prayer as before; then went back and again found them sleeping. Again He awoke them, readmonished them, and once more returned and prayed. Three times this occurred until I was perfectly familiar with His appearance—face, form and movements. He was of noble stature and majestic mien—not at all the weak, effeminate being that some painters have portrayed; but the very God that He was and is, as meek and humble as a little child.

"All at once the circumstances seemed to change, the scene remaining just the same. Instead of before, it was after the crucifixion, and the Savior, with the three apostles, now stood together in a group at my left. They were about to depart and ascend into Heaven. I could endure it no longer. I ran from behind the tree, fell at His feet, clasped Him around the knees and begged Him to take me with Him.

"I shall never forget the kind and gentle manner in which He stooped, raised me up, and embraced me. It was so vivid! So real! I felt the very warmth of His body, as He held me in His arms and said in tenderest tones; 'No, my son; these have finished their work: they can go with me, but you must stay and finish yours.' Still I clung to Him. Gazing up into His face—for he was taller than I— I besought Him fervently; 'Well, promise me that I will come to you at the last.' Smiling sweetly, He said: '*That will depend entirely upon yourself.* I awoke with a sob in my throat, and it was morning."[21]

---

[21]Orson F. Whitney, *Through Memory's Halls, The Life Story of Orson F. Whitney as Told By Himself,* pp. 81-83.

Chapter 15

"The Elders Of The Church . . . Shall . . . Lay Their Hands Upon Them"
(D&C 42:43-44)

And whosoever among you are sick, and have not faith to be healed, but believe, shall be nourished with all tenderness, with herbs and mild food, and that not by the hand of an enemy.

And the elders of the church, two or more, shall be called, and shall pray for and lay their hands upon them in my name; and if they die they shall die unto me, and if they live they shall live unto me.[1]

Background of the revelation

Section 42 of the Doctrine and Covenants is known as the "Law."[2] It contains several laws unto the Church, as the law of preaching the gospel, of morals, of consecration, administration to the sick, sundry duties, of remuneration for services, and concerning transgressors.

Background of the prophetic promise

The two verses of this prophetic promise begin what is known as the law of administration to the sick. The law of consecration preceding it is the socio-economic order to be lived in the New Jerusalem that the saints may show their genuine concern for their fellow Church members and for the Church. A fundamental principle of the gospel on industry immediately precedes the promise: the idle shall not eat the bread of the laborer.

Contents of the promise

(1) The sick who do not have faith to be healed by the power of God should be administered with herbs (medicine) and food. (2) The elders should be called to pray for the

---

[1] D&C 42:43-44.
[2] Ibid., v. 2.

sick by the laying on of hands. (3) If the person dies, believing, he shall die unto the Lord; otherwise, he shall live unto him.

Analysis of the prophetic promise

Anciently, the practice of laying on of hands for the healing of the sick was admonished by the Apostle James. The elders of the Church are counseled to anoint the patient with oil, and "the prayer of faith shall save the sick."[3]

Although the Doctrine and Covenants does not specify oil in the administration of the sick, its use has come down to us from the organization of the Church. The use of olive oil anciently is well known.[4]

"It was the custom to anoint prophets, kings, and holy messengers as a stamp or token of their official calling. In Leviticus, 8:6-12, is an interesting account of the calling of Aaron, and how Moses not only anointed Aaron, but likewise the altar and the vessels, and sanctified them with holy oil. Samuel also anointed Saul and proclaimed him king of Israel, and when Saul transgressed, David was anointed in his stead to be king of Israel. This custom continued in Israel until they were rejected by the Lord and scattered. . . .

"No other kind of oil will do in anointing. It is very apparent that the oil from animal flesh would never do, and there is no other kind of oil that is held so sacredly and is more suited to the anointing than the oil of olive; moreover, the Lord has placed his stamp of approval on it."[5]

Unto members of the Melchizedek Priesthood, the Lord has given the right to perform this ordinance, others may participate but only by the exercise of their faith.[6] The virtue of elders or other members of the Melchizedek

---

[3]James 5:14-15.
[4]Mark 6:7, 12-13.
[5]Joseph Fielding Smith, *Answers to Gospel Questions*, 1:152-153.
[6]*Ibid.*   , pp. 148-150.

Priesthood performing this ordinance is the power which is resident in the Priesthood. Also, of all persons who should have faith to heal, it is the members of that Priesthood.

Not only is the faith of the administrators required in this ordinance, but also that of the patient. If he has "not faith to be healed, but believe," he should be nourished with herbs and food. Latter-day Saints use the services of doctors; in fact, the Prophet Joseph Smith is on record as having medicines administered to him in addition to the administration by the elders.[7] President Brigham Young considered that the use of remedies should be applied in cases of illnesses:

"If we are sick, and ask the Lord to heal us, and to do all for us that is necessary to be done, according to my understanding of the Gospel of salvation, I might as well ask the Lord to cause my wheat and corn to grow, without my plowing the ground and casting in the seed. It appears consistent to me to apply every remedy that comes within the range of my knowledge, and to ask my Father in Heaven, in the name of Jesus Christ, to sanctify that application to the healing of my body; to another this may appear inconsistent."[8] President Young continued to say that if a person were somewhere where remedies or help were not present, then according to his faith, a request might be made of the Lord to send an angel to heal him.[9]

Fulfillment of the prophetic promise

If all of the cases of healing by the administration of the elders of The Church of Jesus Christ of Latter-day Saints were recorded, they would fill volumes. The Lord has said that signs, one of which is healing the sick, should follow the believer, but "they shall not boast themselves of these things, neither speak them before the world."[10] There are times when it is appropriate, if the Spirit impels,

[7]*DHC* 5:126, 209.
[8]*Journal of Discourses*, 4:24.
[9]*Ibid.*
[10]D&C 84:65-73.

for one to express his gratitude to the Lord for receiving such a blessing. The testimony meeting is one of these times, as well as on occasions when it supports and gives evidence of the truth that the gospel has been restored. Recorded in the history of the Church are many accounts of such times. A notable day of healing occurred on July 22, 1839, as reported by Elder Heber C. Kimball, who said about the Prophet Joseph Smith at Nauvoo, Illinois:

"He commenced with the sick in his own house, then visited those who were camping in tents in his own dooryard, commanding the sick in the name of the Lord Jesus Christ to arise from their beds and be whole; when they were healed according to his words. He then went from house to house, and from tent to tent, upon the bank of the river, healing the sick by the power of Israel's God, as he went among them. He did not miss a single house, wagon or tent, and continued this work up to 'the upper stone house,' where he crossed the river in a boat, accompanied by Parley P. Pratt, Orson Pratt, John E. Page, John Taylor and myself, and landed at Montrose [Iowa]. He then walked into the cabin of Brother Brigham Young, who was lying very sick, commanded him in the name of the Lord Jesus Christ to arise and be made whole. He arose, healed of his sickness, and then accompanied Joseph and his brethren of the Twelve, and went in the house of Brother Elijah Fordham, who was insensible, and considered by his family and friends to be in the hands of death. Joseph stepped to his bedside, looked him in the eye for a minute without speaking, then took him by the hand and commanded him in the name of Jesus Christ to arise from his bed and walk. Brother Fordham immediately leaped out of his bed, threw off all of his poultices and bandages, dressed himself, called for a bowl of bread and milk, which he ate, and then followed us into the street. We then went into the house of Joseph B. Noble, who was also very sick, and he was healed in the same manner."[11]

---

[11]Orson F. Whitney, *Life of Heber C. Kimball*, p. 263.

Throughout the dispensation, the healing power of the Priesthood has been manifest. Elder Orson Pratt published as an evidence of the restoration of miracles, many such occurrences, originally published in the *Millennial Star*, under each of these headings: "The Blind Healed," "Healing of One Born Blind," "Bones Set Through Faith," "Leprosy Healed," "Ruptures Healed," "Fevers Rebuked," "A Case of Miraculous Healing," and "Cholera Healed,"[12]

The writer is a witness of many healings; one of these was the healing of a cancer victim.[13] In company with President George Albert Smith, he heard him read on several occasions to interested friends a United Press newspaper account, datelined Honolulu, February 8, 1944. A war correspondent was going into shore toward the Japanese base at Kwajalein Atoll in the South Pacific as the marines were effecting a landing, two wounded marines were picked up out in the water.

"One, from the stain of red around him, we could tell, was wounded badly; the other wounded too, was holding the other's head above water. We picked them up, midst a hail of shot from shore, then pulled back toward safer retreat to render first aid. The one seemed too far gone to need such help, but the other refused aid until his wounded buddy was attended. But our help seemed insufficient, as we soon realized, and we announced our decision to his comrade. Then it happened.

"This young man, the better of the two, bronzed by the tropical sun, clean as a shark's took in the South Seas, slowly got to his knees. His one arm was nearly gone, but with the other, he lifted the head of his unconscious pal into his lap, placed his good hand on the other's pale brow and uttered what to us seemed to be incredible words— words which to this moment are emblazoned in unforgettable letters across the door of my memory: 'In the name of Jesus Christ, and by virtue of the Holy Priesthood which

---

[12]Orson Pratt, *Orson Pratt's Works*, pp. 261-277.
[13]*Deseret News*, "Church Department," (Salt Lake City), June 20, 1931.

I hold, I command you to remain alive until the necessary help can be obtained to secure the preservation of your life.'

"Today the three of us are here in Honolulu and he is still alive. In fact, we walked down the beach together today, as we convalesce. He is the wonder of the medical unit, for—they say—he should be dead. Why he isn't, they don't know—but we do, for we were there, off the shores of Kwajalein."

The healing of the sick by the Lord's servants is an on going event. Elder Harold B. Lee of the Council of the Twelve, related the following in the April 1960 general conference:

"President David O. McKay, I have been a personal witness in these last six months that, as the apostles of old found, we are finding today that the servants of the Living God are going forth, the Lord is working with them confirming the work, with the same signs following. . . .

"I have witnessed the healing of an impotent and crippled child from birth in the Brazilian Mission. I have witnessed the healing of a blind child in the Central American Mission."[14]

Application of the prophetic promise

Death is a part of the eternal plan of the Father. Jacob taught that death "hath passed upon all men, to fulfill the merciful plan of the great Creator."[15] Death opens the door to a life in the spirit world where the purposes of salvation are continued, followed by the next stage in man's everlasting life, the resurrection. Latter-day Saints are assured of continued life; consequently, death does not have a victory. The promise of the Lord is that death will be sweet unto the faithful.[16] This means that through the Holy Ghost they may have the peace of mind that they are going to the reward for which they worked while in this life. On

---

[14]*Conference Report*, April 1960, p. 109.
[15]2 Nephi 9:6.
[16]D&C 42:46.

the other hand, "they that die not in me, wo unto them, for their death is bitter."[17] To be unprepared to meet God will surely bring regret and bitterness. Mormon's lamentation over the fallen Nephites in the last great battle with the Lamanites reminds one of the eternal truth that all must stand before the judgment-seat of Christ where every man will be rewarded according to justice and mercy.[18]

When, because of lack of sufficient faith, or the appointed time to die has come, Latter-day Saints lose a loved one in death, it is well to remember that "thou shalt weep for the loss of them that die, and more especially for those that have not hope of a glorious resurrection."[19]

When sickness comes, the Lord will bless those who call upon the elders, though the blessing may not be readily apparent.

---

[17]*Ibid.*, v. 47.
[18]Mormon 6:16-22.
[19]D&C 42:45.

Chapter 16

"That Ye May Not Be Deceived Seek Ye Earnestly The Best Gifts . . ."

(D&C 46:8-9; 6:10-11; 8:3-5; 11:10-11).

(A) Wherefore, beware lest ye are deceived; and that ye may not be deceived seek ye earnestly the best gifts, always remembering for what they are given;

For verily I say unto you, they are given for the benefit of those who love me and keep all my commandments, and him that seeketh so to do; that all may be benefited that seek or that ask of me, that ask and not for a sign that they may consume it upon their lusts.[1]

(B) Behold thou hast a gift, and blessed art thou because of thy gift. Remember it is sacred and cometh from above—

And if thou wilt inquire, thou shalt know mysteries which are great and marvelous; therefore thou shalt exercise thy gift, that thou mayest find out mysteries, that thou mayest bring many to the knowledge of the truth, yea, convince them of the error of their ways.[2]

(C) Now, behold, this is the spirit of revelation; behold, this is the spirit by which Moses brought the children of Israel through the Red Sea on dry ground.

Therefore this is thy gift; apply unto it, and blessed art thou, for it shall deliver you out of the hands of your enemies, when, if it were not so, they would slay you and bring your soul to destruction.

Oh, remember these words, and keep my commandments. Remember, this is your gift.[3]

(D) Behold, thou hast a gift, or thou shalt have a gift if thou wilt desire of me in faith, with an honest heart, believing in the power of Jesus Christ, or in my power which speaketh unto thee;

For, behold, it is I that speak; behold, I am the light which shineth in darkness, and by my power I give these words unto thee.[4]

Background of the revelations

(A) Section 46 is known because of the gifts of the Holy Ghost enumerated therein. (B) Within a few days of meet-

---

[1]D&C 46:8-9.
[2]D&C 6:10-11.
[3]D&C 8:3-5.
[4]D&C 11:10-11.

ing Joseph Smith, Oliver Cowdery was given a testimony of the calling of the Prophet through Section 6. (C) Oliver Cowdery is given the gifts of translating and of revelation. (D) Hyrum Smith, the brother of the Prophet, desired to participate in the developing kingdom of God, but he is told to wait until he is formally called to the work.

Background of the prophetic promises

(A) The question of non-members attending Church sacrament meetings was raised, whereupon the Lord revealed that they should not be excluded from public meetings. In addition the "confirmation" meeting is mentioned in this same connection, thereby, leading into the information regarding the gifts of the Holy Ghost.

(B) Oliver Cowdery is told to work for the establishment of Zion, not for riches, for the greatest gift is eternal life. His desires will be recognized, provided he keeps the commandments.

(C) The assurance is given to Oliver Cowdery that if he seeks in faith to know concerning the ancient records (Book of Mormon plates), he shall receive a knowledge of them. (See ". . . They Have Been Shown Unto Me By The Power of God"—D&C 5:25; 17:1-4).

(D) "A great and marvelous work is about to come forth . . ." is the opening thought of Section 11. Hyrum Smith is to keep the commandments and help to establish Zion.

Contents of the prophetic promises

(1) To avoid deception, seek for the best gifts of the Spirit. (2) The gifts are given for the benefit of those who keep the commandments, or seek so to do. (3) He who has a gift should remember the source of that gift. (4) Oliver Cowdery is to exercise his gift that he may bring many to repentance. (5) He is told that he has the gift of revelation which would deliver him out of the hands of his enemies. (6) Hyrum Smith is told that faith in Christ and an honest heart will give him a gift.

Analysis of the prophetic promises

The prophecy that a great and marvelous work was about to come forth among the children of men introduces five revelations received before the Church was organized. (See ". . . A Marvelous Work Is About To Come Forth . . ." —D&C 4:1; 6:1; 11:1; 12:1; 14:1).

From Section 46, we learn that the principal purpose for which the gifts of the Holy Ghost are given is that the member of the Church may not be deceived. This promise is given only to one who has affiliated with God's one and only true Church—those who keep the commandments, for one cannot keep the commandments and remain unbaptized. Also, the Lord admonishes his people to remember the gifts "given unto the church."[5] Peter declared that the Holy Ghost is given to them that obey.[6] By the laying on of hands, the gift of the Holy Ghost is bestowed upon the repentant candidate for salvation.[7] Why, to members of the Church only? Because of the commandment, and also because the gifts are bestowed that will secure the person's salvation, if acted upon, that he may not be condemned in accepting the gift of the atonement and later rejecting it.[8]

The gifts of the Holy Ghost are for those who "keep all my commandments, *and him that seeketh so to do.*" The latter clause provides that although perfection is commanded, help is given through the gifts that perfection might eventually be reached.

The mysteries which Oliver Cowdery was told should be known to him are to convince people of error. If this truth is understood in terms of the context of the revelation, the simple principles and ordinances of the gospel were mysteries. He had only been with the Prophet for a few days, and without the benefit of the Book of Mormon, Doctrine and Covenants, and the Pearl of Great Price, to

---

[5]D&C 46:10.
[6]Acts 5:32.
[7]Acts 2:37-39; D&C 33:10-13; 35:6.
[8]3 Nephi 27:16-17; D&C 82:3.

understand the fundamental teachings of the Gospel, most every principle was a "mystery." In fact, the beginner in Gospel principles today is in the same situation—what he does not know is a mystery though not so to the knowledgeable member of the Church.

Fulfillment of the prophetic promises

Two of the prophetic promises are made to Oliver Cowdery.[9] He learned many of the "mysteries" as he was scribe to the Prophet Joseph Smith in the translation of the Book of Mormon. It was upon one of these occasions that a question was raised concerning baptism. Upon inquiring of the Lord, these two brethren were visited by the resurrected John the Baptist, the forerunner of Christ, and they received the Aaronic Priesthood from him. The true nature and purpose of baptism was learned by them on that occasion. Oliver Cowdery was endowed richly with the gift of revelation as indicated. He was also present with the Prophet when they beheld the Savior, Moses, Elias, and Elijah in the Kirtland Temple on April 3, 1836.[10] He learned that the gift of revelation may not be exercised in opposition to the Prophet of the Church. He commanded the Prophet to delete a part of Section 20, but the Prophet convinced him of his error.[11] Not long after this incident Oliver was in error in accepting false teachings, and the Lord said to him:

"But thou shalt not write by way of commandment, but by wisdom;

"And thou shalt not command him who is at thy head, and at the head of the church;

"For I have given him the keys of the mysteries, and the revelations which are sealed, until I shall appoint unto them another in his stead."[12]

By reason of his knowledge of the "mysteries," Oliver was to bring many to a knowledge of the truth. With

---

[9]D&C 6 and 8.
[10]D&C 110.
[11]*DHC* 1:104-105.
[12]D&C 28:5-7.

Parley P. Pratt, David Whitmer, and Ziba Peterson, he was appointed to the first Lamanite mission of the Church. Although they made some progress with the Indians in Ohio and Missouri, their greatest success was with the non-Lamanites in the Ohio Valley. Their success was instantaneous. Hundreds joined the Church, including many men who later took an important part in the Church.

Hyrum Smith was to receive a gift, provided he would seek it in faith. This gift was the Spirit of Christ "which leadeth to do good—yea, to do justly, to walk humbly, to judge righteously."[13] His biographer, Pearson H. Corbett, has provided the following information about him:

"Hyrum's household included as many as twelve to twenty in all. Out of pity the patriarch continually housed and fed certain elderly and unemployable persons."[14]

"Throughout his life Hyrum reflected the family's kindheartedness toward the poverty-stricken. His hospitality knew no bounds. He would divide his substance with the poor even at the risk of starving his own family. Often he would take someone who was old and infirm into his home to be fed and cared for. His faith was that 'the Lord would provide.' "[15]

"Hyrum arose and in his kindly characteristic way spoke on the attributes of the mercy of God, who influences, controls, and conquers, and the propriety and importance of the Saints exercising the same attributes toward their fellows, especially toward the aged and fellow servants in the cause of truth and righteousness. No one, said Hyrum, should be unjustly accused of wrongdoing. And if someone were suspected of any offense there should be ample time allowed to establish fully his innocence or guilt. A person was innocent until proved guilty."[16]

"If you hear of any one on high authority that he is rather inclined to apostasy, don't let prejudice arise, but

    [13]D&C 11:10-12.
    [14]Pearson H. Corbett, *Hyrum Smith Patriarch*, p. 301 footnote.
    [15]*Ibid.* p. 435.
    [16]*Ibid.* p. 312.

pray for him. God may feel after him, and he may return. Never speak reproachfully or disrespectfully; he is in the hands of God. I am one of those peacemakers who take a stand above these little things. . . . If I have difficulty with a man, I will go and settle it.[17]

"The pathos and grandeur of Joseph and Hyrum's relationship is revealed in Joseph's often expressed love for his older brother. At Kirtland when trouble flared between Joseph and William, the soothing influence of Hyrum caused Joseph to exclaim:

" 'And I pray in my heart that all my brethren were like unto my beloved brother Hyrum, who possesses the mildness of a lamb, and the integrity of a Job, and in short, the meekness and humility of Christ; and I love him with that love that is stronger than death, for I never had occasion to rebuke him nor he me.' "[18]

Three years before his martyrdom, the Lord said of Hyrum: "And again, verily I say unto you, blessed is my servant Hyrum Smith; for I, the Lord, love him because of the integrity of his heart, and because he loveth that which is right before me, saith the Lord."[19]

The gifts of the Holy Ghost are given to those who seek them earnestly. The Lord has said that to the bishop and others ordained to watch over the church, there may be given the power to "discern all those gifts lest there shall be any among you professing and yet be not of God."[20] But, to the "head" "it may be given to have all those gifts . . . in order that every member may be profited thereby."[21] That this promise is given to the Prophet and President of the Church is evident from other revelations.[22]

Elder LeGrand Richards of the Council of the Twelve, related the following experience in the Netherlands Mis-

---

[17]*Ibid.* p. 350.
[18]*Ibid,* p. 439.
[19]D&C 124:15.
[20]D&C 46:27.
[21]*Ibid.* v. 29.
[22]D&C 50:25-27; 107:91-92.

sion when he presided over it, indicating this gift to appointed leaders:

". . . one evening the mission secretary and the president of the Rotterdam District had been out visiting investigators together. On their return the mission secretary invited the district president to stay with him at the mission office. This he consented to do. As was customary with the missionaries, they knelt down for prayers together, and retired to bed. The district president seemed very restless and after a few moments he said to the mission secretary, 'I feel impressed that I should return to the district office.' The mission secretary replied, 'If you feel that way about it, I think you had better go.' With that, the district president arose, redressed himself and returned to the district office, which was at the Church in Rotterdam. He arrived just in time to intercept two men carrying his trunk down the front steps which contained the money of the Rotterdam District, amounting to several hundred dollars."[23]

Without much detail, President David O. McKay gave several experiences which attest to the gifts and blessings which attend the servant of the Lord:

"I knew of his protecting care in the Tongan Islands; for when the vessel was submerged by a mountainous wave, we felt peace and security."[24]

"At Papeete, Tahiti, we knew his guiding hand and acknowledged his overruling providence, when replacing our judgment by his inspiration, he moved us to do something which our own judgment had told us not to do, subsequent events proving that the inspiration came in rich abundance in the priesthood meetings with your boys."[25]

Experiences with the gift of interpretation of tongues in President McKay's life are known to many. In New Zealand President McKay spoke to Maori members of

---

[23]Preston Nibley, *Missionary Experiences*, pp. 306-307.
[24]*Gospel Ideals*, p. 554.
[25]*Ibid.*, p. 555.

the Church, many of whom did not know the English language, but when the interpreter repeated his sermon, some of these same Maoris corrected him in his interpretation.[26]

President Heber J. Grant told the following experience: "I have been happy during the twenty-two years that it has fallen to my lot to stand at the head of this Church. I have felt the inspiration of the living God directing me in my labors. From the day that I chose a comparative stranger to be one of the apostles, instead of my lifelong and dearest living friend, I have known as I know that I live, that I am entitled to the light and the inspiration and the guidance of God in directing His work here upon this earth."[27]

Application of the prophetic promises

Membership in the Church does not automatically endow a person with a gift or gifts of the Holy Ghost. It is that person's right to receive gifts, but the Lord says: "seek ye earnestly the best gifts."[28] What might be best for one individual may not be of paramount value to another, though all gifts are useful.[29] The gifts come by faith.[30] President George Q. Cannon asks the following pertinent questions:

"How many of you are seeking for these gifts that God has promised to bestow? How many of you, when you bow before your Heavenly Father in your family circle or in your secret places, contend for these gifts to be bestowed upon you? How many of you ask the Father in the name of Jesus to manifest Himself to you through these powers and these gifts? Or do you go along day by day like a door turning on its hinges, without having any feeling upon the subject, without exercising any faith whatever, content to be baptized and be members of the Church and to rest

---

[26]*Ibid.*, p. 552.
[27]G. Homer Durham (comp.), *Gospel Standards*, pp. 106-107.
[28]D&C 46:8.
[29]*Ibid.*, v. 11.
[30]Moroni 7:37-38.

there, thinking that your salvation is secure because you have done this?"[31]

On the gift of discernment, President Cannon said:

"One of the gifts of the Gospel which the Lord has promised to those who enter into covenant with Him is the gift of discerning of spirits—a gift which is not much thought of by many and probably seldom prayed for; yet it is a gift that is of exceeding value and one that should be enjoyed by every Latter-day Saint. . . . No Latter-day Saint should be without this gift, because there is such a variety of spirits in the world which seek to deceive and lead astray. . . .

"Now, the gift of discernment of spirits not only gives men and women who have it the power to discern the spirit with which others may be possessed or influenced, but it gives them the power to discern the spirit which influences themselves. They are able to detect a false spirit and also to know when the Spirit of God reigns within them."[32]

Latter-day Saints may well consider seriously the following words from the Lord: "For what doth it profit a man if a gift is bestowed upon him, and he receive not the gift? Behold, he rejoices not in that which is given unto him, neither rejoices in him who is the giver of the gift."[33]

---

[31]George Q. Cannon, *Gospel Truths*, pp. 195-196.

[32]*Ibid.*, 198-199.

[33]D&C 88:33.

Chapter 17

" . . . The Lamanites Shall Blossom As The Rose . . ."
(D&C 49:24; 109:65-66)

(A) But before the great day of the Lord shall come, Jacob shall flourish in the wilderness, and the Lamanites shall blossom as the rose.[1]

(B) And cause that the remnants of Jacob, who have been cursed and smitten because of their transgression, be converted from their wild and savage condition to the fulness of the everlasting gospel:

That they may lay down their weapons of bloodshed, and cease their rebellion.[2]

Background of the revelations

(A) Certain elders are assigned to preach to the "Shaking Quakers," a sect having peculiar doctrines and practices from which Leman Copley had been converted to the Church. The true doctrine of Jesus Christ is given in the revelation that the missionaries might be prepared to teach the Quakers. (B) Section 109 of the Doctrine and Covenants is the dedicatory prayer given at the Kirtland Temple, Kirtland, Ohio, on March 27, 1836. Although expressed in prayer language this section was received by revelation.

Background of the prophecies

(A) The "Shaking Quakers" had several communities in the eastern states, including Ohio. By referring to the Lamanites, the revelation indicates that the interest of the Lord's Church is to be in the Indian people. Immediately before this prophecy, reference is made to the cataclismic conditions which will exist when the Savior comes.

(B) The dedicatory prayer of the Kirtland Temple expresses, among other things, the desire that the gathering

---
[1]D&C 49:24.
[2]D&C 109:65, 66.

of Israel might be realized through the acceptance of the Lord's servants by the rulers of the nations. Immediately preceding this prophecy, a plea is made that the children of Judah might begin to return to their homeland, the lands given to Abraham. (See "The Children of Judah—D&C 109:61-64.)

Contents of the prophecies

(A) (1) The prophecy will be fulfilled before the second coming of Christ (2) Jacob (Israel), who is identified in the prophecy as the Lamanite, will flourish in the wilderness and blossom as the rose.

(B) (1) The Lamanites are "remnants of Jacob," according to the Book of Mormon.[3] (2) The Lamanites (American Indian) have been smitten by the gentiles occupying the land of America. (3) They shall be converted to the fulness of the gospel which will bring about a peaceful existence for them.

Book of Mormon facts and prophecies

Prophets upon this continent during the Book of Mormon period of the Nephites and Lamanites (600 B.C.—421 A.D.), reveal the destruction of the Nephite civilization because of their transgressions.[4] With the amalgamation of the Nephites and Lamanites, who were a light-skinned civilized and dark-skinned savage people, respectively, for almost two hundred years during the "short-term millennium" on this continent following the resurrected Savior's visit on this continent, these names took on a different meaning.[5] The Nephites were the true believers in Christ while the Lamanites rejected the gospel.[6] Thus, when the Lamanites survived the great civil war, they, and their descendants were of Lamanite-Nephite lineage. The promise was given to Joseph, son of Lehi, that his

[3]1 Nephi 5:14; 2 Nephi 28:2; Alma 46:23; Mormon 7:10.
[4]Mormon 6; Moroni 8:27-29; 9.
[5]4 Nephi.
[6]4 Nephi vs. 35-39.

seed would not be utterly destroyed for from his fore-
bear, Joseph of Egypt, there would come a seer of the
latter days [Joseph Smith] who would do a work for the
salvation of the seed of Nephi, son of Lehi.[7]

The prophets of the Book of Mormon foresaw the
time (1) when the remnants of Jacob in the last days would
come to know of their Israelitish lineage through the
Book of Mormon and the gospel of Jesus Christ would be
taught them.[8] (2) They were to become a "dark, a filthy,
and a loathsome people" as already indicated in the Doctrine and Covenants prophecy.[9] (3) Their scales of darkness would be removed, and they would become a "white
and delightsome people."[10] (4) The great American nation
would be raised up by the Gentiles, who shall scatter the
Lamanites, but a marvelous work would be performed
among the Gentiles for the Lamanites.[11] (5) The Lamanites are to assist in the building of the New Jerusalem to be built in Jackson County, Missouri.[12]

Fulfillment of the prophecies in the Doctrine and Covenants

The Lord has declared that these are the days preceding the second coming of Christ.[13] After the discovery
of America, four hundred years of persecution, robbing,
and the killing of the Indians on the North and South American continents followed. In South America Cortez and
other conquerors ravaged and despoiled the natives and
killed thousands of them. In the United States the Lamanites were pushed westward until they were placed on government reservations which would hardly sustain life.

For some time it appeared that the Indians would become a vanishing race. Elder Rey L. Pratt, a member of
the First Council of the Seventy in this dispensation, said:

[7] 2 Nephi 3:1-7; D. & C. 3:17; Alma 45:9-14.
[8] 2 Nephi 30:3-5.
[9] Mormon 5:15.
[10] 2 Nephi 30:6.
[11] 1 Nephi 22:6-9.
[12] 3 Nephi 21:20-25; Joseph Fielding Smith, *Doctrines of Salvation*, 2:250-251.
[13] D&C 1:11-14, 34-36; 29:7-11.

"I would like to refer to statistics that reveal the fact that since the coming of the Spanish conquerors among the Indian people—at least speaking of those south of the Rio Grande, clear on through Mexico and down to Central and South America—nine-tenths of them have succumbed. That is in a period of about four hundred years. Mathematically calculating it would not take long for the other one-tenth to be wiped out, for it seems that the same condition of strife and war and blood shed prevails among them. Looking at it naturally it almost looks as though not even a remnant of them might be left. But in this respect, and in order that my faith may not falter, I take courage from the word of the Lord as it came to Nephi concerning this very thing. 'Nevertheless, thou beholdest that the Gentiles who have gone forth out of captivity, and have been lifted up by the power of God above all other nations, upon the face of the land which is choice above all other lands, which is the land that the Lord God hath covenanted with thy father that his seed should have for the land of their inheritance; wherefore, thou seest that the Lord God will not suffer that the Gentiles will utterly destroy the mixture of thy seed, which are among thy brethren.

" 'Neither will he suffer that the Gentiles shall destroy the seed of thy brethren.' "

With the restoration of the fulness of the Gospel of Jesus Christ and his Church, the time came for the Gentiles to bring a new day to the Indians.

Since 1830, when the first Lamanite mission of the dispensation was started with the call of Elder Parley P. Pratt, Ziba Peterson, and Oliver Cowdery to preach to the Indians in New York, Ohio, and Missouri, the Church has endeavored to fulfill its responsibilities to these people.[15]

President Wilford Woodruff quoted the Prophet Joseph Smith as prophesying in 1832 the following about

---

[14]*Conference Report*, April 1929, pp. 75-76.

[15]D. & C. 28:8-10; 30:5-6; Parley P. Pratt, *Autobiography of Parley Parker Pratt*, pp. 49-59.

the activities of the Church which would fill the Rocky Mountains: "There will be tens of thousands of Latter-day Saints who will be gathered in the Rocky Mountains, and there they will open the door for the establishing of the Gospel among the Lamanites, who will receive the Gospel and their endowments and the blessings of God.[16]

In 1841 the Prophet Joseph Smith preached to many Indian chiefs and their people. The Prophet advised them to become a peaceful people in forsaking their warlike ways. His message did not fall upon deaf ears.[17]

When the saints settled in the West, there were periods when large numbers of Indians accepted the gospel in Idaho and Utah Territory. On December 25, 1925, Elder Melvin J. Ballard of the Council of the Twelve, dedicated the land of South America with these words.

". . . I turn the key, unlock, and open the door for the preaching of the gospel in all these South American nations, and rebuke, and command to be stayed, every power that would oppose the preaching of the gospel in these lands. And we do bless and dedicate these nations, and this land for the preaching of the gospel . . ."[18]

When Latter-day Saints think of the descendants of Father Lehi, who brought a colony by divine direction to the American continent and began the Book of Mormon record, they include the natives on the islands of Polynesia, as well as the aborigines of the American continent. A Nephite by the name of Hagoth sailed from this continent about B.C. 50 with men, women and children, but they were never heard of again.[19] Jacob, a Book of Mormon prophet, said: "But great are the promises of the Lord unto them who are upon the isles of the sea; wherefore as it says isles, there must needs be more than this, and they are inhabited also by our brethren."[20]

---

[16]*Conference Report*, April 1898, p. 57.
[17]*DHC* 4:401-412.
[18]*Improvement Era*, April 1926, pp. 575-576.
[19]Alma 63:5-8.
[20]2 Nephi 10:21.

Shortly after World War II, President George Albert Smith appointed Elder Matthew Cowley, Spencer W. Kimball of the Council of the Twelve, and President Antone R. Ivins of the First Council of the Seventy, to constitute a committee to give attention to the problems of the Lamanite. Since that time under the leadership of Elder Spencer W. Kimball, who for many years has directed the work among the Lamanite, the following programs are in operation: (1) The Lamanite Seminary Program is a religious education program to provide training in the teachings of the Gospel of Jesus Christ. Seventy-five percent of the classroom teachers are full-time Latter-day Saint missionaries. In 1967 there were 14,259 Lamanite young people registered in the program. (2) The Lamanite Student Placement Program gives Lamanite children from eight years and over an opportunity for educational, spiritual, social, and cultural advantages in Latter-day Saint homes during the school year. The children return to the homes of their natural parents during the summer. In 1968, there were 3,132 children enrolled in the program in the following places: Utah, Arizona, Idaho, Washington, California, Colorado, Georgia, and Western Canada. Each year since 1949 the number of children in individual homes has increased. (3) The Brigham Young University Lamanite Education Program is to foster in a university environment a comprehensive educational program to meet the individual needs, abilities, and educational objectives of the Lamanites together with the promotion of better relationships and understanding between them and non-Lamanite students. (4) Brigham Young University Institute of Lamanite Research and Services assembles information on every phase of Indian culture, and cooperates with Lamanite leadership in the promotion of self-help programs for the material and cultural advancement of the Lamanites. (Information furnished by Stewart A. Durrant, Secretary to the Latter-day Saint Lamanite Committee.)

Conversions among the Lamanites is very high, with

25 missions in the United States, Canada, Mexico, Central America, South America and Polynesia. In 1952 there were 2,500 baptisms with approximately 45,000 Lamanites on the records of the Church.[21] Convert baptisms among these people have increased over the years. In 1968 there were 13,800, or 5.5 times more in that year than in the year 1952!

What is meant in the prophecy that the Lamanite will "flourish in the wilderness," and "shall blossom as the rose"? Nephi predicted the time when they would be a "white and delightsome people."[22] During Book of Mormon history the Lamanites' "skin became white like unto the Nephites."[23] Elder J. M. Sjodahl gave an answer to the question of the meaning "delightsome," as follows:

"The prophecy in 2 Nephi 30:6 should be compared with Words of Mormon, v. 8, where the inspired author says he prays that his brethren may again 'be a delight-some people;' also with Mormon 5:17, where it is said that the Lamanites 'were once a delightsome people,' and with Moroni 9:12, where the prophet says they had once been a 'civil and a delightsome people.' For these passages, by not mentioning the color of the skin, prove that the principal thought in the expression 'white and delightsome' is centered in the change of disposition, as well as in the complexion."[24]

From the "Apostle to the Lamanites," Elder Spencer W. Kimball, we learn the following:

"The Lamanites must rise in majesty and power. We must look forward to the day when they will be "white and delightsome," sharing the freedoms and blessings which we enjoy; when they shall have economic security, culture, refinement, and education; when they shall be operating farms and businesses and industries and shall be occupied in the professions and in teaching; when they

[21]*Conference Report*, April 1953, p. 107.
[22]2 Nephi 30:6.
[23]3 Nephi 2:15.
[24]J. M. Sjodahl, *An Introduction to the Study of the Book of Mormon*, p. 225.

shall be organized into wards and stakes of Zion, furnishing much of their own leadership; when they shall build and occupy and fill the temples, and serve in them as the natives are now serving in the Hawaiian Temple where I found last year the entire service conducted by them and done perfectly . . . Brothers and sisters, the florescence of the Lamanites is in our hands."[25]

About fifteen years later Elder Kimball gave this report:

"Not only the southwest Indians, but Lamanites in general, are facing an open door to education, culture, refinement, progress, and the gospel of Jesus Christ. The Church has spent its millions in Hawaii and New Zealand and other islands to provide schools for the young Lehites. Surely, no descendants need go now without an education, and schools in Mexico will be followed by schools in other nations. Surely the number of deprived ones is being reduced, and opportunity is knocking at their door. Hundreds of Lamanites are serving in mission fields in both Americas and in the islands of the sea. Lamanites are exercising their priesthood and rearing their families in righteousness. A new world is open to them, and they are grasping the opportunities. God bless the Lamanites and hasten the day of their total emancipation from the thraldom of their yesterday."[26]

Application of the prophecies

The Lord promised Jacob that a branch of his people would migrate to a promised land, which the Book of Mormon identifies as America. Many other rich promises were made to Lehi's descendants, most of which were to find fulfillment in the last days. That day is here; they are flourishing and blossoming, becoming delightsome, as never before in a modern period.

---

[25]*Conference Report*, October 1947, p. 22.
[26]*Conference Report*, October 1960, p. 37.

". . . the florescence of the Lamanites is in our hands." Elder Kimball has provided us with the following information concerning Lamanite needs and Latter-day Saint opportunities:

"This day of the Lamanites brings opportunity. Millions farm the steep hillsides of Andean ranges and market their produce with llamas and horses and burros. They must have the emancipating gospel. Millions serve in menial labor, eke out bare subsistence from soil and toil. They must hear the compelling truths of the gospel. Millions are tied to reservations, deprived, untrained, and less than they could be. They must have the enlightening gospel. It will break their fetters, stir their ambition, increase their vision, and open new worlds of opportunity to them. Their captivity will be at an end—captivity from misconceptions, illiteracy, superstition, fear . . .

"The brighter day has dawned. The scattering has been accomplished; the gathering is in process. May the Lord bless us that we may become nursing fathers and mothers (see Isa. 49:23 and 1 Nephi 21:23) unto our Lamanite brethren and hasten the fulfillment of the great promise made to them . . ."[27]

---

[27]*Conference Report*, October 1965, p. 72.

Chapter 18

"Zion Shall Flourish Upon The . . . Mountains . . ."
(D&C 49:25)

Zion shall flourish upon the hills and rejoice upon the mountains, and shall be assembled together unto the place which I have appointed.[1]

Background of the revelation

This revelation was given for the benefit of several missionaries assigned to teach the United Society of Believers in Christ's Second Appearing, commonly called the Shaking Quakers. Many doctrines of importance are given in refutation of their teachings.

Background of the prophecy

Among the doctrines preceding the prophecy are: Repentance, baptism, and the laying on of hands for the Holy Ghost as necessary for salvation; marriage is ordained of God; meat is good for man; Jesus comes not in the form of a woman nor of a man traveling upon the earth. Immediately preceding verse 25 is the prophecy that the Lamanites are to blossom as a rose, and Israel is to flourish. (See "The Lamanites Shall Blossom As The Rose." —D&C 49:24; 109:65-66).

Contents of the prophecy

(1) Zion will flourish upon the hills and mountains. (2) She shall assemble to the appointed place.

Analysis of the prophecy

Zion is a word of several meanings. It was the name of the Old Jerusalem and its holy mount[2] and the ancient city of Enoch, which was taken into heaven to return in

---

[1]D&C 49:25.
[2]2 Kings 19:21; Psalm 48; Isaiah 8:18; 24:23.

this dispensation.[3] Zion is North and South America, according to the Prophet Joseph Smith.[4] The New Jerusalem to be built in Missouri is also known as the city of Zion.[5] The meaning, however, intended for the prophecy is the "pure in heart" and the Church of Jesus Christ of Latter-day Saints wherein they have membership.[6]

The "hills and mountains" in D&C 49:25, has reference to a mountainous country, comparable to the prophecy mentioned in the Old Testament where the house of the Lord would be built in the last days.[7]

As indicated, Section 49, is a refutation of the teachings of the Shaking Quakers. One might wonder why reference is made to a sojourn of God's true Church in the mountainous area because they were then in the East. The reason seems clear in that the Shaking Quakers had established their communities in the Eastern States; consequently, the Lord was telling the missionaries to tell these people that the gathering place of his people would be in the West and not in the East.

Fulfillment of the prophecy

That the Rocky Mountain area where the saints settled after the martyrdom of the Prophet Joseph Smith and his brother Hyrum, the Patriarch, would be the resting place of the saints was foretold by the Prophet Joseph Smith on August 6, 1842:

"I prophesied that the Saints would continue to suffer much affliction and would be driven to the Rocky Mountains, many would apostatize, others would be put to death by our persecutors or lose their lives in consequence of exposure or disease, and some of you will live to go and assist in making settlements and build cities and see the

---

[3]Moses 7:19, 21; D&C 45:11-14.
[4]*DHC* 6:318-319.
[5]Ether 13:2-11.
[6]D&C 97:21; 105:32; 2 Nephi 26:29-32.
[7]Isaiah 2:2-3; Micah 4:1-2.

Saints become a mighty people in the midst of the Rocky Mountains."[8]

On February 25, 1844, the Prophet made this remarkable prophecy: "I gave instructions and prophesied that within five years we would be out of the power of our enemies, whether they were apostates, or of the world, and told the brethren to record it, that when it comes to pass, they cannot say they had forgotten the saying."[9]

Five years from 1844, the saints had begun to settle the Rocky Mountain area, where their enemies had no power over them.

Upon the testimony of President Wilford Woodruff in 1832, the Prophet predicted that the Church would eventually "fill the Rocky Mountains;" in fact, he said, it would "fill North and South America—it will fill the world." He predicted that in the Rocky Mountains the saints would build temples, and that the Savior would come to them while yet in the mountainous area.[10] The growth of the Church indicates the onward growth of the Church destined to fill the earth. (See "Triumph Of The Kingdom of God"—D&C 103:5-8).

The interpretation and fulfillment of this prophecy concerning Zion flourishing on the hills and mountains is indicated in this commentary: "The Latter-day Saints, it is hardly necessary to say, by their location in the Rocky Mountains and their prosperity, are an irrefutable proof of the truth of the second part of the prophecy (D&C 49:25)."[11]

Application of the prophecy

The application of this prophecy and others given by the Prophet is expressed by President Joseph F. Smith, as follows:

---

[8]*DHC* 5:85.
[9]*DHC* 6:225.
[10]*Conference Report*, April 1898, p. 57.
[11]Hyrum M. Smith and Janne M. Sjodahl, *Doctrine and Covenants Commentary*, p. 287.

"Zion is, indeed, flourishing on the hills, and is rejoicing on the mountains, and we who compose it are gathering and assembling together unto the place appointed. I now ask this congregation if they cannot see that this prediction, (which was made many years before the idea prevailed at all among this people that we should ever migrate and gather out to these mountain valleys), has been and is literally being fulfilled? If there were no other prophecy uttered by Joseph Smith, fulfillment of which could be pointed to, this alone would be sufficient to entitle him to the claim of being a true Prophet."[12]

A prophecy, reserved for another volume on Doctrine and Covenants prophecies and prophetic promises, is the following:

"For, behold, I say unto you that Zion shall flourish, and the glory of the Lord shall be upon her;

"And she shall be an ensign unto the people, and there shall come unto her out of every nation under heaven.

"And the day shall come when the nations of the earth shall tremble because of her, and shall fear because of her terrible ones. The Lord hath spoken it. Amen."[13]

Latter-day Saints are the carriers of that ensign to the nations, provided they live in accordance with the standards of the Gospel of Jesus Christ. It was Ezekiel the Prophet who saw the time in the last days when the people of the world would know the God of Heaven by the lives of those who represented him.[14] As President J. Reuben Clark, a member of the First Presidency of this dispensation, said regarding the descendants of the pioneers who colonized the Rocky Mountain area:

"In living our lives let us never forget that the deeds of our fathers and mothers are theirs, not ours; that their works cannot be counted to our glory; that we can claim no excellence and no place, because of what they did, that we must rise by our own labor, and that labor failing we

---

[12]*Journal of Discourses* 25:97-98.
[13]D&C 64:41-43.
[14]Ezekiel 36:22-24.

shall fail. We may claim no honor, no reward, no respect, nor special position or recognition, no credit because of what our fathers were or what they wrought. We stand upon our own feet in our own shoes. There is no aristocracy of birth in this Church; it belongs, equally to the highest and the lowliest; for as Peter said to Cornelius, the Roman centurion, seeking him:

" '. . . Of a truth I perceive that God is no respecter of persons: But in every nation he that feareth him, and worketh righteousness, is accepted with him.' (Acts 10:24-35).

"So to these humble but great souls, our fathers and mothers, the tools of the Lord, who have, for this great people, hewed the stones and laid the foundations of God's kingdom, solid as the granite mountains from which they carved the rocks for their temple, to these humble souls, great in faith, great in work, great in righteous living, great in fashioning our priceless heritage, I humbly render my love, my respect, my reverent homage. God keep their memories ever fresh among us, their children, to help us meet our duties even as they met theirs, that God's work may grow and prosper till the restored gospel of Jesus Christ rules all nations and all peoples, till peace, Christ's peace, shall fill the whole earth, till 'righteousness shall cover the earth even as the waters cover the mighty deep.' Let us here and now dedicate all that we have and all that we are to this divine work."[15]

---

[15]*Conference Report*, October 1947, p. 160.

Chapter 19

". . . The Covenant . . . They Made Unto Me Has Been Broken . . . It Has Become Void . . ."
(D&C 54:4-6; 82:21; 84:41; 104:4-9)

(A) As has the covenant which they made unto me has been broken, even so it has become void and of none effect.

And wo to him by whom this offense cometh, for it had been better for him that he had been drowned in the depth of the sea.

But blessed are they who have kept the covenant and observed the commandment, for they shall obtain mercy.[1]

(B) And the soul that sins against this covenant, and hardeneth his heart against it, shall be dealt with according to the laws of my church, and shall be delivered over to the buffetings of Satan until the day of redemption.[2]

(C) But whoso breaketh this covenant after he hath received it, and altogether turneth therefrom, shall not have forgiveness of sins in this world nor in the world to come.[3]

(D) Therefore, inasmuch as some of my servants have not kept the commandment, but have broken the covenant through covetousness, and with feigned words, I have cursed them with a very sore and grievous curse.

For I, the Lord, have decreed in my heart, that inasmuch as any man belonging to the order shall be found a transgressor, or, in other words, shall break the covenant with which ye are bound, he shall be cursed in his life, and shall be trodden down by whom I will;

For I, the Lord, am not to be mocked in these things—

And all this that the innocent among you may not be condemned with the unjust; and that the guilty among you may not escape; because I, the Lord, have promised unto you a crown of glory at my right hand.

Therefore, inasmuch as you are found transgressors, you cannot escape my wrath in your lives.

Inasmuch as ye are cut off for transgression, ye cannot escape the buffetings of Satan until the day of redemption.[4]

---

[1] D&C 54:4-6.
[2] *Ibid.*, 82:21.
[3] *Ibid.*, 84:41.
[4] *Ibid.*, 104:4-9.

Background of the revelations

(A) Section 54 was given for the benefit of Newell Knight, who represented the Thompson (Ohio) Branch of the Church, due to some difficulties which had developed regarding the law of consecration.

(B) Section 82 was received at a general council of the Church held in Jackson County, Missouri, April 26, 1832. Matters relating to the order of Enoch were revealed.

(C) On September 22 and 23, 1832, the Prophet received Section 84 for the immediate benefit of some elders who had returned from their missions in the eastern states. It is a Priesthood revelation.

(D) Section 104, received April 23, 1834, is concerned with the United Order, which was to assist the poor of the Church.

Background of the prophetic promises

(A) Newell Knight is told to remain in his office in the branch at Thompson. The members of the Church there were told to repent of their sins if they expected to escape from their enemies.

(B) The prophetic promise in Section 82 is preceded by two pertinent and universal truths regarding the consequences of sinning against knowledge[5] and that when a member of the Church obeys the Lord's law, the Lord will bless him.[6] In the order providing for the needy under the system of stewardships, each was to have equal claims on the property, according to wants which were just. Thus men were asked to improve upon their talents that the Lord's storehouse might be full. Every man was to seek for the interest of his neighbor.

(C) The temple in Jackson County, Missouri, was to be built in this generation. A listing of men who held the Priesthood anciently from Moses to Adam is given. The powers of the Melchizedek Priesthood for exaltation are

---

[5]*Ibid.*, 82:3.
[6]*Ibid.*, v. 10.

given, with emphasis upon the dispensation of Moses. The sons of Moses (Levites) will offer a sacrifice to the Lord in his temple in this dispensation. The importance of the meaning of the oath and covenant of the Higher Priesthood immediately precedes the prophetic promise.

(D) Commandments had been given for the establishment of the order which would help the Church and men in obtaining their salvation. If faithful, men would be blessed.

Contents of the prophetic promises

(1) Wo is pronounced upon those who break the covenant. (2) Their condemnations are: (a) It would have been better to have been drowned in the sea; (b) Shall be dealt with according to the laws of the Church; (c) Delivered over to the buffetings of Satan until the day of redemption; (d) Cursed with a sore and grievous curse; (e) Shall not have forgiveness of sins in this world nor in the world to come; (f) He shall be cursed in this life with the Lord's wrath. (3) Those who keep the covenants are blessed: (a) For they shall obtain mercy; (b) A crown of glory awaits them.

Analysis of the prophetic promises

All of the prophetic promises, except one, were given in relationship to the law of consecration, which was instituted in 1831 primarily to take care of the poor. This socio-economic order provided for a system of stewardships determined by the wants and needs, of the family according to their circumstances.[7] The stewardship was received after the head of the family had consecrated all his belongings to the Church. The surplus from working the stewardship was to be placed into the Bishop's storehouse for the benefit of the Church and for those who did not have stewardships, and for other purposes. The order of Enoch, or United Order, was an inferior law where only a partial consecration was required.

---

[7] *Ibid.,* 51:3.

The exception to the background to these orders was the penalty of altogether turning away from the oath and covenant of the Melchizedek Priesthood (Section 84). The penalty is no forgiveness of sins. The meaning of this penalty is as follows: "This means that all who treat this covenant of the Priesthood with contempt shall never have the privilege of exercising it in the world to come. Therefore they will be barred from celestial exaltation."[8]

A covenant is a contract, an agreement, binding upon both parties to the covenant. The fulness of the Gospel of Jesus Christ is known as the "new and everlasting covenant."[9] Covenants are made in baptism, which are renewable in partaking of the sacrament.[10] Men who are ordained to the Melchizedek Priesthood receive an "oath and covenant."[11] Marriage in the temple is a covenant ordinance.[12]

The condemnations upon the covenant breaker are not only for this life but also for the life to come. The Lord has promised that they who keep their covenants will find rich blessings in this life, and they will also find a place with him in the celestial worlds.

Fulfillment of the prophetic promises

The members of the Church from Colesville, New York, were commanded to settle in Thompson, Ohio, that they might have the privilege of living the law of consecration, recently given to the Church by revelation.[13] The prophetic promise in Section 54, is about this branch of the Church.

Although sufficient information is not available to know exactly why these saints were in transgression, "it is evident that some of the brethren already living at

---

[8]Hyrum M. Smith and Janne M. Sjodahl, *Doctrine and Covenants Commentary*, p. 507.

[9]D&C 45:9.

[10]*Ibid.*, 20:72-79.

[11]*Ibid.*, 84:39-41.

[12]*Ibid.*, 132:15.

[13]D&C 51; 42:30-42.

Thompson, had agreed to enter into the law of consecration and stewardship with the Saints from Colesville; and that afterwards they broke this covenant. Among these brethren were Leman Copley and Ezra Thayre."[14] About Brother Copley, we learn: " 'A man by the name of Copley,' says Newel Knight in his journal, 'had a considerable tract of land there (in Thompson) which he offered to let the Saints occupy. Consequently a contract was agreed upon, and we commenced work in good faith. But in a short time Copley broke the engagement, and I went to Kirtland to see Brother Joseph,' etc. . . Of this matter, John Whitmer, then the Church Historian, writes: 'At this time (the early part of June) the Church at Thompson, Ohio, was involved in difficulty because of the rebellion of Leman Copley, who would not do as he had previously agreed, which thing confused the whole Church, and finally the Lord spake through Joseph the Prophet, saying: 'He then quotes the revelation to Newel Knight given in the text above.' " [Section 54].[15]

From the information just given, it appears that Leman Copley, a convert to the Church from the Shaking Quakers and who at one time testified in court against the Prophet but later repented, was primarily responsible for the difficulties which arose in the Thompson Branch. By his breaking the agreement with the saints, the little group was thrown into confusion. What happened to Leman Copley is presently unknown. Nothing is said about repentance on his part after this time. As fas as church history is concerned, his name does not appear again. He went into oblivion. The judgment day will reveal whether or not he receives the condemnation mentioned in the prophetic promise.

The case of Ezra Thayre is different. According to what is known about his part in the problem in the Thompson Branch, we are informed that he made a covenant for

---

[14]*DHC* 1:180.
[15]*Ibid.*, 1:180-181, footnote.

the Church to use his land for which he would receive
compensation. He attempted to repudiate this contract,
and thus came under condemnation.[16] The Lord extended
to Brother Thayer the opportunity to repent of his "pride,
and of his selfishness."[17] If he repented, he was to go with
the saints to Missouri; if not he should be paid in accordance with the agreement, and be cut off the Church.[18]

Ezra Thayre repented and remained active in the
Kingdom, participating in several missions. He was a
member of a stake High Council, and also a member of
Zion's Camp. The condemnations pronounced upon him
were apparently set aside by his repentance.

In Sections 82 and 104, where instructions are given
concerning the Order of Enoch, or United Order, condemnations are pronounced upon those who break the
covenants of these orders. In verse 11 of Section 82 the
uncommon names of nine men who were to enter this order
in Jackson County, Missouri, are given. The names of five
of these brethren are shown in parenthesis, printed in the
revelation after the need to keep their names secret had
passed away. The names are: Newel K. Whitney, Sidney
Rigdon, Joseph Smith, Oliver Cowdery, and Martin Harris. The following testimony of Orson Pratt pertains to
Sections 82 and 104 and Jackson County:

"Therefore when I speak of the Order of Enoch, I
do not mean the order of ancient Enoch, I mean the Order
that was given to Joseph Smith in 1832-3-4, which is a
law inferior to the celestial law, because the celestial law
required the consecration of all that a man had. The law
of Enoch only required a part. The law of consecration
in full required that all the people should consecrate everything that they had; and none were exempt. The law of
Enoch called upon certain men only to consecrate.

"Now did the people keep this second law—inferior
to the first? The Lord picked out some of the best men

16*Ibid.*, 1:188, footnote.
17D&C 56:8.
18*Ibid.*, vs. 9-11.

in the Church, and tried them if they would keep it. 'Now I will,' says he, 'try the best men I have in the Church, not with the celestial law, but they shall consecrate in part, and have a common stock property among them.' And in order to stir them up to diligence, he fixed certain penalties to this law, such as, He shall be delivered up to the buffeting of Satan; sins that have been remitted shall return to him and be answered upon his head. How did they get along then? The Lord tells us that the covenant had been broken. Consequently, it remained with him to do with them as seemed to him good. Many have apostatized since that day; Sidney Rigdon for one, Oliver Cowdery for another, and John Johnson for another. Why have they apostatized? They did not comply with the covenant that they made in regard to the law given to Joseph Smith, that was afterwards called the law of Enoch."[19]

Application of the prophetic promises

The overriding lesson from these experiences in our early Church history and the revelations is the need to keep the covenants entered into with the Lord. As an authoritative commentary on Section 104 states: "Some of those who were called to become members of the United Order entered into covenants, as required, but soon broke their pledges because of covetousness (v. 4). Over these the wrath of God hovered as a thunder cloud; they might be destroyed by the enemy at any time (v. 5). Transgressors were to be cut off from the Order, for the protection of the innocent (v. 7), and when they were cut off, the adversary had power over them (v. 10)."[20]

One of the prophetic promises stated that if a person hardens his heart against a covenant, he should be dealt with according to the laws of the Church.[21] In some of the cases mentioned, the individual repented, and was thereby brought back into Church activity, as for example,

---

[19]*Journal of Discourses* 16:156.

[20]Hyrum M. Smith and Janne M. Sjodahl, *Doctrine and Covenants Commentary*, pp. 669-670.

[21]D&C 82:21.

Ezra Thayer. There are occasions, however, when repentance did not always return a person to his former position. (See "Pray Always Lest You. . .Lose Your Reward" —D&C 31:12; 61:39; 10:5; 93:49).

To transgress and fall away from the Church after making covenants with the Lord is severely condemned in the revelations.[22] The severity of the punishment is contingent upon the character of the covenant, and the person making the covenant because: "For of him unto whom much is given much is required; and he who sins against the greater light shall receive the greater condemnation."[23]

We are in this earth life to be proved. Each person is to remain faithful in all things, whether he "will abide in my covenant, even unto death, that you may be found worthy. . . ." and "if ye will not abide in my covenant ye are not worthy of me."[24] Covenants may be made, and covenants may be voided by the Lord. He has said that when men do not obey, they receive not the blessing. It is then that some complain that the Lord has failed in his promises, but their reward "lurketh beneath, and not from above."[25] Toward the end of the Prophet's ministry, the Lord revealed: "For behold, I reveal unto you a new and everlasting covenant; and if ye abide not that covenant, then are ye damned; for no one can reject this covenant and be permitted to enter into my glory.

"For all who will have a blessing at my hands shall abide the law which was appointed for that blessing, and the conditons thereof, as were instituted from before the foundation of the world."[26]

The word of the Lord to his saints is: "Verily I say unto you, all among them who know their hearts are honest, and are broken, and their spirits contrite, and are

---

[22]*Ibi   d.*, 56:1.
[23]*Ibid.*, 82:3.
[24]*Ibid.*, 98:14-15.
[25]*Ibid.*, 58:30-33.
[26]*Ibid.*, 132:4-5.

willing to observe their covenants by sacrifice—yea, every sacrifice which I, the Lord, shall command—they are accepted of me."[27] President Brigham Young gave counsel in the following passage that should cause every member of the Church to consider carefully his relationship to the covenants into which he has entered:

"Now, you Elders who understand the principles of the kingdom of God, what would you not give, or sacrifice, to assist in building up His kingdom upon the earth? Says one, 'I would do anything in my power, anything that the Lord would help me to do, to build up his kingdom'. Says another, 'I would sacrifice all my property,' Wonderful indeed! Do you not know that the possession of your property is like a shadow, or the dew of the morning before the noon-day sun, that you cannot have any assurance of its control for a single moment! It is the unseen hand of Providence that controls it. In short, what would you not sacrifice? The Saints sacrificed everything; but, strictly speaking, there is no sacrifice about it. If you give a penny for a million of gold! a handful of earth for a planet! a temporary worn out tenement for one glorified, that will exist, abide, and continue to increase throughout a never ending eternity, what a sacrifice to be sure!"[28]

---

[27] *Ibid.*, 98:8.
[28] *Journal of Discourses* 1:114.

Chapter 20

". . . After Much Tribulation . . ."
(D&C 58:3-5)

Ye cannot behold with your natural eyes, for the present time, the design of your God concerning those things which shall come hereafter, and the glory which shall follow after much tribulation.

For after much tribulation come the blessings. Wherefore the day cometh that ye shall be crowned with much glory; the hour is not yet, but is nigh at hand.

Remember this, which I tell you before that you may lay it to heart, and receive that which is to follow.[1]

Background of the revelation

Within a week of the arrival of the Prophet Joseph Smith and his party in Jackson County, Missouri, Section 58 of the Doctrine and Covenants was received. This area had been designated by revelation as the site of the New Jerusalem, or City of Zion, predicted by the prophets.[2]

Background of the prophecy

Inasmuch as this revelation gives the reasons for the saints being commanded to settle in Missouri,[3] there is reason for letting them know that this place of residence might not be their permanent abode. The prophets had predicted glorious things to result from this latter-day objective.[4]

With the beginning of this dispensation of the gospel, persecution began to develop. Following the First Vision, the persecution commenced[5] and was the Prophet's heritage.[6]

---

[1]D&C 58:3-5.
[2]Ibid., 57.
[3]Ibid., vs. 6-12.
[4]Ether 13:2-11; Micah 4:1-2; Joel 3:16; Zephaniah 3:14-16.
[5]Joseph Smith 2:33.
[6]Ibid., vs. 22-27.

Contents of the prophecy

(1) The natural eye does not permit man to see the things of the hereafter. (2) Glory is to be received after much tribulation; in fact, after much tribulation come the blessings. (3) The hour is not yet when the saints are to receive great glory. (4) Members of the Church should keep in mind that tribulation and glory will follow.

Fulfillment of the prophecy

Although the location of the New Jerusalem was known and some of the saints had arrived in the promised land away from their original persecutors, they might well have believed that this was the place where they could rest. By the summer of 1833, two years later, storm clouds burst upon the saints. A mob announced that they were to move from the community or suffer the consequences. The Lord had said that they could not then behold what was in store for them in their new land, but glory would be theirs "after much tribulation."[7] Many members of the Church were killed, savagely wounded or mistreated during the persecutions in Jackson County. Although they moved into other counties of Missouri, their persecutions became more severe until they were expelled into Illinois in 1839. As a party of members, including Elder Heber C. Kimball, were on the bank of the Mississippi River looking toward Commerce, Illinois, later named Nauvoo, Brother Kimball said: "It is a very pretty place, but not a long abiding home for the Saints," Brother Rigdon, upon learning of this remark and since he had had as much persecution as he could stand, said: "I should suppose that Elder Kimball had passed through sufferings and privations and mobbings and drivings enough, to learn to prophesy good concerning Israel." Elder Kimball replied, with a mixture of humor and meekness: "President Rigdon, I'll prophesy good concerning you all the time—if you can get it."

[7]D&C 58:3.

But the saints did not have surcease from tribulation, for Satan's emissaries fought against them and drove them from the state of Illinois. In the winter of 1846, the saints built a beautiful city with a population of about 20,000 inhabitants at a time when Chicago had only a population of 3,000. They settled on the prairies of Iowa. "Here in these humble prairie settlements, surrounded by Indians, hopeful and even happy, though enduring much sickness and privation, which resulted in many deaths, the pilgrim Mormons passed the winter of 1846-7."[9]

"After much tribulation"—pioneer life in the far West was hard, oftentimes scarcity of food, even famine, severe climatic conditions, and hostile Indians, together with persecution by Federal officers in the days of plural marriage—was the lot of the saints of God.

Application of the prophecy

There is no assurance that tribulation is over for the members of the Church, whether they are faithful or whether they adhere to the commandments. (See "Upon My House Shall It Begin" —D&C 112:23-26). Success in this life and in the eternal worlds is dependent upon faithfulness to the Lord's word as given through his prophets. The observations and testimony of Elder Abraham O. Woodruff, a member of the Council of the Twelve in this dispensation, are pertinent to this subject:

"The Latter-day Saints, as a rule, are not easily shaken by conditions, however trying they may be. The experience of the past has shown us that the few men who have fallen by the wayside, because they were filled with fear when trouble arose, have signally failed in their efforts to lead others from the Church. The majority of the people of God today are not easily moved nor frightened; their hearts do not sink within them when clouds appear upon our horizon. I believe it is pleasing in the sight of

---

[8]Orson F. Whitney, *Life of Heber C. Kimball*, pp. 256-257.

[9]Orson F. Whitney, *History of Utah*, pp. 298-299.

the Lord when His people have sufficient faith not to be easily moved, so that when any difficulties arise, or whenever they are beset by the enemies of righteousness, they do not feel that the whole work is going to pieces, and that the Church can no longer make the remarkable progress it has made up to the present time. Our past history should be a strength unto us, and a hope for the future. It should stimulate our faith in God. Indeed, in the minds of those who have a testimony of the truth, there is no doubt whatever in regard to the outcome of this work. They know it will triumph over all its adversaries, no matter how powerful they may be. Whatever agencies are organized to oppose the work, they know that God is all-powerful, and that He rules the destinies of men and nations, and He will bring His work to victory in the end. So the Latter-day Saints who are doing their duty are not easily moved. On the other hand, whenever anything has arisen in the shape of opposition, and whenever the clouds have been dark and threatening, those who were weak, because they were not doing their duty and keeping the commandments of the Lord, have always been the ones who thought the work was going to pieces, and that 'the bottom was falling out of Mormonism.' Whenever members of the Church have such feelings within them it is an evidence of their own weakness, and of the fact that they are not keeping the commandments of God, because of which they have not the assurance regarding the final victory of this work that a faithful man possesses. We expect there will be opposition, but at the same time we confidently expect that God, in the future as in the past, will deliver us if we will only do our duty. We never intend to so shape our faith and belief that it will please the adversary, or the world."[10]

"For after much tribulation, as I have said unto you in a former commandment, cometh the blessing.

"Behold, this is the blessing which I have promised

---

[10]*Conference Report*, April 1904, pp. 34-35.

after your tribulations, and the tribulations of your brethren—your redemption, and the redemption of your brethren, even their restoration to the land of Zion, to be established, no more to be thrown down.

"Nevertheless, if they pollute their inheritances they shall be thrown down; for I will not spare them if they pollute their inheritances." (See ". . . This Is The Blessing Which I Have Promised . . ." —D&C 103:12-14).

Chapter 21

". . .Even Peace In This World. . ."
(D&C 59:23; 19:23)

(A) But learn that he who doeth the works of righteousness shall receive his reward, even peace in this world, and eternal life in the world to come.[1]

(B) Learn of me, and listen to my words; walk in the meekness of my Spirit, and you shall have peace in me.[2]

Background of the revelations

(A) On Sunday, August 7, 1831, Section 59 was re-received. It is the modern revelation establishing Sunday as the Lord's day, and giving instructions on observance of the Sabbath day.

(B) One of the early doctrinal revelations is Section 19, received in March 1830. The principal subject revealed is eternal or everlasting punishment, including the intense suffering of Jesus Christ for the sins of man.

Background of the prophetic promises

(A) Following the instructions on observance of the Sabbath day, the blessings of keeping this commandment are given, followed by the truth that they who neither confess the Lord's hand in all things nor keep his commandments, offend God.

(B) Martin Harris is called to repentance lest he receive the punishment mentioned in the preceding verses. He is reminded of the time when the Lord withdrew his Spirit from him, presumably referring to the occasion when he lost the 116 pages of translated manuscript from the gold plates.

Contents of the prophetic promises

(1) If one does the works of righteousness, his reward will be peace in this world, and eternal life in the world

---

[1]D&C 59:23.
[2]Ibid. 19:23.

to come. (2) To receive peace one must learn of the Lord, listen to his words, and be meek.

Analysis of the prophetic promises

Righteousness is defined in the *Doctrine and Covenants Commentary* as: ". . .such conduct as will stand the scrutiny of a just and competent judge. . .God must be the judge; not man."[3]

To be in God's presence and to be exalted in the celestial kingdom is eternal life. The Lord declared that Eternal is his name; therefore, to receive eternal life is to have God's life.[4] The greatest gift God bestows upon man is this blessing, for this purpose the Lord established his work.[5]

The meek are those who conform their lives to the commandments, thus submitting their wills and desires to God's. The expression "meekness of my Spirit" means to be led by the Holy Ghost in righteous paths.

The revelations are plain that peace, or surcease from political unrest and warfare will not come to the world until the second coming of Christ when the millennial reign of peace begins. (See "Peace Shall Be Taken From The Earth"—D&C 1:35). President George Albert Smith said:

"Now, if there is any doubt in the minds of the people of this Church as to when peace shall come into the world again, I want to emphasize by reading again the word of the Lord wherein he says: 'The Lord's scourge shall pass over by night and by day, and the report thereof shall vex all people; yea, it shall not be stayed until the Lord come;

" 'For the indignation of the Lord is kindled against their abominations and all their wicked works.' " (D&C 97:23-24).[6] (See "Zion Shall Escape If . . ."—D&C 97:22-28).

---

[3]Hyrum M. Smith and Janne M. Sjodahl, *Doctrine and Covenants Commentary*, pp. 137-138.

[4]D&C 19:10-12.

[5]*Ibid.* 14:7; Moses 1:39.

[6]*Conference Report*, October 1917, pp. 44-45.

Fulfillment of the prophetic promises

The promise is made that he who does the works of righteousness will have peace in this world. Jesus promised his disciples: "Peace I leave with you, my peace I give unto you: not as the world giveth, give I unto you. . ."[7] An indication of the meaning of this peace is given in the next part of the verse: "Let not your heart be troubled, neither let it be afraid."

Fear is an instrument of the devil. If he can plant uncertainty of the truth, of the fact that there is no life after death, or that it is impossible to overcome one's weaknesses, he has won a tremendous victory. Fear replaces faith in Christ when sin enters, and when the person does not accept the atonement of Christ with a living faith in him, which leads to repentance of sin. The comforting message of the Savior to his Church is: "Therefore whosoever belongeth to my church need not fear, for such shall inherit the kingdom of heaven."[8]

Peace of mind, assurance that Jesus Christ is the Son of God, the Savior and Redeemer of men, comes from the Holy Ghost.[9] Expressed in the language of President Charles W. Penrose:

"In that certainty, there is peace, something to rely on; something dependable; something that doesn't need any quibbling or questioning or doubt or uncertainty, but the full conviction of my soul of the truth to others and that very certainty that sounded in my voice has carried conviction, thank the Lord, to many others in my travels and labors in the ministry."[10]

The peace spoken of is neither earned by accepting the ways of the world nor by being free of tribulation. Adversities are a part of earth life, and the soul that does not experience pain, sorrow, disappointment, and so forth,

---

[7] John 14:27.
[8] D&C 10:55.
[9] *Ibid.* 36:2.
[10] *Conference Report*, October 1916, p. 21.

is not the fortunate one.[11] From the Prince of Peace we learn the following: "These things I have spoken unto you, that in me ye might have peace. In the world ye shall have tribulation: but be of good cheer; I have overcome the world."[12]

If Jesus Christ is the only source of peace in this world, then his Church on the earth is the organization in which men may find the peace that surpasseth all understanding. Elder Marion G. Romney, of the Council of the Twelve, said:

"We know that the gospel of Jesus Christ, of which this Church is the repository, is the one and only way of peace. We know that to everyone who accepts and lives it there comes peace—peace in his heart—even in the midst of turmoil in the world. We know that if the people of the world would accept it and live it, we would have peace in all the world."[13]

An experience of receiving the conviction and the peace the Holy Ghost imparts is related by President Anthony W. Ivins, counselor to President Heber J. Grant, because of his earnest desire to know the truth:

"It was my custom while making these investigations, to go to a remote place which I had selected, and there pray to the Lord for wisdom that I might understand the things which I read. On one of these occasions, after reading the Book of Mormon, the testimony which I desired came to me. A great joy filled my soul, I was very happy. I felt that my transgressions were forgiven, and I loved and forgave every one. That my Redeemer lived and had restored His Gospel through the instrumentality of Joseph Smith, the great prophet of this dispensation, seemed as certain to me as my own existence."[14]

Elder Marion G. Romney gave the Church an ex-

---

[11]D&C 122:1-9.

[12]John 16:33.

[13]*Conference Report*, April 1961, p. 117.

[14]*Testimonies of the Divinity of the Church of Jesus Christ of Latter-day Saints by Its Leaders*, p. 100.

planation of eternal life spoken of in the prophetic promise:

"This gift of eternal life in the world to come may
not, of course, be fully realized during earth life. An assurance that it will be obtained in the world to come
may, however, be had in this world. As a matter of fact,
the blessings of the celestial kingdom are promised only
to those who have such an assurance. According to the
vision, a successful candidate for these blessings must qualify on three counts: First, he must have '. . .received the
testimony of Jesus, and believed on his name' and been
'. . .baptized after the manner of his burial'; second, he
must have received 'the Holy Spirit by the laying on of
hands of him who is ordained and sealed unto this power';
and third, he must be 'sealed by the Holy Spirit of promise.' "[15]

Application of the prophetic promises

Faithful members of The Church of Jesus Christ of
Latter-day Saints know that the mission of the Church is
to establish peace. But peace today comes from the Holy
Ghost to individuals, not to groups or nations. Peace of
mind brings contentment, joy and satisfaction, and an
assurance of the truth that God's will is to be done as
prophesied by the prophets. In the words of the First
Presidency, consisting of Brigham Young, Heber C. Kimball, and Jedemiah M. Grant:

"Incomparable delight and happiness fill the soul of
the faithful Saint, who has the testimony of Jesus and the
Spirit of the living God to enlighten his understanding.
Happiness supreme and love divine fill his bosom, as he
seeks to impart the gladsome intelligence to his fellow
species, that they may also be partakers with him in the
glorious cause, and share in its blessings. Thus our holy
religion absorbs every feeling, desire, ambition, motive,
and action of our natures, and renders every association in

---

[15]*Conference Report*, September 1949, p. 41.

life tributary thereto; it forms the vitality of our very
existence; it enters not only into our spiritual but also
into our temporal organization, and controls us in all our
affairs. This is true of every person who has tasted the
good work of life, has received the Holy Ghost, and continues to walk in the light, and be led by its gentle influence. This is salvation in the kingdom of God, it is glory
celestial, and exaltation. This is the work that makes angry
the adversary, who fears the overthrow of his kingdom
and power upon the earth, that causes Satan to rage and
seek to destroy the Saints of the Most High, as he did in
the days of Jesus and of his Apostles and followers."[16]

If one desires to have the assurance and peace spoken
of by President John Taylor in the following statement,
he may receive it by doing the works of righteousness:

"Some in speaking of war and troubles, will say, are
you not afraid? No, I am a servant of God, and this is
enough, for Father is at the helm. It is for me to be as
clay in the hands of the potter, to be pliable and walking
in the light of the countenance of the Spirit of the Lord,
and then no matter what comes. Let the lightnings flash
and the earthquakes follow, God is at the helm. . ."[17]

Finally, Elder Marion G. Romney's counsel to all:

"The Prophet Joseph Smith taught that one so sealed
[by the Holy Spirit of promise, which is the Holy Ghost]
would have within himself an assurance born of the spirit,
that he would obtain eternal life in the world to come.
He urgently and repeatedly admonished the Saints of
his day to obtain such an assurance by making their calling and election sure. It is this assurance within a person
which brings to him the peace in this world which will
sustain him in every tribulation."[18]

---

[16]Roy W. Doxey, *The Latter-day Prophets and the Doctrine and Covenants*,
Vol. 1, p. 434.

[17]*Journal of Discourses* 10:58.

[18]*Conference Report*, September 1949, p. 42.

Chapter 22

A Stronghold In Kirtland, Ohio, And Also A Scourge.
(D&C 64:21-22; 124:82-83)

(A) I will not that my servant Frederick G. Williams should sell his farm, for I, the Lord, will to retain a strong hold in the land of Kirtland, for the space of five years, in the which I will not overthrow the wicked, that thereby I may save some.

And after that day, I, the Lord, will not hold any guilty that shall go with an open heart up to the land of Zion; for I, the Lord, require the hearts of the children of men.[1]

(B) Let my servant William Law pay stock into that house, for himself and his seed after him, from generation to generation.

If he will do my will let him not take his family unto the eastern lands, even unto Kirtland; nevertheless, I, the Lord, will build up Kirtland, but I, the Lord, have a scourge prepared for the inhabitants thereof.[2]

Background of the revelations

(A) Section 64 was received in Kirtland, Ohio, September 11, 1831. Some of the brethren were making preparations for a journey to Jackson County, Missouri, the following month.

(B) Section 124 was received on January 19, 1841, in Nauvoo, Illinois, where the saints had settled after the Missouri persecutions. This city became the headquarters of the Church.

Background of the prophecies

(A) The principle of forgiveness is discussed. The Lord's former disciples were not always forgiving of each other; consequently, they were chastened and afflicted. The Lord will forgive whom he will forgive, but we are to forgive all men. Excommunication from the Church does

---

[1]D&C 64:21-22.
[2]*Ibid.* 124:82-83.

not mean that the officers administering the penalty are not forgiving. Information and instructions are given concerning several brethren. Among these was Isaac Morley, who was told to sell his farm, but Brother Williams was to retain his farm for five years.

(B) The prophecy in Section 124 is preceded by instructions concerning the Nauvoo House, a place where the weary traveler might find rest in contemplating the glories of Zion. The Prophet and his descendants were to live in this house also. Among the stockholders in the house was William Law.

Contents of the prophecies

(1) Frederick G. Williams was to retain his farm in Kirtland for the space of five years. (2) During this period the wicked were not to be overthrown. (3) After the five years those who left Kirtland for Missouri could do so. (4) The Lord requires the hearts of men. (5) William Law was to purchase stock in the Nauvoo House. (6) A scourge is prepared for the inhabitants of Kirtland. (7) The Lord says that he will build up Kirtland.

Analysis of the prophecies

Brother Williams became an influential member of the Kirtland community. Later when the First Presidency was organized with Joseph Smith as president, he was appointed a counselor.[3] Although he was excommunicated from the Church in 1839, he was later admitted to membership and died October 10, 1842.

William Law became a counselor in the First Presidency when Hyrum Smith was appointed Patriarch to the Church.[4] He, because of apostasy, was excommunicated from the Church in 1844, and joined with others who were instigators and abettors of the murder of Joseph Smith and his brother.

---

[3]*Ibid.* 90:6.
[4]*Ibid.* 124:91.

Fulfillment of the prophecies

Not often does a prophecy give a specific time or date as does the one in Section 64. (See "A Prophecy With A Date"—D&C 118:4-6). When Frederick G. Williams was told not to sell his farm in Kirtland until five years had passed, a contribution to the success in building the first temple in this dispensation was begun. The promised land of Missouri had been designated as the place where the city of Zion, or the New Jerusalem, would be built.[5] Some of the saints had been commanded to gather to the area of Jackson County. (See ". . .The Covenant. . .They Made Unto Me Has Been Broken. . .It Has Become Void. . ." —D&C 54:4-6; 82:21; 84:41; 104:4-9). One imbued with the spirit of enjoying the blessings of the center-place of Zion would probably find it difficult to remain away from that favored place. In fact, Sister Polly Knight, too ill to travel but possessed with the desire to be in Zion, passed away soon after her arrival, which gave rise to the introduction to Section 58 of the Doctrine and Covenants.[6] Elders Newel K, Whitney and Sidney Gilbert were counseled that they should also remain in Kirtland.[7] These brethren, and we assume others in Kirtland, were to be "on the Lord's errand" in doing "the Lord's business."[8]

The building of the temple in Kirtland was the major business of the saints.[9] The urgency with which the saints should undertake this commandment is indicated in the fact that six months later, they were severely chastized for not being about "the Lord's business."[10] Success was achieved by March 1836, when the temple was dedicated.[11] Prophecies given in the dedicatory prayer are being literally fulfilled. (See "The Children of Judah"—D&C 109:61-

---

[5]*DHC* 4:609-610; Ether 13:2-11.
[6]D&C 58:1-2.
[7]*Ibid.* 54:26.
[8]*Ibid.* vs. 29.
[9]*Ibid.* 88:119-120.
[10]*Ibid.* 95.
[11]*Ibid.* 109.

64; "The Lamanites Shall Blossom As The Rose"—D&C 49:24; 109:65-66; "The Scattered Remnants Of Israel" —D&C 109:67).

The true purpose for which the Kirtland Temple was erected was to receive the Lord Jesus Christ and the restoration of Priesthood keys.[12] Five years from September 1831 [Section 64], the temple was completed and dedicated, thus the prophecy was fulfilled—"in the which I will not overthrow the wicked, that thereby I may save some."[13]

The fulfillment of the second prophecy concerning Kirtland came because of the "wicked" in that area. The Prophet was told by vision of the wickedness among the members of the Church and even the attempt to kill him. Jarrings and discord developed in great magnitude, even in the House of the Lord. Within two years of the dedication of the temple, a general exodus of the saints took place. Eventually, the Kirtland Temple was repudiated by the Lord. (See "Yea The Hearts Of Tens Of Thousands Shall. . .Rejoice. . .And The Fame Of This House Shall Spread. . ."—D&C 110:7-10; 88:119-120).

The month following the prophecy in Section 124 (B), Hyrum Smith, Patriarch to the Church, addressed a letter to the remaining saints in Kirtland who desired to publish a Church paper and perform other functions, in which he told them to leave the area. He wrote:

"All the Saints that dwell in that land are commanded to come away, for this is 'Thus saith the Lord;' therefore pay out no moneys, nor properties for houses, nor lands in that country, for if you do you will lose them, for the time shall come, that you shall not possess them in peace, but shall be scourged with a sore scourge; yet your children may possess them, but not until many years shall pass away;. . .and then I will send forth and build up Kirtland, and it shall be polished and refined according

---

[12] *Ibid.* 110.

[13] *Ibid.* 64:21.

to my word; therefore your doings and your organizations and designs in printing, or any of your councils, are not of me, saith the Lord, even so. Amen."[14]

The following information is taken from an article written by Artel Ricks:

"On the afternoon of February 4, 1842, a tornado swept out of the heavens and pointed a finger at Kirtland and neighboring townships. Houses and barns were demolished. In Kirtland one child was reported killed, and the Presbyterian church was blown down. Accompanied by rain, hail, 'vivid flashes of lightening, and severe claps of thunder,' it must have been a fearsome sight. 'In some places the timber was completely leveled with the ground, and even apple trees, some that had weathered the storms of many years, were torn up by the roots. . . .(Painsville Telegraph, February 9, 1842)."[15]

The scourge that overtook Kirtland was not only a material destruction, but also an economic one, for the population decreased to a number fewer than when the saints moved there in 1831. Also, it, with Lake County, did not develop industrially as once believed possible, although it is one of the beautiful areas of Ohio. Probably the real scourge which afflicted the area was the spirit of bitterness and apostasy which took hold of the inhabitants. "The Saint Louis *Luminary* on February 17, 1855, published an article containing this statement:

'We called at Kirtland—found some tolerably good Saints considering circumstances, and many apostates. They have all become 'rappers' and deny the Christ. They have taken possession of the temple, and they are no better off than thieves and robbers.' " (Temples of the Most High, p. 45).[16]

"Hyrum's prophecy was not limited to the members in Kirtland township or the county of which it is a part.

---

[14]*DHC* 4:443-444.

[15]*Improvement Era*, May 1956, p. 307.

[16]*Ibid.* pp. 340-341.

It appears to have applied to the entire Kirtland Stake, most of the branches of which were in northeastern Ohio in an area about one-sixth the size of the state of Utah. Suffice it to say that the Church disappeared from the entire region.

"Are we now entering the second phase of Hyrum's prophecy?"[17]

The second phase is as follows: ". . .yet your children may possess them, but not until many years shall pass away;

". . .and then will I send forth and build up Kirtland, and it shall be polished and refined according to my word. . .." The Lord said also: ". . .I, the Lord, will build up Kirtland. . ."[18]

Brother Ricks continues: "Most of the branches of the Kirtland Stake were situated in an area corresponding roughly with the North Ohio District of the Great Lakes Mission. In this area today there are over a thousand members."[19]

According to data from the Church Historian's office, the literalness with which this prophecy is being fulfilled is indicated in the increase in The Church of Jesus Christ of Latter-day Saint membership in that area today. There were about 14,500 members of the Church residing in this same area at the end of 1968.

---

[17]*Ibid.* p. 343.
[18]D&C 124:83.
[19]*Improvement Era*, May 1956, p. 343.

Chapter 23

"The Keys of the Kingdom of God. . ."
(D&C 65:2; 109:72)

(A) The keys of the kingdom of God are committed unto man on the earth, and from thence shall the gospel roll forth unto the ends of the earth, as the stone which is cut out of the mountain without hands shall roll forth, until it has filled the whole earth.[1]

(B) Remember all thy church, O Lord, with all their families, and all their immediate connections, with all their sick and afflicted ones, with all the poor and meek of the earth; that the kingdom, which thou hast set up without hands, may become a great mountain and fill the whole earth;[2]

Background of the revelations

(A) Section 65 is designated as a prayer, received at Hiram, Ohio, October 1831. (B) The prayer offered at the dedication of the Kirtland Temple on March 27, 1836, is Section 109 of the Doctrine and Covenants. As is also true of Section 65, though a prayer, this section was received by revelation.

Background of the prophecies

(A) The opening verse of this revelation is a command to prepare the way of the Lord by making his paths straight. To make paths straight for the King is an oriental imagery referring to the practice of sending messengers in advance of his coming to make crooked paths straight and smooth. A similar expression is found in Isaiah 40:3 and Malachi 3:1.[3] (B) Before this prophecy, the dedicatory prayer includes the following: Judgments of the last days are enumerated; prayers for the rulers of the earth should be offered; the extension of the Church by stakes;

---

[1]D&C 65:2.

[2]*Ibid.* 109:72.

[3]Hyrum M. Smith and Janne M. Sjodahl, *Doctrine and Covenants Commentary,* p. 398.

the return of the Jew to the Holy Land; the Lamanites to be converted; and scattered Israel is to be gathered.

Contents of the prophecies

(A) (1) The keys of the kingdom of God are on the earth. (2) The gospel is to roll forth to the ends of the earth as the stone cut out of the mountain without hands.

(B) (1) The plea is made that the Lord remember the church members, their relatives, and also the poor and meek on the earth. (2) The kingdom set up on the earth is to fill the whole earth.

Analysis of the prophecies

The reference to the stone cut out of the mountain without hands is found in Daniel's prophecy.[4] Elder B. H. Roberts gave the Church an analysis of this ancient prophecy and its fulfillment in the latter days. Briefly, the dream of King Nebuchadnezzar as interpreted by Daniel indicated that his kingdom, Babylonia, was the first world power mentioned (the 6th and 5th century B.C.); to be replaced by the Medo-Persian kingdom (from about 538 B.C. to 330 B.C.); followed by the Greco-Macedonian kingdom (from about 330 B.C. to 160 B.C.), with the Roman empire immediately following and ending in the fifth century A.D. Each one of the foregoing kingdoms was symbolized by a metal of the great image which the King dreamed; the golden head—Babylonia; the silver breast and arms—Medes and Persians; the brazen belly and thighs the Greco-Macedonian kingdom; the legs of iron—Roman empire; and the feet of iron and clay which eventually were broken to be replaced by the kingdom of God. This last kingdom was not man-made, as the other kingdoms represented by the image, for it came without the use of man's hands.[5]

---

[4]Daniel 2:37-45.

[5]*DHC* Introduction: XXXVI-XLI.

Fulfillment of the prophecies

The Gospel of Jesus Christ is being taught to the nations of the earth by The Church of Jesus Christ of Latter-day Saints, which is the prophesied Kingdom of God. In the 44th verse of Daniel chapter 2, it is said that in the days of the fifth kingdom, represented by the feet of clay and iron, the God of heaven should set up his kingdom. The days of "these kings" refer to the times of the modern kingdoms that resulted from the break-up of the Roman empire. Some Latter-day Saints believed that the tenth kingdom (representing the tenth toe of the feet) was the modern kingdom of Greece established in 1829. This may be true, but from other parts of the metal image there are not the same number of members of the body to agree with the kingdoms which arose, as for example the Medes and Persians, represented by the breast and arms, making three parts and not one nor two arms only. The important fact is that there would be modern kingdoms in existence when the Kingdom of God was organized by divine direction in the last days.

The keys of the Kingdom of God were restored through the ministry of angels. The power to officiate in holy ordinances, to preach the gospel, to receive communication from the King of Heaven, to spread the word of God throughout the world, were restored to the earth by John the Baptist, and Peter, James and John, in the year 1829.[6] Subsequently, other powers were returned to the earth in the Kirtland Temple on April 3, 1836, by the ancient prophets Moses, Elias, and Elijah.[7]

The Church with its officers, principles, ordinances, powers, and privileges, comprising a divine organization, a kingdom, exists upon the earth directed by the authority restored by angelic beings.[8] A comparison with the New Testament Church and The Church of Jesus Christ

---

[6]D&C 27:5-14.
[7]*Ibid.* 110.
[8]*Ibid.* 20; 21; 107.

of Latter-day Saints shows that the latter is the same as the former divine church, with some additional parts, as revealed from the heavens.

Latter-day Saints accept the following words of the Prophet Joseph Smith regarding Daniel's prophecy:

"The ancient prophets declared that in the last days the God of heaven should set up a kingdom which should never be destroyed, nor left to other people; and the very time that was calculated on, this people were struggling to bring it out. . .I calculate to be one of the instruments of setting up the kingdom of Daniel by the word of the Lord, and I intend to lay a foundation that will revolutionize the whole world. I once offered my life to the Missouri mob as a sacrifice for my people, and here I am. It will not be by sword or gun that this kingdom will roll on; the power of truth is such that all nations will be under the necessity of obeying the Gospel."[9]

Two points upon which the Prophet spoke suggest the following observations: (1) Ancient prophets saw the day when the kingdom of God would be organized upon the earth. (2) The Gospel and Church will revolutionize the whole world.

Regarding the first, Daniel was not the only prophet to foresee the restoration of the gospel in the last days. Peter predicted that there would be a restitution of all things spoken of by the prophets from the presence of the Lord.[10] Paul said that a new dispensation—the fulness of times—would be restored to gather together all things in Christ.[11] The Revelator, John, saw that in the hour of God's judgments (last days) the gospel would be restored by an angel.[12] Other prophets foretold events which have had their fulfillment in The Church of Jesus Christ of Latter-day Saints: the coming forth of the Book of Mor-

---

[9]*DHC* 6:364-365.
[10]Acts 3:19-21.
[11]Ephesians 1:9-10.
[12]Revelations 14:6-7.

mon;[13] temple building as a part of the divine program;[14] the gathering of Israel from the nations of the earth (See "The Scattered Remnants of Israel"—D&C 109:67); and the Lamanites to become a blessed people through the Gospel (See "The Lamanites Shall Blossom as the Rose" —D&C 49:24; 109:65-66).

The Gospel of Jesus Christ as restored will eventually revolutionize the religious world. This may be accomplished in two ways: (a) by men's thoughts being changed concerning religious truths, and (b) by the number of adherants to the true Gospel, changes will come into the lives of these converts. Some of the elders of the Church have pointed out some of the changes in religious thought since the restoration of the gospel. Elder James E. Talmage calls attention to the doctrine of God from that of a Spirit only to a personal being; that children who die unbaptized are not condemned; the teaching of hell fire and brimstone into which the wicked are cast forever.[15] Some of these and other teachings are mentioned by President David O. McKay.[16] As the kingdom rolls on to greater increases in membership, the effects of the true gospel will be more widely felt among men. (It should be borne in mind also that as the wickedness of men increases so also men shall become more godless, but as far as the "Christian" teachings extant in Joseph Smith's day, changes have come in the theologies, but more particularly in the minds of men).

It should not be expected that the kingdom of God will fill the whole earth until after the second coming of Christ when the Millennium will begin and conditions will exist that honorable men might live in peace and prosperity. This fact is indicated in the verses which follow number 72 of Section 109; for, the Church will come into the

---

[13]Isaiah 29; Ezekiel 37:15-28.
[14]Malachi 3:1; Isaiah 2:2-3.
[15]*Improvement Era* 33:478-479.
[16]*Gospel Ideals*, pp. 27-32.

fulness of beauty and power among men when the mountains flow down at the Lord's presence and the valleys are exalted at the time of the resurrection of the faithful.[17]

The destiny of this Church was given by the Prophet Joseph Smith, as reported by President Wilford Woodruff, as follows:

". . . it is only a little handful of Priesthood you see here tonight, but this Church will fill North and South America—it will fill the world. . . . It will fill the Rocky Mountains. There will be tens of thousands of Latter-day Saints who will be gathered in the Rocky Mountains . . .

"I name these things because I want to bear testimony before God, angels and men that mine eyes behold the day, and have beheld for the last fifty years of my life, the fulfillment of that prophecy."[18]

That kingdom when once established following the Millennium will be the kind of kingdom mentioned in the following passage from President Brigham Young:

"It may be asked what I mean by the Kingdom of God. The Church of Jesus Christ has been established now for many years, and the Kingdom of God has got to be established, even that kingdom which will circumscribe all the kingdoms of this world. It will yet give laws to every nation that exists upon the earth. This is the Kingdom that Daniel, the Prophet, saw should be set up in the last days."[19] "When the Kingdom of God is fully set up and established on the face of the earth, and takes the preeminence over all other nations and kingdoms it will protect the people in the enjoyment of all their rights, no matter what they believe, what they profess, or what they worship. If they wish to worship a god of their own workmanship, instead of the true and living God, all right, if they will mind their own business and let other people alone."[20]

[17]D&C 109:73-76.
[18]Conference Report, April 1898, p. 57.
[19]Journal of Discourses 11:275.
[20]Ibid. 2:310.

Application of the prophesies

The crux of these prophecies is that the kingdom of God (Church) now on the earth will never be taken from the earth as it has in the past. In Daniel's prophecy the following characteristics are given: (1) it will never be destroyed; (2) it will not be left to other people; (3) it will overcome all other kingdoms; and (4) it will stand forever, because it is set up by the God of heaven. (Dan. 2:44).

Expressed in the language of President Brigham Young, we learn:

"When the wicked have power to blow out the sun, that it shines no more; when they have power to bring to a conclusion the operations of the elements, suspend the whole system of nature, and make a footstool of the throne of the Almighty, they may then think to check 'Mormonism' in its course, and thwart the unalterable purposes of heaven. . . . it will stand as firm and immovable in the midst of it all as the pillars of eternity. . . . 'Mormonism' stands upon the eternal basis of omnipotence. Jehovah is the 'Mormonism' of this people, their Priesthood and their power; and all who adhere to it, will, in the appointed day, come up into the presence of the King Eternal, and receive a crown of life."[21]

The place of calling upon the Lord in prayer and works is found in the following verses:

"Pray unto the Lord, call upon his holy name, make known his wonderful works among the people.

"Call upon the Lord, that his kingdom may go forth upon the earth, that the inhabitants there may receive it, and be prepared for the days to come, in the which the Son of Man shall come down in heaven, clothed in the brightness of his glory, to meet the kingdom of God which is set up on the earth."[22]

---

[21]*Ibid.* 1:88-89.
[22]D&C 65:4-5.

Chapter 24

"... You Shall See Me And Know That I Am ..."
(D&C 67:10-14; 88:66-68)

(A) And again, verily I say unto you that it is your privilege, and a promise I give unto you that have been ordained unto this ministry, that inasmuch as you strip yourselves from jealousies and fears, and humble yourselves before me, for ye are not sufficiently humble, the veil shall be rent and you shall see me and know that I am—not with the carnal neither natural mind, but with the spiritual.

For no man has seen God at any time in the flesh, except quickened by the Spirit of God.

Neither can any natural man abide the presence of God, neither after the carnal mind.

Ye are not able to abide the presence of God now, neither the ministering of angels, wherefore, continue in patience until ye are perfected.

Let not your minds turn back; and when ye are worthy, in mine own due time, ye shall see and know that which was conferred upon you by the hands of my servant Joseph Smith, Jun. Amen.[1]

(B) And if your eye be single to my glory, your whole bodies shall be filled with light, and there shall be no darkness in you; and that body which is filled with light comprehendeth all things.

Therefore, sanctify yourselves that your minds become single to God, and the days will come that you shall see him; for he will unveil his face unto you, and it shall be in his own time, and in his own way, and according to his own will.[2] (See "Inasmuch As My People Build A House Unto Me ..." —D&C 97:15-20); (See "... From Him Shall Be Taken Even The Light Which He Has Received." —D&C 1:31-33; 50:23-24; 88:67).

Background of the revelations

(A) At the November 1831, conference consideration was given to the publishing of the revelations as "A Book of Commandments."[3] A question was raised in the conference regarding the authenticity of the revelations because

---

[1] D&C 67:10-14.
[2] *Ibid.* 88:67-68.
[3] *Ibid.* 1:6.

of the Prophet's language; consequently, the Lord challenged any one to take the least of the revelations and write one like unto it.

(B) Section 88 is known as the "Olive Leaf" because it speaks peace to the saints through its teachings.

Background of the prophetic promises

(A) The elders in the conference were told that the critic of the revelations should write a revelation to match even the least in the compilation of revelations, but if unsuccessful, he would have to acknowledge the truth of the revelations. They were told, however, that there is no unrighteousness in them, for they came from God.

(B) The promise is given in Section 88 that the day will come when "you shall comprehend even God." God's majesty and power are known by his created earths, many of which are populated. If one draws near to the Lord, the Lord will draw near to him. (See "Pray Always . . . And Great Shall Be Your Blessing . . ." —(D&C 19:38; 90:24; 112:10; 88:63-65).

Contents of the prophetic promises

(1) One may see God, provided he is spiritual, for he cannot be known by the carnal or natural mind. (2) Only when quickened by the Spirit of God can man see him while in the flesh. (3) A carnal person cannot abide the presence of angels. (4) Patience is enjoined until perfection is reached. (5) By becoming worthy, the full potential of God's teachings may be fulfilled. (6) If one's eye is single to God's glory, his body will be filled with light which comprehendeth all things. (7) Through sanctification, one's mind may become single to God and then he will reveal himself, but in his own time, way, and will.

Analysis of the prophetic promises

The revelations refer to mortals seeing God, and also the purified seeing him in the life after death.[4] The promises

---

[4]*Ibid.* 97:15-17; 38:7-8.

herein discussed pertain to the privilege of men in the flesh seeing God.

The carnal, or natural mind, is possessed by one who has not been "born again" by the Holy Ghost.[5] His desires are to satisfy his sensual nature. The natural man may become spiritual by accepting the atonement of Christ through membership in his Church, and become a saint.[6] Membership in Christ's Church does not make a person spiritual, but obedience to the teachings of Christ will do so. All members of the Church may not be "spiritually born of God", taught Alma.[7] In this dispensation, the Lord has counseled his people to sanctify themselves that they might receive the blessing of being with God.[8]

On another occasion, I wrote the following about keeping one's mind single to God:

"Keeping one's mind single to God is the way to sanctification. Such single mindedness involves (a) walking uprightly before the Lord, seeking to know his will through study, praying unceasingly, recognizing that salvation comes only through Jesus Christ; (b) doing one's duty to bring about a change from the carnal to the spiritual state. To be "born again" by the Spirit (Holy Ghost) is a qualification to be sanctified. To become a new creature in Christ Jesus is essential to "inherit the kingdom of God." (Mosiah 27:25-26).[9]

To see God while in the flesh requires not only worthiness, as indicated, but also to be quickened by the Holy Ghost during that experience. Moses had such an experience, as did other prophets.[10] Elder Orson F. Whitney, an apostle of this dispensation, discusses this subject, as follows:

"Let it not be supposed, however, that to see spirit-

---

[5] Mosiah 27:25.
[6] *Ibid.* 3:19.
[7] Alma 5:14-32.
[8] D&C 88:66-68; 105:35-37; 88:2.
[9] Roy W. Doxey, *Zion in the Last Days*, p. 40.
[10] Moses 1:11

ually is not to see literally. Vision is not fancy, not imagination. The object is actually beheld, though not with the natural eye. We all have spirit eyes, of which our natural or outward eyes are the counterpart. All man's organs and faculties are firstly spiritual, the body being but the clothing of the spirit. In our first estate, the spirit life, we 'walked by sight.' Therefore we had eyes. But they were not our natural eyes, for these are not given until the spirit tabernacles in mortality. All men have a spirit sight, but all are not permitted to use it under existing conditions. Even those thus privileged can only use it when quickened by the Spirit of the Lord. Without that, no man can know the things of God, 'because they are spiritually discerned.' Much less can he look upon the Highest unspiritually, with carnal mind or with natural vision. 'No man' —no natural man— 'hath seen God at any time.' (John 1:18). But men at divers times have seen him as Moses saw him—not with the natural but with the spiritual eye, quickened by the power that seeth and knoweth all things.

"The seeric faculty, possessed in greater degree by some than by others, is the original spirit sight reinforced or moved upon by the power of the Holy Ghost . . . Joseph Smith possessed this ability—this gift, but it was the Spirit of the Lord that enabled him to use it. By that Spirit he beheld the Father and the Son . . ."[11]

The Melchizedek Priesthood is also necessary to prepare people to see God. "And without the ordinances thereof, and the authority of the priesthood, the power of godliness is not manifest unto men in the flesh;

"For without this no man can see the face of God, even the Father, and live."[12]

Joseph Smith was foreordained in the premortal world to his calling in this life. When the Priesthood was not on the earth, he saw God and Jesus Christ. May we not,

---

[11]Orson F. Whitney, *Saturday Night Thoughts*, pp. 40-41.
[12]D&C 84:21-22.

therefore, believe that he saw them with his spirit eyes by the aid of the Priesthood he held in that other world?

The doctrine of the second Comforter, mentioned by Jesus as "another Comforter" is the actual presence of God the Father and his Son Jesus Christ.[13] The Prophet Joseph Smith explained that this blessing is received by those who receive baptism into the Lord's Church and then

". . . continue to humble himself before God, hungering and thirsting after righteousness, and living by every word of God, and the Lord will soon say unto him, Son, thou shalt be exalted. When the Lord has thoroughly proved him and finds that the man is determined to serve Him at all hazards, then the man will find his calling and election made sure, then it will be his privilege to receive the other Comforter . . .

"Now what is this other Comforter? It is no more or less than Jesus Christ himself; and this is the sum and substance of the whole matter; that when any man obtains this last Comforter, he will have the personage of Jesus Christ to attend him, or appear unto him from time to time, and even he will manifest the Father unto him, and they will take up their abode with him, and the visions of the heavens will be opened unto him, and the Lord will teach him face to face, and he may have the perfect knowledge of the mysteries of the Kingdom of God . . ."[14]

Fulfillment of the prophetic promises

One of the testimonies of the validity of the Church of Jesus Christ of Latter-day Saints is that the same blessings bestowed upon men in past dispensations of the gospel are present in this dispensation. If God and his Son Jesus Christ did not reveal themselves today as they did anciently, serious doubts could be raised concerning the truth of the work initiated by Joseph Smith. The testimony of many of this generation verify that God has revealed himself in

---

[13]John 14:16-18, 21, 23.
[14]*DHC* 3:380-381.

his own way and in his own time. Recorded in a modern book of scripture, we find the First Vision, in which Joseph beheld the Father and the Son.[15] In the Doctrine and Covenants there are recorded the vision of God, his Son, and angels by Sidney Rigdon and Joseph Smith.[16] Recorded also is the appearance of the Savior to Oliver Cowdery and Joseph Smith in the Kirtland (Ohio) Temple on April 3, 1836.[17]

Without enumerating all recorded accounts of manifestations of this character, examples of various ways in which the Lord has revealed himself will be mentioned. The following account was related by Elder George A. Smith:

"On the first day of the dedication (of the Kirtland Temple), President Frederick G. Williams, one of the Council of the Prophet, and who occupied the upper pulpit, bore testimony that the Savior, dressed in his vesture without seam, came into the stand and accepted of the dedication of the house, that he saw him, and gave a description of his clothing and all things pertaining to it."[18]

President George Q. Cannon received a sight-knowledge testimony of the Savior,[19] as did President Lorenzo Snow. (See, "Inasmuch As My People Build A House Unto Me . . ." —D&C 97:15-20).

Elder George F. Richards, president of the Council of the Twelve at his death, reported the following in general conference:

"The Lord has revealed to me, by dreams, something more about the love for God and the love for fellow men. I believe in dreams, brethren and sisters. The Lord has given me dreams, which to me, are just as real and as much from God as was the dream of King Nebuchadnezzar

---

[15]Pearl of Great Price, Joseph Smith 2:7-20.
[16]D&C 76:19-24.
[17]*Ibid.* 110:1-10.
[18]*Journal of Discourses* 11:10.
[19]George Q. Cannon, *Gospel Truths*, p. 134.

which was the means of saving a nation from starvation, or the dream of Lehi who through a dream led his colony out of the old country, across the mighty deep to this promised land, or any other dreams that we read of in scripture.

"It is not out of place for us to have important dreams, for we read in the scriptures: 'And it shall come to pass in the last days, saith God, I will pour out of my Spirit upon all flesh: and your sons and your daughters shall prophesy, and your young men shall see visions, and your old men shall dream dreams.'[20]

"More than forty years ago I had a dream, which I am sure was from the Lord. In this dream I was in the presence of my Savior as he stood in mid-air. He spoke no word to me, but my love for him was such that I have not words to explain. I know that no mortal man can love the Lord as I experienced that love for the Savior unless God reveals it unto him. I would have remained in his presence, but there was a power drawing me away from him, and as a result of that dream I had this feeling, that no matter what might be required at my hands, what the gospel might entail unto me, I would do what I should be asked to do, even to the laying down of my life.

"And so when we read in the scriptures what the Savior said to his disciples: 'In my Father's house are many mansions: . . . I go to prepare a place for you . . . that where I am, there ye may be also.'[21]

"I think that is where I want to be. If only I can be with my Savior and have the same sense of love that I had in that dream, it will be the goal of my existence, the desire of my life.'[22]

Elder Melvin J. Ballard in general conference gave the following experience:

"I know, as well as I know that I live and look into your faces, that Jesus Christ lives, and he is the Redeemer

[20]Acts 2:17.
[21]John 14:2, 3.
[22]*Conference Report*, October 1946, p. 139.

of the world, that he arose from the dead with a tangible body, and still has that real body which Thomas touched when he thrust his hands into his side and felt that wound of the spear, and also the prints of the nails in his hands.[23] I know by the witness and the revelations of God to me that Thomas told the truth. I know by witness that Joseph Smith told the truth, for mine eyes have seen. For in the visions of the Lord to my soul, I have seen Christ's face, I have heard his voice. I know that he lives, that he is the Redeemer of the World, and that as he arose from the dead, a tangible and real individual, so shall all men arise in the resurrection from the dead."[24]

Application of the prophetic promises

The Lord's promise that some of this dispensation will see him has been amply fulfilled, but it has been "in his own time, and in his own way, and according to his own will." And so it will always be in this life.

Sight-knowledge of God, or by dreams, or in other ways, does not insure salvation to the recipient. To know God by the Holy Ghost is more substantial and far-reaching, and then if the Lord gives the further witness by revealing himself, the latter becomes a powerful influence. If, however, the beholder of spiritual manifestations sins, as he may, the blessing condemns him. Great trials often follow these experiences, and the true conversion of the individual is then tested. The seeking of signs and wonders for faith is condemned by the Lord.[25]

The sure way of salvation is to be "born again" by the Holy Ghost. Strength and power are then the qualities of the possessor. But, even the sanctified may fall away into darkness.[26]

Would you sin if you were in God's presence? Perhaps the words of the Savior to the prophet would be helpful as a reminder of the nearness of his presence:

---

[23]John 20:26-29.
[24]*Conference Report,* April 1920, pp. 40-41.
[25]D&C 63:7-12.
[26]*Ibid.* 20:31-34.

"But behold, verily, verily, I say unto you that mine eyes are upon you. I am in your midst and ye cannot see me;

"But the day soon cometh that ye shall see me, and know that I am; for the veil of darkness shall soon be rent, and he that is not purified shall not abide the day."[27]

27*Ibid.* 38:7-8.

Chapter 25

"They Are They . . . Who Have Received Of His Fullness, And Of His Glory . . ."
(D&C 76:50-60; 132:4-5; 131:1-4; 132:15-22).

(A) And again we bear record—for we saw and heard, and this is the testimony of the gospel of Christ concerning them who shall come forth in the resurrection of the just—

They are they who received the testimony of Jesus, and believed on his name and were baptized after the manner of his burial, being buried in the water in his name, and this according to the commandment which he has given—

That by keeping the commandments they might be washed and cleansed from all their sins, and receive the Holy Spirit by the laying on of the hands of him who is ordained and sealed unto this power;

And who overcome by faith, and are sealed by the Holy Spirit of promise, which the Father sheds forth upon all those who are just and true.

They are they who are the church of the Firstborn.

They are they into whose hands the Father has given all things—

They are they who are priests and kings, who have received of his fulness, and of his glory;

And are priests of the Most High, after the order of Melchizedek, which was after the order Enoch, which was after the order of the Only Begotten Son.

Wherefore, as it is written, they are gods, even the sons of God—

Wherefore, all things are theirs, whether life or death, or things present, or things to come, all are theirs and they are Christ's, and Christ is God's.

And they shall overcome all things.[1]

(B) For behold, I reveal unto you a new and an everlasting covenant; and if ye abide not that covenant, then are ye damned; for no one can reject this covenant and be permitted to enter into my glory.

For all who will have a blessing at my hands shall abide the law which was appointed for that blessing, and the conditions thereof, as were instituted from before the foundation of the world.[2]

(C) In the celestial glory there are three heavens or degrees;

---

[1]D&C 76:50-60.
[2]Ibid., 132:4-5.

And in order to obtain the highest, a man must enter into this order of the priesthood [meaning the new and everlasting covenant of marriage];

And if he does not, he cannot obtain it.

He may enter into the other, but that is the end of his kingdom; he cannot have an increase.[3]

(D) Therefore, if a man marry him a wife in the world, and he marry her not by me nor by my word, and he covenant with her so long as he is in the world and she with him, their covenant and marriage are not of force when they are dead, and when they are out of the world; therefore, they are not bound by any law when they are out of the world.

Therefore, when they are out of the world they neither marry nor are given in marriage; but are appointed angels in heaven; which angels are ministering servants, to minister for those who are worthy of a far more, and an exceeding, and an eternal weight of glory.

For these angels did not abide my law; therefore, they cannot be enlarged, but remain separately and singly, without exaltation, in their saved condition, to all eternity; and from henceforth are not gods, but are angels of God forever and ever.

And again, verily I say unto you, if a man marry a wife, and make a covenant with her for time and for all eternity, if that covenant is not by me or by my word, which is my law, and is not sealed by the Holy Spirit of promise, through him whom I have anointed and appointed unto this power, then it is not valid neither of force when they are out of the world, because they are not joined by me, saith the Lord, neither by my word; when they are out of the world it cannot be received there, because the angels and the gods are appointed there, by whom they cannot pass; they cannot, therefore, inherit my glory; for my house is a house of order, saith the Lord God.

And again, verily I say unto you, if a man marry a wife by my word, which is my law, and by the new and everlasting covenant, and it is sealed unto them by the Holy Spirit of promise, by him who is anointed, unto whom I have appointed this power and the keys of this priesthood; and it shall be said unto them—Ye shall come forth in the first resurrection; and if it be after the first resurrection, in the next resurrection; and shall inherit thrones, kingdoms, principalities, and powers, dominions, all heights and depths—then shall it be written in the Lamb's Book of Life, that he shall commit no murder whereby to shed innocent blood, it shall be done unto them in all things whatsoever my servant hath put upon them, in time, and through all eternity; and shall be of full force when they are out of world; and they shall pass by the angels, and the gods, which are set

[3]*Ibid.*, 131:1-4.

there, to their exaltation and glory in all things, as hath been sealed
upon their heads, which glory shall be a fulness and a continuation of
the seeds forever and ever.

Then shall they be gods, because they have no end; therefore
shall they be from everlasting to everlasting, because they continue;
then shall they be above all, because all things are subject unto them.
Then shall they be gods, because they have all power, and the angels
are subject unto them.

Verily, verily, I say unto you, except ye abide my law ye cannot attain to this glory.

For strait is the gate, and narrow the way that leadeth unto the
exaltation and continuation of the lives, and few there be that find
it, because ye receive me not in the world neither do ye know me.[4]

Background of the revelations

(A) Section 76 is known as the "Vision," and was received by Joseph Smith and Sidney Rigdon on February
16, 1832. It is a revelation concerning the four kingdoms
following the resurrection into which all of mankind will
go.

(B, D) Section 132 is the revelation on celestial marriage for time and for all eternity and also plural marriage.

(C) Section 131 consists of doctrinal instructions given
by the Prophet Joseph Smith in May 1843.

Background of the prophetic promises

(A) The revelation on the future kingdoms following
the resurrection contains the doctrine of eternal progression;[5] the origin of the "Vision"; sight-knowledge of God
and Christ;[6] and Satan and the sons of perdition.[7]

(B) Section 132 opens with a reference that Joseph
Smith had inquired about Abraham, Isaac, Jacob, Moses,
David and Solomon, "my servants," having wives and con-
cubines.

(C) The prophetic promise in Section 131 begins the
revelation.

---

[4]*Ibid.*, 132:15-22.
[5]*Ibid.*, 76:1-10.
[6]*Ibid.*, vs. 11-24.
[7]*Ibid.*, vs. 25-49.

(D) After the introduction of Section 132 (B), the doctrine of celestial marriage is the subject until verse 34, which begins the subject of plural marriage.

Contents of the prophetic promises

(1) They who shall come forth in the resurrection of the just are those who: (a) accept Jesus Christ in baptism by immersion; (b) keep the commandments that they might receive a remission of sins; (c) receive the Holy Spirit by the laying on of hands; (d) overcome by faith and are sealed by the Holy Spirit of promise. (2) These persons become members of the church of the Firstborn to receive all that the Father hath, priests and kings forever, for they are gods. (3) A new and everlasting covenant is revealed which must be received in obedience to the law which will permit them to receive the Lord's glory. (4) In order to receive the highest degree of the celestial kingdom and have eternal increase, it is necessary to receive the new and everlasting covenant of marriage. (5) Covenants between husbands and wives, not by the Lord, are of no force when the parties are dead. (6) Those who do not abide the law of celestial marriage are appointed angels in the future life to minister for those in a higher degree of heaven. (7) If marriage contracts are not entered into by the word of the Lord through his servant and sealed by the Holy Spirit of promise, they are not of force and the participants remain single, without exaltation, though saved, throughout the eternities as angels, not gods. (8) If, however, the sealing is by the Holy Spirit of promise, they shall inherit all powers, provided they do not commit murder, and they shall have a continuation of the seed forever. (9) Strait is the way which leadeth to the exaltation and continuation of the lives and few find it, because they are not obedient to the full law.

Analysis of the prophetic promises

The resurrection of the just is the first general resurrection which begins at the second coming of Christ. The

just are those who are defined in the prophetic promise
as members of Christ's Church through baptism and receiving the Holy Ghost by an authorized servant of the
Lord. They become clean from sin by keeping the commandments, and they are sealed by the Holy Spirit of
promise.

The Holy Spirit of promise is the Holy Ghost. The
expression means: the Holy Ghost with the promise of
eternal life.[8]

The Church of the Firstborn is the Church which will
exist after the resurrection when faithful people have received eternal life (exaltation) in the celestial kingdom.[9]

A new and everlasting covenant is marriage for eternity solemnized in the House of the Lord by one who is
ordained to this power. It is one of the covenants belonging to the new and everlasting covenant, the Gospel of
Jesus Christ.

In the celestial kingdom there are three degrees of
glory and to receive the highest (exaltation) one must receive the covenant of eternal marriage. This blessing, received by the faithful, provides for the power to have
eternal increase. Eternal increase is the same as continuation of the seeds or lives, or to have the ability to beget
spirit children following the resurrection.

Those who do not abide this law are not entitled to the
exaltation, but they become angels in one of the three
kingdoms of glory. Those angels who are entitled to the
celestial kingdom because of obedience to the celestial law,
except marriage for eternity, serve the exalted in that kingdom. These angels remain single, without marriage, throughout the eternities, having had the opportunity for the
fulness of the Gospel in the earth life or in the spirit world
after death.

If a couple have obeyed the fulness of the law and been
sealed by the Holy Spirit of promise after their obedience

---

[8]*Ibid.,*   88:3-4.
[9]*Ibid.,* 76:54-60.

to gospel covenants and sin, as apparently all people do, but they do not commit murder in the shedding of innocent blood or deny the Holy Ghost, they may eventually receive the blessing of exaltation. This blessing is dependent upon the conditions given in verse 26 of Section 132, about which the *Doctrine and Covenants Commentary* says:

"This verse has been greatly misunderstood and by some grossly abused. Unfortunately there are some who seem to think that after they are married for time and all eternity, the Lord, in this passage, grants them immunity against sin, as long as they do not shed innocent blood or deny the Holy Ghost. It should be remembered that the Lord taught during his ministry this same doctrine as given in the Doctrine and Covenants. (Matt. 12:31-32). He has never granted to any person the privilege of sinning wilfully and then obtaining the reward of faithfulness without repentance. John said:

" 'If any man see his brother sin a sin which is not unto death, he shall ask, and he shall give him life for them that sin not unto death. There is a sin unto death; I do not say that he should pray for it.' (I John 5:16).

"In this passage we are taught that all manner of sin which is forgiveable on repentance, or 'not unto death,' may be forgiven on repentance, but some sins may call for a most dreadful punishment even then—the destruction in the flesh and being turned over to the buffetings of Satan until the day of redemption. This punishment is most severe. The Lord has not at any time contradicted Himself, and he has said: 'And no unclean thing can enter into his kingdom; therefore nothing entereth into his rest save it be those who have washed their garments in my blood, because of their faith, and the repentance of all their sins, and their faithfulness unto the end.' (3 Nephi 27:19). The wilful sinners who remain in their sins, 'shall return unto God, and behold his face, and remain in their sins.' (2 Nephi 9:38. Compare Mormon 9:3-4)."[10]

---

[10]Hyrum M. Smith and Janne M. Sjodahl, *The Doctrine and Covenants Commentary*, p. 829.

Innocent blood, according to the revelations, is the blood (life) of the Lord's servants. Joseph and Hyrum Smith are examples, as also Abinadi, of persons of innocent blood.[11]

In the following statement Elder Melvin J. Ballard, an apostle of this dispensation, provides this information about the resurrection and marrying and giving in marriage:

"In the resurrection there is neither marriage nor giving in marriage, for this Church teaches the doctrine that every ceremony, marriage or baptism, must be fulfilled upon this earth, and that any man or woman who is entitled to these ceremonies will have the privilege of either receiving them or rejecting them before the resurrection. That is why it is going to take one thousand years after the first resurrection until the last can happen. If any of them prove themselves worthy of baptism or worthy of sealing to husband or wife, it will all take place before the resurrection, for after the resureection, or at the time of the resurrection, every man or woman's status is fixed. It all has to be done here. They are privileged to be experienced before the resurrection. It will be preached to them in the spirit world, and if they are worthy, these same blessings will be administered to them, for the power to bind and seal is here."[12]

Fulfillment of the prophetic promises

The fulfillment of these promises is planned for the future; that is, after faithful men and women have received the final judgment. This blessing comes only after the resurrection, though they may have the assurance of this glory while in the spirit world, and some may know it in the earth life. The Prophet Joseph Smith said:

"Except a man and his wife enter into an everlasting covenant and be married for eternity, while in this probation, by the power and authority of the Holy Priesthood,

---

[11]D&C 135:7; 136:36; Mosiah 17:10.

[12]Bryant S. Hinckley, *Sermons and Missionary Services of Melvin Joseph Ballard*, p. 232.

they will cease to increase when they die; that is, they will not have any children after the resurrection."[13]

The testimony of Elder Melvin J. Ballard regarding the forming of marriage arrangements in the spirit world after death, even for children, is possible:

"You mothers worry about your little children. We do not perform sealings for them. I lost a son six years of age, and I saw him a man in the spirit world after his death, and I saw how he had exercised his own freedom of choice and would obtain of his own will and volition a companionship, and in due time to him and all those who are worthy of it, shall come all of the blessings and sealing privileges of the house of the Lord. Do not worry over it. They are safe; they are all right."[14]

In general conference, President Rudger Clawson, a president of the Twelve Apostles of this dispensation, related the following experience received by a friend:

" 'Upon one occasion I saw in vision my father and mother who were not members of the Church, who had not received the gospel in life, and I discovered that they were living separate and apart in the spirit world, and when I asked them how it was that they were so, my father said, 'This is an enforced separation, and you are the only individual who can bring us together. You can do this work. Will you do it?'—meaning that he should go into the House of the Lord and there officiate for his parents who were dead, and by the ordinance of sealing bring them together and unite them in the family relation beyond the veil. And he informed me that he had attended to the work, and I rejoiced with him and congratulated him.' "[15]

The tender sympathy and assurance of life after death in the knowledge of the reunion of loved ones is illustrated in the following personal experience of President Heber J.

---

[13]*DHC* 5:391.

[14]Bryant S. Hinckley, *Sermons and Missionary Services of Melvin Joseph Ballard*, p. 260.

[15]*Conference Report*, October 1908, p. 74.

Grant, seventh president of the Church, after relating that his twelve year old daughter expressed faith that her father could heal her mother by the power of the Priesthood, as he had done on other occasions:

"I told my little girl that we all had to die sometime, and that I felt assured in my heart that her mother's time had arrived. She and the rest of the children left the room.

"I then knelt down by the bed of my wife (who by this time had lost consciousness) and I told the Lord I acknowledged His hand in life, in death, in joy, in sorrow, in prosperity, or adversity. I thanked Him for the knowledge I had that my wife belonged to me for all eternity, that the gospel of Jesus Christ had been restored, that I knew that by the power and authority of the Priesthood here on the earth that I could and would have my wife forever if I were only faithful as she had been. But I told the Lord that I lacked the strength to have my wife die and to have it affect the faith of my little children in the ordinances of the gospel of Jesus Christ; and I supplicated the Lord with all the strength that I possessed, that He would give to that little girl of mine a knowledge that it was His mind and His will that her mama should die."

"Within an hour my wife passed away, and I called the children back into the room. My little boy about five and a half or six years of age was weeping bitterly, and the little girl twelve years of age took him in her arms and said: 'Do not weep, do not cry Heber; since we went out of this room the voice of the Lord from heaven has said to me, 'In the death of your mama the will of the Lord shall be done.' "

"Tell me, my friends, that I do not know that God hears and answers prayers! Tell me that I do not know that in the hour of adversity the Latter-day Saints are comforted and blessed and consoled as no other people are!"[16]

From President Joseph F. Smith we have this testimony:

---

[16]G. Homer Durham (comp.), *Gospel Standards*, p. 361.

"Why did he teach us the principle of eternal union of man and wife? Because God knew that we were his children here, to remain his children forever and ever and that we were just as truly individuals, and that our individuality was as identical as that of the Son of God, and would therefore continue, worlds without end, so that the man receiving his wife by the power of God, for time and for all eternity, would have the right to claim her and she to claim her husband, in the world to come. Neither would be changed, except from mortality to immortality; neither would be other than himself or herself, but they will have their identity in the world to come precisely as they exercise their individuality and enjoy their identity here. God has revealed this principle, and it has its bearings upon the evidence that we possess of the actual, literal resurrection of the body, just as it is and as the prophets have declared it in the Book of Mormon."[17]

Application of the prophetic promises

The purpose of this earth life is that we might receive eternal life, or exaltation, in the celestial kingdom. To receive this blessing, one must enter into the new and everlasting covenant of marriage in the temple. If one does not follow this commandment from the Lord, the principal purpose for which this life is planned will be averted. But this applies to the individual, for though there may be few who will receive the exaltation, this number will no doubt be many. Already, the Lord has said that some have entered into this blessing.[18]

---

[17]Joseph F. Smith, *Gospel Doctrine*, p. 277.
[18]D&C 132:37.

Chapter 26

". . . *The Laborer Is Worthy of His Hire.*"
(D&C 84:79-91)

Behold, I send you out to prove the world, and the laborer is worthy of his hire.

And any man that shall go and preach this gospel of the kingdom, and fail not to continue faithful in all things, shall not be weary in mind, neither darkened, neither in body, limb, nor joint; and a hair of his head shall not fall to the ground unnoticed. And they shall not go hungry, neither athirst.

Therefore, take ye no thought for the morrow, for what ye shall eat, or what ye shall drink, or wherewithal ye shall be clothed.

For, consider the lilies of the field, how they grow, they toil not, neither do they spin; and the kingdoms of the world, in all their glory, are not arrayed like one of these.

For your Father, who is in heaven, knoweth that you have need of all these things.

Therefore, let the morrow take thought for the things of itself.

Neither take ye thought beforehand what ye shall say; but treasure up in your minds continually the words of life, and it shall be given you in the very hour that portion that shall be meted unto every man.

Therefore, let no man among you, for this commandment is unto all the faithful who are called of God in the church unto the ministry, from this hour take purse or scrip, that goeth forth to proclaim this gospel of the kingdom.

Behold, I send you out to reprove the world of all their unrighteous deeds, and to teach them of a judgment which is to come.

And whoso receiveth you, there I will be also, for I will go before your face. I will be on your right hand and on your left, and my Spirit shall be in your hearts, and mine angels round about, to bear you up.

Whoso receiveth you receiveth me; and the same will feed you, and clothe you, and give you money.

And he who feeds you, or clothes you, or gives you money, shall in no wise lose his reward.

And he that doeth not these things is not my disciple; by this you may know my disciples.[1]

---

[1]D&C 84:79-91.

Background of the revelation

This revelation is known as a Priesthood revelation because of the information about the place of the Priesthood in the plan of salvation. The word of the Lord is given regarding the temple in the New Jerusalem; the relationship of the Aaronic to the Melchizedek Priesthoods, and many other important subjects pertaining to the missionary work of the Church.

Background of the promise

The need to know what the Lord revealed to the Book of Mormon people as well as the present-day revelations is emphasized. To those who serve in the mission field special instructions are given concerning the miracles which may be performed by the Priesthood; the need for baptism of water and the Spirit to be saved is given.

Contents of the promise

(1) The missionary is sent out to prove the world, for, he, the laborer, is worthy of his hire. (2) The faithful in this calling will find material as well as spiritual blessings. (3) He need not be concerned about what or when he eats, for the Lord is mindful of the welfare of his servants. (4) He should treasure eternal truths in his mind that the Spirit may draw them forth in a time of need. (5) The missionary should not take purse or scrip. (6) He should reprove the world of their unrighteous deeds and teach a judgment to come. (7) The Lord will be with him in his labors. (8) He who befriends the Lord's servants will receive his reward, but on the other hand, he who will not feed or furnish money to them will not be the Lord's servants.

Analysis of the promise

These verses are a prophetic promise of what will be received by the *faithful* missionary and those who sustain him. They who will not befriend the Lord's servant will not be his disciple.

The "laborer is worthy of his hire" summarizes what

may be called the Law of Remuneration for Services. This law is enunciated in Section 42, given in February 1831, as the law to the Church.[2] This law of remuneration is also mentioned in other revelations.[3] When a person gives full time service in the kingdom, he is to receive assistance in providing his material necessities. By and large, the ministry of the Church is not included in this category; for example, the missionary who serves a two-year period sustains himself, but the general authority and other full-time workers are included in this law.

To be "faithful in all things" means to seek for and obtain the spirit of one's calling as a missionary. This is accomplished only by righteousness in thought and deed. It means dedicated and loyal service at all times.

Emphasis is placed in this promise that in order to be a faithful servant one must study the gospel that when the need arises, the full mind will draw forth the necessary information—a dry well will not produce water.

The commandment to take purse and scrip in the early part of the dispensation was the same commandment given by the Savior to his disciples in the meridian dispensation.[4] When conditions changed, as they have in our dispensation when laws and other factors made it unfeasible to go without money and baggage, the meaning of purse and scrip, the disciples were commanded to take them.[5] Once again we find an example of the same teachings and practices of the earlier dispensation a part of the restoration of all things.[6]

An essential message of the servants of the Lord is that the judgment after death will be faced by every man. Also, the revelations are clear concerning judgments in this life in the form of natural calamities and wars. (See "The

---

[2]*Ibid.* 42:70-73.
[3]*Ibid.* 31:5; 70:12; 106:3.
[4]Luke 9:1-4; 10:1-5.
[5]*Ibid.* 22:35-36.
[6]Acts 3:19-21.

Wars That Shall Shortly Come to Pass"—Part II—Conditions after the American Civil War"—D&C 87:4-8; "And The Voice of Warning Shall be Unto All People"—D&C 1:2-5). Under some circumstances, the message of judgments should not be mentioned.[7]

In this same Priesthood revelation we learn that they who receive the Lord's servants receive the Savior, and in receiving him they receive the Father.[8] When a person helps a missionary with food, or other necessaries of life, he does not "receive" the Lord in the fullest sense given in this instruction. Only he who accepts the Lord fully through baptism and remains faithful will receive all that the Father hath, as indicated in these verses.[9]

Fulfillment of the promise

At the beginning of the dispensation missionaries of The Church of Jesus Christ of Latter-day Saints went out under the commandment that purse and scrip should not be used. They labored under adverse conditions sometimes, but always the Lord was with his faithful servants, raising up friends in time of need. The fulfillment of this prophetic promise is known throughout the Church by the posterity of those who labored without money and baggage. In 1863, President Heber C. Kimball said the time had come when the Gospel was to be preached to all nations and to be taught more quickly than it had ever before; therefore, the elders were to take purse and scrip.[10] There were times after that day that elders continued to labor without such means but, by and large, the taking of some means of subsistence was followed.

Testimonies of the Lord's goodness to his servants, who faithfully discharged their duties, are many. What impelled these men to travel in such a manner? President Brigham Young testified, as follows:

[7] D&C 105:24.
[8] *Ibid.* vs. 35-37.
[9] *Ibid.* vs. 38-39.
[10] *Journal of Discourses* 10:168.

"It has never been considered a hard thing by the Elders of this Church to pursue that course. Inspired by the Spirit of God they feel as God feels towards the human family—a desire to bless, comfort, and instruct and to lead them in the paths of life. God places this principle in the hearts of his servants—it emanates from him and is part of his nature; and inasmuch as the Elders are dictated by this spirit in their acts insomuch do they resemble their heavenly Father, who is full of benevolence and 'causes his sun to rise on the evil and on the good, and makes the rain to descend on the just and on the unjust;' and hence whenever we become acquainted with the principles of life ourselves we feel a desire to communicate the same unto others, and I see those all around me, here in this assembly, who, as well as myself, have traveled thousands of miles—I have traveled thousands of miles—on the same principle as the ancient disciples did, trusting in God for sustenance while proclaiming the principles of life to the people."[11]

President John Taylor said:

"We used to be in the habit of going without purse and scrip. That is the way I have travelled hundreds and thousands of miles, but then we felt as the disciples of old did. When we returned, if asked if we had lacked anything, we could say verily no. . . . At that time we were the poorest people in the world, but now we are better off than the generality of mankind, and we are able to help one another, and there is no necessity for our missionaries to go under the circumstances they have done heretofore . . ."[12]

The power of conviction went with these brethren in those early days, as it does now, but under different circumstances. President Wilford Woodruff relates the experiences of some members of the Quorum of the Twelve under the commandment of going without purse or scrip.

---

[11] *Ibid.* 15:285.
[12] *Ibid.* 12:48.

He said:

". . . I want to make a little statement of my experience in those days concerning circumstances that took place with me. When Brother Brigham [Young] left home he told me that all his family had was one barrel of rotten flour. Two hundred cents would have bought every pound of provision I left with my family when I left home. But we left our wives, for we had the commandment of God upon us, we were either going to obey it, or die trying. That was the spirit of the elders of Israel; and I blessed my wife and child and left them in the hands of God, and to the tender mercies of our noble bishops, and those who were acquainted with them know how it was in those days . . . . I mention this just to show our position. We traveled without purse and scrip, and we preached without money and without price. Why? Because the God in heaven had called upon us to go forth and warn the world."[13]

Application of the promise

When the Lord calls men into his service through his appointed leaders, there come blessings with faithful service. It was so with the early missionaries, their wants were supplied, and the persons receiving their ministrations were benefited with the words of salvation and also material blessings. When the ambassadors of the Lord give of their time, talents, and means to help build the kingdom of God on the earth, they receive bounteous blessings in fulfillment of commandments, one of which is that of peace in this world.[14] In addition, God's power is with his missionaries and his saints who are endeavoring to make their contributions in ward and stake positions. The Spirit of the Lord is with those who follow this commandment: "And again, I say unto you, I give unto you a commandment, that every man, both elder, priest, teacher, and also member, go to with his might, with the labor

---

[13]*Ibid.* 18:124-125.
[14]D&C 59:23.

of his hands, to prepare and accomplish the things which I have commanded."[15]

Although the commandment of no purse or scrip is no longer in force, the service performed by missionaries under a different set of circumstances is just as beneficial. The same Priesthood functions for guidance, instruction, and salvation ordinances, as formerly.

---

[15]*Ibid.* 38:40.

Chapter 27

". . . Ye Are Lawful Heirs . . . Blessed Are Ye If Ye Continue In My Goodness . . ."
(D&C 86:8-11)

Therefore, thus saith the Lord unto you, with whom the priesthood hath continued through the lineage of your fathers—

For ye are lawful heirs, according to the flesh, and have been hid from the world with Christ in God—

Therefore your life and the priesthood have remained, and must needs remain through you and your lineage until the restoration of all things spoken by the mouths of all the holy prophets since the world began.

Therefore, blessed are ye if ye continue in my goodness, a light unto the Gentiles, and through this priesthood, a savior unto my people Israel. The Lord hath said it. Amen.[1]

Background of the revelation

This revelation was given through the Prophet Joseph Smith at Kirtland, Ohio, December 6, 1832. It is an explanation of the parable of the Wheat and the Tares, given by the Savior.[2]

Background of the prophetic promise

The verses under consideration are preceded by the Parable of the Wheat and the Tares. The Lord's counsel was to permit the tares to grow with the wheat until the time of harvest (gathering), and then the tares would be burned. The relationship between the parable and the prophetic promise seems to be that the lawful heirs to the priesthood will be the gatherers in the last days, but if they do not fulfill their responsibilities they may be as the tares in the parable.

---

[1]D&C 86:8-11.
[2]Matthew 13:24-43.

Contents of the prophetic promise

(1) The priesthood has continued through the lineage of the fathers. (2) Ye [elders] are lawful heirs according to the flesh. (3) These lawful heirs have been hid from the world. (4) The priesthood must remain through these elders and their lineage until the restoration of all things has been completed. (5) Blessed are those who continue in goodness, a light unto the Gentiles, and a savior of Israel.

Analysis of the prophetic promise

The "you" of verse 8, "ye" of verses 9 and 11 and "your life" of verse 10, refer to the Elders of the Church, "my servants," and not to Joseph Smith alone.[3]

The Holy Priesthood did not come down to our dispensation from one person to another, as it does today; but it has come down from the fathers. This means that the Priesthood has come down from those who held it anciently; in fact, ancient prophets restored the priesthood to Joseph Smith and Oliver Cowdery. This priesthood must remain through the lineage of the elders, as promised.

The promise is given, however, that this authority will continue with the faithful members of the Church. The elders are lawful heirs to the priesthood, because they are literally of the lineage of Joseph, son of Jacob, and most often of the tribe of Ephraim. In fact, the priesthood will continue in this lineage until all that is necessary for the salvation of man on this earth has been accomplished.

Fulfillment of the prophetic promise

The testimonies received by the Holy Ghost are convincing evidence of the truth that Latter-day Saints are literally and lawfully heirs to the priesthood. President Wilford Woodruff said the following:

"I say to the brethren and sisters—you have your appointment; the Lord has raised up these Elders of Israel, and I can prove from the Book of Doctrine and Covenants that you received the Priesthood from eternity, and your

---

[3]Joseph Fielding Smith, *Origin of the "Reorganized" Church*, p. 55.

lives have been hid with Christ in God, and you knew it not. You are literally and lawfully heirs of the Priesthood through the lineage of your fathers, and that Priesthood will continue throughout eternity; therefore, you have received your appointment, and the Lord looks to you to build up his Zion and kingdom upon the earth."[4]

Elder Franklin D. Richards, an apostle and Church Historian of this dispensation, in reference to the prophetic promise said: "What a glorious development! What! the Priesthood came down from the days of the ancients . . . Yes, certainly. It is evident the eye of God has been over us, and the eyes of His angels have watched over the continuation of the fathers down through the generations that have come unto us."[5]

About the Prophet Joseph Smith, President Brigham Young said:

"It was decreed in the councils of eternity, long before the foundations of the earth were laid, that he should be the man, in the last dispensation of this world, to bring forth the word of God to the people, and receive the fulness of the keys and power of the Priesthood of the Son of God. The Lord had his eye upon him, and upon his father, and upon his father's father, and upon their progenitors clear back to Abraham, and from Abraham to the flood, from the flood to Enoch, and from Enoch to Adam. He has watched that family and that blood as it has circulated from its fountain to the birth of that man. He was foreordained in eternity to preside over this last dispensation . . ."[6]

It is a remarkable fact that many families of The Church of Jesus Christ of Latter-day Saints have common ancestors. The late Archibald F. Bennett, probably the greatest genealogist the Church has produced, said that during their lifetime the knowledge of the progenitors of some

---

[4]*Journal of Discourses* 18:120.
[5]*Millennial Star* 56:402-403.
[6]*Journal of Discourses* 7:289-290.

early leading families was very meagre. For example, Heber
C. Kimball did not know the names of his grandparents,
and Brigham Young knew no further than his great-grand-
parents.[7] With recent information available, Brother
Bennett traced many genealogies and learned of relationships with the Prophet Joseph Smith. The Prophet and
Brigham Young were 6th cousins; Heber C. Kimball and
the Prophet were 5th cousins, and from Zaccheus Gould,
an ancestor of the Prophet, "have come, in addition to
the Prophet, Hyrum Smith, Joseph F. Smith, and President
George Albert Smith, and such other progeny as Willard
Richards, Franklin D. Richards, George F. Richards, Le-
Grand Richards, and Orson F. Whitney," all of whom were
general authorities of the Church.[8]

Sometimes the Lord reveals genealogical connections
by dreams and visions when genealogical information is
not available. So it was with the Orson and Parley P.
Pratt family. The writer has in his possession a photostat
copy of a letter given him by Mrs. Una Pratt Giles, grand-
daughter of Parley P. Pratt, written on October 11, 1853,
to Parley from his brother Orson. An excerpt follows:

"I have published the history and genealogy of Joseph
Smith as written before his death: this includes six or
seven generations of his ancestry. You will recollect that
Joseph had a vision and saw that our fathers and his
all sprang from the same man a few generations ago. I
should be pleased to trace both genealogies back to their
junction, if it be possible."

About the relationship of the Smith and Pratt families,
Brother Bennett, who quoted the aforementioned vision
wrote:

"Another of her [Lucy Mack Smith, the Prophet's
mother] ancestors was Rev. John Lathrop, a Puritan
preacher who was thrust into prison for the principles he
taught. . . .

---

[7] Archibald F. Bennett, *Saviors on Mount Zion*, p. 87.
[8] *Ibid.* p. 88.

"Only in recent years has the name of his wife who died in England been discovered, so that her memory can be honored. She also was the daughter of a minister. Of their children, a son Samuel Lathrop the 4th great-grandfather of President Wilford Woodruff and also of Parley P. Pratt and Orson Pratt; a daughter Jane is the 4th great-grandmother of the Prophet. Thus was the Prophet's statement of his relationship to the Pratts verified."[9]

Joseph Loomis, an ancestor of the Prophet Joseph Smith, was also the progenitor of President Lorenzo Snow, President George Albert Smith, and Elder Joseph F. Merrill, among others.[10]

Brother Archibald F. Bennett, who was also a member of the Brigham Young University faculty, once told the writer that he believed that in time a very great many Latter-day Saint families would find a common progenitor not too far removed from them. Through patriarchal blessings, members of the Church have learned that they have a common progenitor a long, long time ago, in Joseph, son of Jacob, and father of Ephraim and Manasseh because they are "lawful heirs, according to the flesh, and have been hid from the world with Christ in God." The Prophet Joseph Smith taught that the gentiles, not of Israel, are adopted into the house of Israel when they receive the Holy Ghost by the laying on of hands.[11]

Application of the prophetic promise

Our fathers (Adam and his descendants, the prophets) received the priesthood, and we are of their lineage (Israel); therefore, we are lawful heirs for Abraham was promised that his seed would bear the priesthood through the generations of time.[12] Our fathers, during the great apostasy from the gospel, were "hid from the world" by Christ, but in the last dispensation, we Latter-day Saints are revealed to the

---

[9]*Ibid.* pp. 89-90.
[10]*Ibid.* pp. 87-88.
[11]Joseph Fielding Smith, *Teachings of the Prophet Joseph Smith*, pp. 149-150.
[12]Abraham 2:8-11.

world as descendants of Israel who have a legal claim to
the priesthood. Because we are of the royal lineage of
Abraham, we have the commission to become saviors to our
fellowmen in assisting the Savior. We have a destiny given
us of the Father. Some may not accept and carry forward
that commission, but each is under obligation to perform
the Lord's work.

Unto the Twelve Apostles, the Lord said: "For verily
I say unto you, the keys of the dispensation, which ye
have received, have come down from the fathers, and
last of all, being sent down from heaven unto you."[13]

Elder Franklin D. Richards said:

". . . the Lord has cared for a lineage which has
given you and me the right to the Holy Priesthood, and
has awakened our souls to trace back that lineage as far
as it can be discovered by records, or dreams, or visions,
or revelation, or by Urim and Thummim, until we go back
with our labors on that lineage, and thus return the only
grateful acknowledgment we can make to them for being
our fathers and mothers and giving us such honorable birth,
and at such a period of time, when the Priesthood is
revealed again, and that we can receive blessings of un-
told worth, that we never ourselves shall know the full
or, until we overcome this mortality, put on immortality
and enter into the exaltation which is promised unto the
faithful."[14]

Another Prophet has said:

"What are we? We are the agents of God, himself,
through the Holy Order of the Priesthood of the Son of
God. I wonder if we think of that. I wonder if that is on
our minds when we deal with one another, when we
deal with our families, with our neighbors, and with our
friends. We hold these powers with which out of his abundance God has endowed us, that we might be able to carry

---

[13]D&C 112:32.
[14]*Millennial Star* 56:403.

on the mission with which we were charged when we came here."[15]

---
[15]*Conference Report*, October 1955, pp. 87-88.

Chapter 28

"The Wars That Will Shortly Come to Pass"
(Part I)—The American Civil War
(D&C 87:1-3; 130:12-13)

(A) Verily, thus saith the Lord concerning the wars that will shortly come to pass, beginning at the rebellion of South Carolina, which will eventually terminate in the death and misery of many souls;

And the time will come that war will be poured out upon all nations, beginning at this place.

For behold, the Southern States shall be divided against the Northern States, and the Southern States will call on other nations, even the nation of Great Britain, as it is called, and they shall also call upon other nations, in order to defend themselves against other nations; and then war shall be poured out upon all nations.

(B) I prophesy, in the name of the Lord God, that the commencement of the difficulties which will cause much bloodshed previous to the coming of the Son of Man will be in South Carolina.

It may probably arise through the slave question. This a voice declared to me, while I was praying earnestly on the subject, December 25th, 1832.[2]

Background of the revelation

(A) In commenting upon conditions at the time Section 87 was received, the Prophet referred to plagues in India, cholera in other parts of the world, and the threatened dissolution of the Union due to South Carolina declaring itself free from the United States. President Jackson issued a proclamation against this measure and quelled this rebellion.[3]

(B) Section 130 consists of a series of doctrinal instructions correcting some statements made by Elder Orson Hyde in April 1843.

---

[1]D&C 87:1-3.
[2]*Ibid.*, 130:12-13.
[3]*DHC* 1:301.

The revelation on wars was first printed in the first edition of the Pearl of Great Price, 1851. The first time it appeared in the Doctrine and Covenants was in 1876. In addition, a number of the elders carried a copy of the revelation and read it to congregations long before the Civil War commenced.

Background of the prophecies

(A) Several years before 1832, discontent was manifest in the South over Federal tariff laws which protected the industrialists of the North while the Southern planters suffered. The tariff act of 1828 was called a tariff of abominations in the South, and the one of 1832 was also considered with equal or greater abhorrence. This discontent led South Carolina to favor the nullification of the Federal tariff laws, and, if necessary, to withdraw from the Union. President Andrew Jackson issued his proclamation of Nullification on December 10, 1832, which denied to any State the power to secede from the Union. Although South Carolina appealed to the other states for support, it was not forthcoming. Virginia and Georgia were sympathetic to the cause, but would do nothing for South Carolina.[5] Although a crisis had developed in the Nation, the ingredients to bring about an armed conflict between the States were not there. New tariff legislation in 1833 indicated a conciliatory attitude on the part of the South and the North.

(B) Two prophetic verses in the Doctrine and Covenants received at the beginning of 1831, herald the coming American Civil War: (1) "Ye hear of wars in far countries, and you say that there will soon be great wars in far countries, but ye know not the hearts of men in your own land."[6] (2) "Ye hear of wars in foreign lands; but, behold, I say unto you, they are nigh, even at your doors, and not many years hence ye shall hear of wars in your own lands."[7]

---

[4] Roy W. Doxey, *The Latter-day Prophets and the Doctrine and Covenants* 3:140-142.

[5] William B. Hesseltine, *The South in American History*, p. 198.

[6] D&C 38:29.

[7] *Ibid.*, 45:63.

On January 4, 1833, The Prophet made the following prophecy: "And now I am prepared to say by the authority of Jesus Christ, that not many years shall pass away before the United States shall present such a scene of *bloodshed* as has not been paralleled in the history of our nation."[8]

Contents of the prophecy

(1) The wars of the last days would commence with the rebellion of South Carolina. (2) This war would terminate in the death and misery of many souls. (3) The Southern States would be divided against the Northern States. (4) The South would call upon Great Britain for help. (5) The conflict between North and the South would probably arise through the slave question.

Analysis of the prophecies

On the same day Section 87 was received, Christmas, 1832, a "voice" declared to the Prophet that the war between the North and the South would "probably arise through the slave question."[9] Significant in this prophecy is the word "through", not because of slavery, but that slavery would be a contributing cause. Historians have differed in their understanding of the cause of the Civil War, some advocating one cause—slavery, while others believed that other causes in addition to slavery was the reason.[10]

Fulfillment of the prophecies

South Carolina rebelled against the Federal Government, and war commenced on April 12, 1861, with twenty-two Northern States against eleven Southern States. The war was long and costly in human life and material. "The death and misery of many souls"—is affirmed by a correspondent in these words: The Americans "have certainly fought more desperately, for a longer time, and with more

---

[8]*DHC* 1:301.

[9]D&C 130:12.

[10]Edwin C. Rozwenec (ed.), *Slavery As A Cause of the Civil War.*

dreadful slaughter, than any nation before them!" The war ended in 1865 with victory won by the North.[11]

"As measured by anything in Europe's past, the American Civil War is astronomical in its statistics. The theater of operations embraced an area so vast that a single flanking movement covered a distance of 800 miles. More than 2,000 combats took place, of which 149 were engagements of enough importance to be called battles. Half a million soldiers gave their lives, either on the battlefield or as a direct consequence of the campaigns. The cost in money to the North alone amounted to nearly five billion dollars; and the South did not admit defeat until every resource, both moral and material, had been exhausted."[12]

The Southern States did call upon Great Britain for aid, but that nation did not enter the conflict. Britain allowed Southern cruisers to be fitted out in her shipyards, resulting in the payment of $15,000,000 damage claim to the Union after the War.

The American Civil War was the first of modern wars, as prophesied.

"The first of the unlimited industrialized wars was the Civil War in America. It was the first great conflict of the steam age, and the aim of the Northern, or Federal, states was unconditional surrender—that is, total victory. Its character was, therefore, that of a crusade, and because of this, as well as because it put to the test the military developments of the Industrial Revolution, it opened a radically new chapter in the history of war."[13]

"In its tactics as well as weapons this struggle is the first in history which can readily be identified with the warfare of the present day. The railway and telegraph at last came into their own, after having confused and annoyed the professional soldiers of Europe. Hundreds of steamships,

---

[11]Roy W. Doxey, *The Latter-day Prophets and the Doctrine and Covenants* 3:143.

[12]Lynn Montross, *War Through the Ages* (Harper and Brothers Publishers: New York and London, 1944), p. 591.

[13]J.F.C. Fuller, *A Military History of the Western World*, Vol. 3, p. 6.

plying the great rivers and the 3,500-mile coast line, supplied and transported the armies of both sides. Eli Whitney,
the father of mass production in arms, had inadvertently
helped to bring on the strife by his invention of the cotton
gin, which provided the Confederates with the sinews of
war. Cyrus McCormick's reaper, by opening up the prairies
of the West, added enormously to the strength of the Federal cause.

"The first duel between ironclad warships was followed
by the first railway gun, the first electrically exploded tor-
pedo and the first recorded instance of a vessel being sunk
by a submarine. The first metallic cartridges were invented
for the first breech-loading repeating rifles to meet the test
of war. The machine gun had its first demonstration on the
battlefield, and wire entanglements made their first appearance.

"To this list might be added such recent arms as the
revolver and rifled cannon, neither of which had as yet
proved its worth in largescale operations. Nearly as much
originality was shown in the adaptation of weapons which
had been thought obsolete. Among these revivals were the
military observation balloon, lamp and flag signaling, the
land mine and the hand grenade."[14]

Application of the prophecy

The prophecy about the American Civil War is an
outstanding example of the prophetic powers possessed by
the Prophet Joseph Smith. Its importance to the Latter-day
Saint is not only in this connection, but also because it is a
direct answer to the Prophet's prayer. In addition, the
background of the prophecy in Section 38, as a prelude to
Section 87, is also one received as an answer to prayer. In
the context to that prophecy we read: "I tell you these
things because of your prayers; wherefore, treasure up
wisdom in your bosoms, lest the wickedness of men reveal
these things unto you by their wickedness, in a manner
which shall speak in your ears with a voice louder than

---

[14]Lynn Montross, *War Through the Ages*, pp. 591-592.

that which shall shake the earth; but if ye are prepared ye shall not fear."[15]

Not only the Prophet but others had prayed for guidance in view of European troubled conditions in 1830 and 1831. The answer to the prayers came through the Prophet. Latter-day Saints may take a valuable lesson from this experience. Look to the Prophet for guidance in a troubled time! Your prayers may have been answered in the scriptures already given or received by the living Prophet!

---

[15]D&C 38:30.

Chapter 29

"The Wars That Will Shortly Come to Pass" (Part II)—Conditions After the American Civil War (D&C 87:4-8)

. . . and the Southern States will call on other nations, even the nation of Great Britain, as it is called, and they shall also call upon other nations, in order to defend themselves against other nations, and then war shall be poured out upon all nations.

And it shall come to pass, after many days, slaves shall rise up against their masters, who shall be marshaled and disciplined for war.

And it shall come to pass also that the remnants who are left of the land will marshal themselves, and shall become exceedingly angry, and shall vex the Gentiles with a sore vexation.

And thus, with the sword and by bloodshed the inhabitants of the earth shall mourn; and with famine, and plague, and earthquake, and the thunder of heaven, and the fierce and vivid lightning also, shall the inhabitants of the earth be made to feel the wrath, and indignation, and chastening hand of an Almighty God, until the consumption decreed hath made a full end of all nations;

That the cry of the saints, and of the blood of the saints, shall cease to come up into the ears of the Lord of Sabaoth, from the earth, to be avenged of their enemies.

Wherefore, stand ye in holy places, and be not moved, until the day of the Lord come; for behold, it cometh quickly, saith the Lord. Amen.[1]

Background of the revelation

Two times during the year 1831, January and March, the Lord revealed that war would come to the United States.[2] Then, on December 25, 1832, he revealed details concerning the war between the North and the South.[3] (See Part I of "The Wars That Will Shortly Come to Pass.")

Background of the prophecy

Not only did the revelation say that the North would be divided against the South, but that the conflict would

---

[1]D&C 87:3-8.
[2]Ibid. 38:29; 45:63.
[3]Ibid. 87:1-3.

begin with the rebellion of South Carolina. Also, it would result in the death and misery of many souls, and that the South would call upon Great Britain for assistance, all of which came literally true.

Contents of the prophecy

(1) Great Britain would call upon nations to assist her when she would be required to defend herself against other nations. When this happened war would be poured out upon all nations. (2) Some time after this conflict, slaves would be marshalled for war against their masters. (3) The "remnants" of the land would become angry with the Gentiles, afflicting them with a sore vexation. (4) Then the inhabitants of the earth would mourn because of war, famine, plague, and earthquake, bringing about the dissolution of nations. (5) Thus the cries of the saints who had been martyred would cease. (6) In the meantime, the saints were commanded to remain in holy places until the Lord comes.

Fulfillment of the Prophecy

Some of the prophetic events mentioned in this revelation have been fulfilled, while others are yet future. (1) A careful reading of verse 3 of Section 87 indicates that when Great Britain would be required to ask other nations to help her against her enemies, then war would be poured out upon all nations. When the revelation was received, Great Britain was the dominant power in Europe and the world. The industrialization of Germany brought a competitor for the leadership of Europe. When Germany defeated France in the Franco-Prussian War of 1870, Great Britain developed a friendship for France that she might have a balance of power in Europe. Germany challenged the economic leadership of Great Britain. With the powerful rise of Japanese imperialism in the east and with the defeat of Russia, the rise of the United States to a world power, and the further development of Great Britain, France, and Germany, the scene was being set for a world conflict.

When Great Britain called upon her allies, including the United States, and the involvement of other countries then "the war became global and not a single greater Power was left free to act as its arbiter."[4]

(2) Slaves are to rise up against their masters. (a) Some Latter-day Saints have considered that this part of the prophecy pertains to the Civil War because nearly 200,000 Negroes were marshalled by the North against the South. (b) The future fulfillment concerning slaves may arise out of the agitation of the civil rights movement in the United States, but if a person thinks of a world-wide fulfillment it might be the struggle of people in communist nations seeking their freedom.[5]

(3) The American Indian is referred to in the Book of Mormon as a remnant of Israel.[6] President Daniel H. Wells, counselor to President Brigham Young, taught that the remnant spoken of in this prophecy was the American Indian who would one day vex the gentile nation, the United States, with a sore vexation.[7]

(4) Verse 6 of the prophecy indicates that the day would come when the inhabitants of the earth would mourn because of war, famine, plague, and earthquake. These calamities would bring an end to the nations. All of these calamitous events are but a prelude to the second coming of Christ when the reigns of government will be taken by him.[8]

(5) John the Revelator saw the souls of the martyrs who were slain for the word of God crying for vengeance.[9] Similarly, the saints of this dispensation who have died for the truth will be avenged. When the Lord's servants are rejected, killed, there is no escape from judgment for those who are responsible. The rejection of Alma and Amulek by

---

[4]J.F.C. Fuller, *A Military History of the Western World*, Vol. 3, p. 182.
[5]F.P. Chambers, C.P. Harns, C.C. Bagley, *This Age of Conflict*, preface.
[6]2 Nephi 28:2; Alma 46:23; 3 Nephi 15:12; 21:21-24.
[7]*Millennial Star* 27:186-187.
[8]D&C 38:21-22.
[9]Revelation 6:9-11.

the apostate Nephites in Ammonihah brought quick destruction.[10] (See "I Will Fight Your Battles,"—D&C 105:14-15).

(6) Preservation from the judgments of the last days is promised the faithful saints. When they were scattered from the center place of Zion, the Lord commanded that they gather into the stakes of Zion for refuge.[11] The Saints have the assurance that all things will work for the good of those who walk uprightly before the Lord. (See "I Will Raise Up Unto Myself A Pure People"—D&C 100:15-17).

Application of the prophecy

The revelation on wars (Section 87), was literally fulfilled although it was received almost thirty years before the American Civil War which was prophesied in some detail. In addition, as pointed out in this discussion, war among the nations has also come to pass.

Not only has the world experienced one world war, but World War II engulfed the world in far greater conflict in terms of nations involved and loss of life and material. War continues day by day. It was hoped that after each World War peace had come, but it is evident that World War I began a series of conflicts. The following commentary is meaningful in this regard:

"The two World Wars, and the intervening wars, revolutions, and crises, are now realized to be episodes in a single Age of Conflict, as it might be called, which began in 1914 and has not yet run its course. Exactly what that age portends in ultimate terms no one yet knows. It has certainly brought the world more change and tragedy than any other equal span of events in recorded time."[13]

In view of the fulfillment of this part of the prophecy, Latter-day Saints may be assured that those elements of the prophecy yet future will also be literally fulfilled. The appli-

---

[10]Alma 14:17-29; 15:1; 16:9-11.
[11]D&C 101:17-24.
[12]Ibid. 100:15-17.
[13]F.P. Chambers, C.P. Harris, C.C. Bagley, This Age of Conflict, Preface.

cation of the article in this series entitled "Peace Shall Be Taken From the Earth," is meaningful in this quotation: ". . . if ye are prepared ye shall not fear."[14]

---

[14]D&C 38:29.

Chapter 30

"... Conspiring Men In The Last Days ..."
(D&C 89:4)

Behold, verily, thus saith the Lord unto you: In consequence of evils and designs which do and will exist in the hearts of conspiring men in the last days, I have warned you, and forewarn you, by giving unto you this word of wisdom by revelation—.[1]

Background of the revelation

President Brigham Young related the circumstances which made the Prophet Joseph Smith inquire of the Lord regarding the use of tobacco. He said that the Prophet instructed a school of brethren, in a small room attached to the store of Bishop Newel K. Whitney in Kirtland, Ohio. During these sessions some of the men would smoke and chew tobacco and expectorate on the floor creating a situation which he did not like and about which his wife complained. The revelation known to the Church as the Word of Wisdom was received on February 27, 1833.

Background of the prophecy

This revelation is addressed to the council of high priests in Kirtland, the church, and also the saints in Zion, not as a commandment but a revelation expressing the will of God in the temporal salvation of all saints. Subsequently, the Church in general conference accepted this revelation as binding upon its members; therefore, the revelation became a commandment, or the will of the Lord.[2]

Contents of the prophecy

This prophecy may not be worded like others, but nonetheless it carries the same prophetic intent. The words:

---

[1]D&C 89:4.

[2]Roy W. Doxey, *The Latter-day Prophets and the Doctrine and Covenants*, Vol. 3, pp. 227-228. (Quotations from Brigham Young, Jr., Francis M. Lyman, and Joseph F. Smith.)

"In consequence of evils and designs . . ." clearly sets the meaning for what will happen in the future. (1) Evils and designs do and will exist in the hearts of conspiring men in the last days. (2) The efforts of designing men would be concentrated upon fostering the use of the items mentioned in the revelation—hot drinks (tea and coffee), tobacco, and strong drink. These things are declared by the Lord to be "not good for man."[3] Because of these evil efforts of men, the Lord provided his people with counsel and commandment that their salvation might be complete by obedience to his word.

Fulfillment of the prophecy

It took years after this prophecy was received for science to affirm its truth. There will no doubt be further information discovered that will certify these harmful products as "not good for man." Many Latter-day Saint writers have brought together the research of science to show how tea, coffee, tobacco, and liquor are definitely harmful to one's health.[4]

Probably the most damaging conclusion which is known against cigarette smoking is its association with lung cancer. About twenty years ago, researchers deduced that there was an association of cancer and tobacco-tar condensates. Further studies have shown that lung cancer is a contributing factor in the death of cigarette smokers. Conclusions reached by the Advisory Committee to the Surgeon General of the United States Public Health Service, in a report issued in 1964, verify not only that cigarette smoking is causally related to lung cancer, but also to chronic bronchitis, coronary artery disease, as well as being associated with accidental deaths from fires in the home.[5]

---

[3]D&C 89:5-9.

[4]John H. Widtsoe and Leah D. Widtsoe, *The Word Of Wisdom, A Modern Interpretation*, 1939; L. Weston Oaks, *The Word of Wisdom and You*, 1958; currently a series of articles on this subject is being published in the *Church News* by Dr. Lindsay Curtis.

[5]*Smoking and Health*, pp. 232, 302, 327, 345.

Despite this evidence the advertising of cigarettes continues with millions of dollars being spent annually to encourage people to smoke. In 1958, a sub-committee of the Committee on Government Operations of the United States House of Representatives, reported that when the tobacco-lung cancer "scare" hit the public in 1953 there was a considerable decline in cigarette sales.[6] The tobacco companies have recouped these losses and increased their profits by introducing the filter-tip cigarette. The conclusions of the Committee, however, speak for themselves regarding their false advertising:

"In view of the publicized health hazards a strange though completely explicable transformation has occurred in the filter cigarette since its introduction. Many smokers apparently found the filters to be less satisfying (as in the case of Kents) than their old regular cigarettes. They tried different brands, presumably in search of a filter cigarette which not only afforded health protection but also (as one brand advertised) 'tastes good like a cigarette should.'

"The cigarette manufacturers obliged—at least with respect to taste. Unfortunately, the much advertised health protection—that is, less nicotine and tar—was an unpublicized casualty. The filter cigarette smoker is, in most cases, getting as much or more nicotine and tar from the filter than he would get from the regular cigarette the advertisers have persuaded him to abandon—for his health's sake."[7]

"Evidence submitted to the subcommitte showed how the cigarette industry accomplished the feat of achieving a higher level of nicotine and tar in cigarette smoke despite the filter.

"First the filters were loosened to permit a larger number of smoke particles to get through. Second, the

---

[6]"False and Misleading Advertising," *Twentieth Report of the Committee On Government Operations*, 1958, p. 13.

[7]*Ibid.* p. 15.

blend was changed to include more of the stronger, heavier-bodied tobaccos. This 'switch' to the 'low grade' darker leaves has turned the tobacco market upside down. The mild, light, bright tobaccos, the most desirable of tobacco in the pre-filter period, are accumulating as surplus in Government warehouses, while the low grades of former years have moved rapidly into the hands of the cigarette manufacturers."[8]

In its final conclusions the Committee Report without knowing it, affirmed the prophecy in the Word of Wisdom by testifying in this manner:

"1. The cigarette manufacturers have deceived the American public through their advertising of filter-tip cigarettes.

"Ironically, while denying the alleged health hazards of cigarette smoking, the cigarette industry has, in its advertising, made these charges appear true.

"Without specifically claiming that the filter tip removes the agents alleged to contribute to heart disease or lung cancer, the advertising has emphasized such claims as 'clean smoking,' 'snowy white,' 'pure,' 'miracle tip,' '20,000 filter traps,' 'gives you more of what you changed to a filter for' and other phrases implying health protection, when actually most filter cigarettes produce as much or more nicotine and tar as cigarettes without filters.

"2. The effectiveness of this deceptive advertising is evidenced by the rise in filter-cigarette sales from 1.4 percent of total cigarette sales in 1952 to 40 percent in 1957. The American public have paid premium prices of 2 to 6 cents per pack for filter cigarettes for 'protection' they did not receive. . . ."[9]

Liquor advertising today suggests that benefits are derived from drinking—sociability, good cheer, and happiness. These claims are made despite the damaging effects

---

[8]*Ibid.* p. 18.
[9]*Ibid.* pp. 24-25.

of the use of alcohol. Dr. L. Weston Oaks gives the following summation of the use of alcohol:

"A study of alcohol's effects upon the human body reveals undeniable evidence that the drug is derogatory to our best welfare; that its use precludes our enjoyment of the highest intellectual, spiritual, physical or social life."[10]

A motivational research agency provided the coffee industry with some suggestions on how to best sell their product after determining in some depth interviews the attitudes of coffee drinkers toward their consumption of this beverage. It was discovered that there were lingering feelings of sin and punishment associated with this habit. It was considered by these coffee drinkers as a drug-provoking habit, a dangerous drink because of its overstimulating the heart and other organs of the body, and it was accused of aiding in laziness! The task of the industry was to change this sinful and escapist attitude to a beneficial and life-accepting one. Suggestions were made whereby coffee would be dramatized as a positive helper in life! The initiation of children to the use of coffee was advocated by using it as a symbol of initiation into maturity, a small amount in milk to be increased as a part of the growing up process was recommended.[11]

Application of the prophecy

Latter-day Saints have come to recognize in recent years that their faith in the Prophet Joseph Smith's mission has been vindicated by science in the Word of Wisdom. They have come to realize better that the efforts of men to promote the use of deleterious substances and liquids fulfills the prophecy concerning these efforts which are evil and designing. President David O. McKay once expressed gratitude that the Lord did not say, "Strong drink to excess is not good;" nor "Drunkenness is not good. . . ." But like other eternal truths it stands unqualified; *strong*

---

[10]L. Weston Oaks, *The Word of Wisdom and You*, p. 148.
[11]Neil H. Borden and Martin V. Marshall, Advertising Management, pp. 606-609.

drink is not good."[12] Social drinking, the taking of a cocktail or a small quantity of liquor, is damaging to the brain! Dr. Melvin H. Knisely, chairman of the department of anatomy at the Medical College of South Carolina reported that social drinking may result in a "great deal of damage to the brain." The brain consists of between 10 billion to 18 billion cells, but if only as few as 10,000 cells were destroyed at a time by heavy drinking this could be significant over a long period of time.[13]

---

[12]*Conference Report*, April 1911, pp. 61-62.

[13]"Social Drink—It May Destroy the Brain," *The Deseret News*, September 19, 1968.

Chapter 31

"And All Saints . . . Shall Find Wisdom And Great Treasures of Knowledge . . ."
(D&C 89:18-21)

And all saints who remember to keep and do these sayings, walking in obedience to the commandments, shall receive health in their navel and marrow to their bones;

And shall find wisdom and great treasures of knowledge, even hidden treasures;

And shall run and not be weary, and shall walk and not faint.

And I, the Lord, give unto them a promise, that the destroying angel shall pass by them, as the children of Israel, and not slay them. Amen.[1]

Background of the revelation

Section 89 of the Doctrine and Covenants is known as the Word of Wisdom. During the winter of 1833, a school of the prophets held in Kirtland, Ohio, was conducted in a room occupied by the Prophet Joseph Smith and his family. Due to the brethren using tobacco, the Prophet inquired of the Lord regarding this practice, and the Word of Wisdom was received.[2]

Background of the prophetic promise

The Word of Wisdom contains instruction on food and drink which are beneficial and also food and drink which are harmful to one's health. It antedated scientific data regarding much of its contents. In fact, there is a prophecy in it regarding the evils and designs of men to foster harmful products on the public. (See "Conspiring Men In The Last Days."—D&C 89:4). Among the beverages which are condemned are: tea, coffee, and alcoholic drinks. Tobacco is also singled out as harmful. Foods which are prescribed

---

[1]D&C 89:18-21.

[2]Brigham Young, *Journal of Discourses* 12:158.

for man's use are: wholesome herbs, fruits in the season thereof, meat used sparingly, and grains.

Contents of the prophetic promise

(1) Saints who obey the Word of Wisdom, and who walk in obedience to the commandments shall receive health. (2) They shall find wisdom and treasures of knowledge, "even hidden treasures." (3) They shall run and neither be weary nor faint. (4) The destroying angel shall pass them by.

Analysis of the prophetic promise

The word "saint" means "a holy one"; consequently, members of The Church of Jesus Christ of Latter-day Saints profess to be holy ones. This does not mean that the member of the Church is without blemish or blame, but it does mean, as one definition suggests, that "holy" applies to exclusive service in the cause of God. In other words, the "saint" or "holy one" is set apart from the world as one of God.[3]

Special notice should be taken of the qualification that those who receive the blessings of the Word of Wisdom, must walk in "obedience to the commandments," and not only those who "keep and do these sayings."

From Dr. L. Weston Oaks, the following is given:

"The expression, 'health in the navel,' is of clear-cut significance, not only for those of us who live now, but especially for those who are to become our posterity. For individuals who have passed their natal day, the navel or umbilicus has little importance, save that it testifies of one's having come into the world in the natural way. In the fetus and unborn baby all nourishment, fluids, regulating materials such as hormones, enzymes and chemicals—as well as every bit of waste materials to be carried away—during the growth and preparation of the infant body to sustain itself after birth, must pass through this portal. . . .

---

[3] 1 Peter 1:12-16.

". . . if his prenatal development is hampered by parents who break the rules of health laid down, he becomes the innocent victim of their ignorance and carelessness. Since every poison which enters the mother's bloodstream, whether it be alcohol, nicotine, caffeine, poisons generated by acute infection, or the insidious toxins of chronic disease, readily passes from the blood of the mother to that of the unborn child, there is little indeed that nature can do to protect him against what she does."[4]

From the same source the following is pertinent: ". . . 'marrow to the bones' is likewise of major significance in human health. Bone marrow may be yellow—as seen in the marrow cavities of long bones—or red. Yellow marrow consists of fat cells, blood vessels and a framework of cells and fibers. Red marrow, which is present even in the long bones of the newborn infant, contains many mature blood cells of all kinds, along with countless immature forms which are in the course of completing development, and which later will find their way into the circulation. As an individual grows in years, red bone marrow becomes more fatty, and by one's twentieth birthday almost the entire marrow content of long bones has become yellow in type.

"So long as it is adequate for the job, bone marrow manufactures the various blood cells to replace those millions destroyed in our daily activities, or by such things as acute infections, choronic anemias, and especially by accidents or illness associated with hemorrhage. . . .

". . . 'marrow to their bones' is clearly a significant promise, in this day when anemias of severe grade are more common than ever before."[5]

Elder Marion G. Romney, of the Council of the Twelve, gave this discussion of the "destroying angel" mentioned in this prophetic promise:

"From this promise in the Word of Wisdom and other scriptures, it appears that there are destroying angels who

---

[4]L. Weston Oaks, *The Word of Wisdom and You*, pp. 39-40.
[5]*Ibid.* pp. 41-42.

have a work to do among the peoples of the earth in this last dispensation. (D&C 86:4-7). The Lord told the Prophet Joseph Smith that because all flesh was corrupted before him, and the powers of darkness prevailed upon the earth, these angels were 'waiting the great command to reap down the earth, to gather the tares that they may be burned.' (Sec. 38:11-12). That was in 1831. In 1894, President Woodruff said: 'God has held the angels of destruction for many years lest they should reap down the wheat with the tares. But I want to tell you now, those angels have left the portals of heaven, and they stand over this people and this nation now, and are hovering over the earth waiting to pour out the judgments. And from this very day they shall be poured out. Calamities and troubles are increasing in the earth, and there is a meaning to these things.' (IE 17:1165).

"Now . . . in view of this revealed knowledge and understanding which the Lord has given concerning what is transpiring about us, is it not a glorious thing to have the assurance that if we will clothe ourselves with bodies purified through observance of the Word of Wisdom, these destroying angels will pass us by, as they did the children of Israel, and not slay us? Well, this is one of the blessings to follow observance of the Word of Wisdom."[6]

Fulfillment of the prophecy

Data are not available regarding the number of members of the Church who live the Word of Wisdom. It is probably safe to say that most members of the Church to some degree live it. President Heber J. Grant said:

"I would like it known that if we as a people never used a particle of tea or coffee or of tobacco or of liquor, we would become one of the most wealthy people in the world. Why? Because we would have increased vigor of body, increased vigor of mind; we would grow spiritually;

---

[6]*Conference Report*, October 1952, pp. 32-33.

we would have a more direct line of communication with God, our Heavenly Father."[7]

Elder John A. Widtsoe and Leah D. Widtsoe gave these four rewards for faithfully obeying the Word of Wisdom: "First, strength and vigor of body; second, protection against disease; and third, the possession of knowledge and wisdom, even 'hidden treasures of knowledge.' A fourth reward is implied, namely 'temporal salvation,' in which may be included economic welfare."[8] Though this book was written over 30 years ago, the published information on Latter-day Saint birth rates covers the period from 1900 to 1936, making it a useful source of information. The writers indicate that bodily vigor might be shown in the Latter-day Saint birth rates which are consistently higher than the United States population. For the period 1960 through 1967, except 1961 for which there was no United States information, from 23.7 births per thousand (1960) in the United States to a low of 17.8 in 1967, with each year decreasing.[9] In The Church of Jesus Christ of Latter-day Saints, the highest birth rate per thousand was 35.00 in 1960, with a low of 25.23 in 1966. There has been a general decrease of births in the Church, but not consistently each year.[10] On the average during the seven year period, the Church has had an additional 10 births more per thousand than the United States. Death rates per thousand in the Church were 4 persons less than in the United States for the period 1960 through 1967, except 1961. Also, for the years 1927 and 1928, the death rate was strikingly lower than the rate in twenty-five nations. "The death rates from specific diseases, among Latter-day Saints are low compared with other large groups of people."[11]

---

[7]G. Homer Durham (comp.), *Gospel Standards*, p. 50.

[8]John A. Widtsoe and Leah D. Widtsoe, *The Word of Wisdom, A Modern Interpretation*, pp. 235-236.

[9]*Statistical Abstract of the United States*, 1968, p. 47.

[10]*Conference Report*, April, 1960, 1966.

[11]John A. Widtsoe and Leah D. Widtsoe, *The Word of Wisdom, A Modern Interpretation*, p. 239.

The living of the Word of Wisdom and the other commandments opens the door for opportunities in acquiring "wisdom and great treasures of knowledge, even hidden treasures." Because Latter-day Saints are the only people who may receive the gift of the Holy Ghost, they may seek for these rich treasures. Elder Harold B. Lee related the experience of Elder Don B. Colton, who was also a Sunday School teacher in Washington, D.C., while serving in the house of Representatives and who was asked by members of his class why the Latter-day student was not academically ahead of students who did not observe the Word of Wisdom. The answer was not then available to Brother Colton, but during the week, while at lunch with a non-member of the Church, his friend said:

" 'Congressman Colton, I've been out in your state. While I was there I was a guest of some of the members of your Church, and they invited me in to attend your meetings, and one of these meetings you hold is called a fast and testimony meeting.' And he said, 'I sat there and heard young men and women get up and bear testimony that I knew, and the sincerity with which they spoke their testimonies left no doubt that they knew the gospel was true; they knew that Jesus was the Savior of the world.' And then he said, 'Gentlemen, those people out there have hidden treasures of knowledge that the rest of us don't have.' And Brother Colton said, 'Think of it. I had to have a non-member colleague of mine tell me what the Lord meant in the Word of Wisdom, that we would find great treasures of knowledge, the depths of the mysteries of godliness.' The great undiscovered truths can only be perceived by the spirit. We put ourselves in spiritual tune when we keep God's commandments."[12]

In addition to the personal testimonies of God's existence and Jesus Christ as the Son of God, that Joseph Smith is a prophet and his successors divinely appointed, the Latter-day Saint has a living knowledge of questions which

---

[12]Harold B. Lee, "Faith," *Y Speeches of the Year,* June 28, 1955.

learned men have pondered over the centuries. They have "hidden knowledge" answering the questions of Where did I come from? Why am I here? and Where do I go at death? These and many more questions for which answers are not available in the world are in the theology of The Church of Jesus Christ of Latter-day Saints.

The living of the commandments provide a person with wisdom to assist him in his temporal welfare. "A wise person will conserve his economic resources. Adherence to the Word of Wisdom reduces the cost of living—the main economic problem of our day—by the larger use of the less expensive foods, such as grains, vegetables and fruits, and by saving the huge sums expended elsewhere for harmful alcoholic beverages, tobacco, tea and coffee."[13]

One criterion of the high degree of spirituality possessed by those who keep the commandments, including the Word of Wisdom, is the Church activity in which Latter-day Saints engage. The four Priesthood programs—Home Teaching, Welfare, Missionary, and Genealogy—promote this important aspect of religious life. There is ample opportunity for saints to be active participants in Church activity throughout their lives.

Application of the prophecy

Every Latter-day Saint rejoices in the increased information available to sustain the Word of Wisdom as an authentic guide to living. In recent years the scientific research into tobacco and alcohol evidence the truth of this revelation. (See ". . . Conspiring Men in the Last Days . . ." —D&C 89:4).

Sometimes members of the Church are not sure as to what constitutes wisdom in the living of this law of health. In addition to the specifics mentioned in the revelation, the following from President Joseph Fielding Smith should help these inquirers:

"A safe guide to each and all is this: If in doubt as to

---

[13]John A. widtsoe and Leah D. Widtsoe, *The Word Of Wisdom, A Modern Interpretation*, p. 242.

any food or drink, whether it is good or harmful, let it alone until you have learned the truth in regard to it. If anything offered is habit-forming, we will be safe in concluding that it contains some ingredients that are harmful to the body and should be avoided."[14]

The Word of Wisdom is a commandment, having been accepted as such by the Church.[15] Where is there a Latter-day Saint who does not need wisdom, even hidden treasure of knowledge, in this day of uncertainty?

Although good health is a highly desirable blessing, the Word of Wisdom is intended to contribute to one's spirituality. No commandment is temporal only, but all commandments are spiritual.[16] The blessings of the eternities are contingent upon the rebirth by the Holy Spirit through accepting the laws by which that birth is possible. The body is the temple of the Holy Spirit and must be clean to inherit this blessing.[17]

---

[14]*Improvement Era* 59:78-79.

[15]Roy W. Doxey, *The Latter-day Prophets and the Doctrine and Covenants,* Vol. 3, pp. 226-230.

[16]D&C 29:34-35.

[17]1 Corinthians 3:16-17.

Chapter 32

"... Through You Shall The Oracles Be Given ... Even Unto The Church."

(D&C 90:1-4)

Thus saith the Lord, verily, verily I say unto you my son, thy sins are forgiven thee, according to thy petition, for thy prayers and the prayers of thy brethren have come up into my ears.

Therefore, thou art blessed from henceforth that bear the keys of the kingdom given unto you; which kingdom is coming forth for the last time.

Verily I say unto you, the keys of this kingdom shall never be taken from you, while thou art in the world, neither in the world to come;

Nevertheless, through you shall the oracles be given to another, yea, even unto the church.[1]

Background of the revelation

This revelation was received at Kirtland, Ohio, on March 8, 1833. Up to this time, the presiding authorities in the Church were Joseph Smith, First Elder, and Oliver Cowdery, Second Elder. In the evolution of Church organization, Section 90 sets up a presidency of three, with Joseph Smith as President of the Church and Sidney Rigdon and Frederick G. Williams, as counselors.

Background of the prophecy

This prophecy opens Section 90.

Contents of the prophecy

(1) Joseph Smith's sins are forgiven. (2) The Prophet is blessed in holding the keys of the kingdom. (3) This kingdom is coming forth for the last time. (4) The keys of the kingdom are to remain with the Prophet as long as he lives in mortality and in the life after death. (5) These powers are to be given to the Church.

---

[1]D&C 90:1-4.

Analysis of the prophecy

Although the statement that Joseph Smith's sins are forgiven is not a pertinent part of the prophecy, its relationship to the prophecy itself is indicated in the words, "Therefore, thou art . . ."

As an authoritative source says, this declaration is confirmation of the ordinance at the January 1833 conference of washing of feet that the brethren might be clean from the blood of this generation.[2]

Verse 6 of Section 60 indicates that Sidney Rigdon and Frederick G. Williams had their sins remitted also. To forestall any thought that these brethren were rank sinners we read:

> Neither the Prophet Joseph, nor his brethren, had any great transgressions, as measured by worldly standards, on their consciences, but no mortal is entirely free from sin. The fact is that, the nearer a man draws to the presence of God, the more keenly he feels his imperfections and shortcomings, and the more natural it is to exclaim with Peter, 'Depart from me; for I am a sinful man, O Lord!' (Luke 5:8). It is not surprising, therefore, to learn that the Prophet and his brethren, coming, as it were, from the very presence of the Lord, engaged in prayers for the forgiveness of their sins and received the assurance quoted."[3]

The keys of the kingdom are those powers bestowed upon the Prophet by angelic personages in the beginning of the dispensation. When Peter, James, and John conferred the Melchizedek Priesthood upon him and Oliver Cowdery, they gave them the keys of the apostleship.[4] The keys of the Priesthood mean the power to direct the affairs of the Church (kingdom).

The kingdom was continuing to develop at the time Section 90 was given, for in this revelation a First Presidency was directed to be organized. Also, other keys, or authorities, were restored three years later in the Kirtland

---

[2]*Ibid.* 88:138-141; Hyrum M. Smith and Janne M. Sjodahl, *Doctrine and Covenants Commentary*, p. 576.

[3]*Ibid.* 576-577.

[4]D&C 27:12-13.

Temple.[5] There is sufficient authority on the earth to provide the means for men and women to be exalted in the celestial kingdom, but the kingdom will continue to develop until the Lord's work is accomplished for the salvation of people in this world.

Joseph Smith was true to the work assigned him— the initiator and restorer of the fulness of the Gospel of Jesus Christ in the Latter days. He was foreordained to this position in the premortal worlds. The Lord knew before Joseph Smith was born that he would be true and faithful to his calling. He inspired Joseph, son of Jacob, to know this fact.[6]

In 1831, the Lord revealed that if Joseph Smith were to fall, he would have the power to select his successor, because only through the Prophet could revelation come for the Church.[7] It appears that the Lord was testing the Prophet at that time, but by 1833, he was told in the prophecy that he would hold the keys forever.

The "oracles" will be given to another, even unto the church. The word "oracles" means the revelations given by God.[8] Therefore, the keys of the kingdom are to be received from Joseph Smith and given to others, that the keys might remain in the Church forever. As indicated, only by the keys may revelation be received for the Church.

Fulfillment of the prophecy

By divine revelation, the Lord has said that the First Presidency of the Church hold all of the keys of the kingdom, with power to regulate the affairs of the Church.[9] The second quorum in authority is the Council of the Twelve Apostles.These brethren form a quorum "equal in

---

[5]*Ibid.* 110.
[6]2 Nephi 3:6-11.
[7]D&C 43:1-7.
[8]Hyrum M. Smith and Janne M. Sjodahl, *Doctrine and Covenants Commentary,* p. 577.
[9]D&C 90:6; 107:18-19, 22.

authority and power" to the First Presidency.[10] When the Quorum of the First Presidency is disorganized by the death of the President of the Church, the President of the Twelve Apostles becomes the President of the Church, for he is the presiding officer of the Quorum which holds the keys of the kingdom, and he has the right to receive revelation for the Church. (An example is Section 136, received by President Brigham Young as President of the Twelve Apostles.)

The Prophet Joseph Smith conferred upon the Twelve Apostles the keys which he had received from messengers of God.[11]

Upon the death of the Prophet Joseph Smith, concern was indicated by some as to whom should lead the Church. President Sidney Rigdon maintained that he should be appointed the guardian of the Church.[12] When the members of the Twelve arrived in Nauvoo, a meeting of the Twelve Apostles, high council, and high priests convened to consider the claims of Brother Rigdon. Following his presentation, President Brigham Young said, in part: "I have the keys and the means of obtaining the mind of God on the subject. . . .

"Joseph conferred upon our heads all the keys and powers belonging to the Apostleship which he himself held before he was taken away, and no man or set of men can get between Joseph and the Twelve in this world or in the world to come.

"How often has Joseph said to the Twelve, 'I have laid the foundation and you must build thereon, for upon your shoulders the kingdom rests.' "[13]

On August 8, 1844, the Church met for the purpose of hearing from the claimants to the Presidency of the Church. Sidney Rigdon presented his claims. Seven of the Quorum of the Twelve were present, John Taylor was

[10]*Ibid.* 107:23-24.
[11]*Times and Seasons* 5:651, 664, 698; *Millennial Star* 10:115.
[12]DHC 7:224-225.
[13]*Ibid.* pp. 229-230.

recovering from wounds received in Carthage jail; four others had not arrived in Nauvoo. President Brigham Young asked the congregation if they wanted a guardian for the Church to which the Church replied negatively. He then presented the claim of the Twelve, about which he said: "They stand next to Joseph, and are as the First Presidency of the Church."[14]

Confirmation of the authority of the Twelve, as presented by President Young, was his transformation in voice, person and manner to that of Joseph Smith.

The late President George Q. Cannon of this event said:

"If Joseph had arisen from the dead and again spoken in their hearing, the effect could not have been more startling than it was to many present at that meeting; it was the voice of Joseph himself; and not only was it the voice of Joseph which was heard, but it seemed in the eyes of the people as if it were the very person of Joseph which stood before them. A more wonderful and miraculous event than was wrought that day in the presence of that congregation we never heard of. The Lord gave his people a testimony that left no room for doubt as to who was the man chosen to lead them."[15]

In the Journal of Elder Wm. C. Staines of the date of August 8, 1844, the following statement is recorded: "Brigham Young said: 'I will tell you who your leaders or guardians will be—the Twelve—I at their head.' This was with the voice like the voice of the Prophet Joseph. I thought it was he, and so did thousands who heard it. This was very satisfactory to the people, and a vote was taken to sustain the Twelve in their office, which with a few dissenting voices, was passed.

"Wilford Woodruff described the event as follows: 'If I had seen him with my own eyes, there is no one that could have convinced me that it was not Joseph Smith, and any-

---

[14]*Ibid.* p. 233.
[15]Tullidge, *Life of Brigham Young*, 1877, p. 115.

one can testify to this who was acquainted with these two men" (*Deseret Evening News*, March 12, 1892)."[16]

The conference sustained the Twelve Apostles, "the First Presidency of the Church, and at the head of this kingdom in all the world," with President Brigham Young as President of the body to direct the Church.[17] The Twelve Apostles continued to direct the Church until October 8, 1848, when the First Presidency was sustained as follows: Brigham Young, President; Heber C. Kimball and Willard Richards, counselors.[18]

In the aforementioned manner the keys of the kingdom were given "unto the Church" through the Twelve Apostles, who received them from the Prophet Joseph Smith. This was confirmed when this Quorum was sustained as the rightful successors to the Prophet.

Application of the prophecy

Whenever the Quorum of the First Presidency is re-organized upon the death of the President of the Church, the Twelve Apostles have reorganized that Quorum by the authority each apostle received when he was ordained to the apostleship.

Each Latter-day Saint is under covenant to accept the new First Presidency as appointed by revelation through the Council of the Twelve. The history of the Church shows that the saints have sustained the action of the Twelve, and they have "upheld [the First Presidency] by the confidence, faith, and prayer of the church."[19]

Because this method of continuing the keys of the kingdom was established by revelation, the Church has continued to grow in membership, awaiting the day when it shall fill the whole earth. The keys of the kingdom will always reside in God's true Church begun by the Prophet

[16]*DHC* 7:236, footnote.
[17]*Ibid.* p. 240.
[18]*Ibid.* p. 628.
[19]D&C 107:22.

Joseph Smith. The words of the Lord to Oliver Cowdery
are applicable to all members of the Church;

"And thou shalt not command him who is at thy head,
and at the head of the church;

"For I have given him the keys of the mysteries, and
the revelations which are sealed, until I shall appoint unto
them another in his stead."[20]

---

[20]*Ibid.* 28:6-7.

Chapter 33

"Inasmuch As My People Build A House Unto Me . . ."
(D&C 97:15-20; 84:4-5)

(A) And inasmuch as my people build a house unto me in the name of the Lord, and do not suffer any unclean thing to come into it, that it be not defiled, my glory shall rest upon it;

Yea, and my presence shall be there, for I will come into it, and all the pure in heart that come into it shall see God.

But if it be defiled I will not come into it, and my glory shall not be there; for I will not come into unholy temples.

And, now, behold, if Zion do these things she shall prosper, and spread herself and become very glorious, very great, and very terrible.

And the nations of the earth shall honor her, and shall say: Surely Zion is the city of our God, and surely Zion cannot fall, neither be moved out of her place, for God is there, and the hand of the Lord is there;

And he hath sworn by the power of his might to be her salvation and her high tower.[1]

(B) Verily this is the word of the Lord, that the city New Jerusalem shall be built by the gathering of the saints, beginning at this place, even the place of the temple, which temple shall be reared in this generation.

For verily this generation shall not all pass away until an house shall be built unto the Lord, and a cloud shall rest upon it, which cloud shall be even the glory of the Lord, which shall fill the house.[2]

Background of the revelations

(A) This revelation is concerned primarily with temple building in Zion (Jackson County, Missouri). A School of Elders conducted by Elder Parley P. Pratt was commended. Ten days before, August 2, 1833, the cornerstones of the Kirtland Temple were laid.

(B) A number of missionaries had returned to Kirtland in September 1832. "It was while they were together in

---

[1] D&C 97:15-20.
[2] Ibid., 84:4-5.

this season of joy that the following communication was received. The Prophet designates it a Revelation on Priesthood."[3]

Background of the prophecies

(A) Section 97 contains the commandment to build speedily the temple in Zion, the site of which had been dedicated on August 2, 1831.[4] Immediately before the prophecy the reason is given for this House of the Lord: a place of thanksgiving, instruction for those who are called to the work of the ministry that they may be perfected in their callings, in doctrine and in all things pertaining to the kingdom of God.[5]

(B) The opening verses of Section 84 indicate that a purpose of the Church of Jesus Christ of Latter-day Saints is to gather the saints together to the city of New Jerusalem.[6] Furthermore, this city will be built at the temple site in the western boundaries of the State of Missouri.[7]

Contents of the prophecies

(A) (1) The Lord's glory will rest upon his temples, provided no unclean thing enters therein. (2) The presence of the Lord will be in his House. (3) If Zion will follow these commandments, she shall prosper in becoming very great and glorious. (4) Eventually the nations of the earth will honor her because they will know that Zion is the city of God, which shall never be moved out of her place, for God shall be there.

(B) (1) The New Jerusalem will be built by the gathering of the saints. (2) The temple will be reared in this generation. (3) This generation will not pass away until the temple is built, and the glory of the Lord rests upon it.

---

[3]*Ibid.*, 84: Introduction.
[4]*Ibid.*, 97:10-11.
[5]*Ibid.*,   vs. 12-14.
[6]*Ibid.*, 84:2.
[7]*Ibid.*, v. 3.

The Significance of Temples

The Lord commanded his people to build a tabernacle for their travels in the wilderness that therein he might reveal salvation ordinances to them.[8] Subsequently, three temples were erected in the land of Palestine by the Israelites. It is apparent, however, that the Lord revealed to Adam and the patriarchs before Moses, certain ordinances and information, as stated in the Pearl of Great Price, which can be received only in the temple.[9] The importance of the temple in the eternal plan is indicated in the fact that the Prophet Joseph Smith said that the most important reason for the gathering of God's people together in any dispensation is to build temples.[10] Bible prophecies indicate that in the last dispensation of the gospel there would be a restoration of the principles and practices of former dispensations, which, of course, includes the important activity of temple building and the ordinances therein.[11]

The temple serves many purposes: where the Lord's presence may be known; where he may come to visit his people, for the temple is the House of the Lord; where salvation ordinances are received for the exaltation of the faithful that the people might receive spiritual power over the adversary.

The power and influence of the temple is indicated in the following statement from the *Doctrine and Covenants Commentary:*

"The history of Temples teaches us that the people of God have been strong, or weak, in proportion to the faithfulness with which they have attended to their sanctuaries. The history of the Temple of Jerusalem is, as Dr. Joseph Angus, in his *Bible Handbook*, notes, 'an index to the history of the Jews. When it fell, they were scattered;

---

[8]*Ibid.,* 124:38.
[9]Abraham, Facsimile No. 2.
[10]Joseph Fielding Smith, *Teachings of the Prophet Joseph Smith,* pp. 307-308.
[11]Acts 3:19-21; Ephesians 1:9-10; Micah 4:1-2.

as it rose from its ruins, they gathered round it again; and history dates the captivity, with equal accuracy, from the destruction of the Temple, or from the first capture of Jerusalem.' Speaking of the Temples in this dispensation, someone has declared that the completion of the Nauvoo Temple was the salvation of the Church from annihilation, although the Saints were forced to flee into the desert. . . ."[12]

From the same source we learn of the intent of Satan and also the power which may be with the Church when the temple is in operation:

"The rearing of a Temple of God in the world is the construction of a citadel by the followers of Prince Immanuel in the territory claimed by Diabolus. Hence his rage when the people of God build Temples. But the Temple in Kirtland served its divine purpose, as did that in Nauvoo, though both were abandoned. In it the Saints received that power from on high which enabled the Church to withstand, successfully, the attacks of all enemies. Owing to the baptism by the Holy Spirit received in the Temples, the Church, notwithstanding persecution, exile, and apostasy, has grown in spiritual power and become able to make itself felt in the world as a regenerating force. But for the Temples and the communion with God established through the Temple service, the Church might have been overwhelmed in the persecutions of Missouri and Illinois, just as the Primitive Church might have perished in the early persecutions but for the power it received on the day of Pentecost. Comp. Acts 1:8."[13]

President Heber C. Kimball predicted that when the Salt Lake Temple reached the square the powers of evil would rage and the Saints would suffer persecution. In November 1882, the temple reached the square, and shortly thereafter the Edmunds law against plural marriage was enacted. Within two years Elder Rudger Clawson was

---

[12]Hyrum M. Smith and Janne M. Sjodahl, *Doctrine and Covenants Commentary*, p. 612.

[13]*Ibid.*, pp. 722-723.

sentenced to the penitentiary for polygamy. This began the anti-Mormon crusade, "which, for bitterness and cruelty, takes rank in the history of religious persecution with the deeds of the dark ages."[14]

Fulfillment of the prophecy

The saints did not speedily build the Jackson County temple as commanded. On December 16, 1833, the Lord revealed a parable about Zion.[15] The temple, if built, would have been the tower of the parable from which the movements of the enemy could have been observed by inspiration, but the people did not do as commanded in speedily building this house. Instead they questioned whether or not the tower should be built, with the query: "And what need hath my Lord of this tower, seeing this is a time of peace?"[16] As a result, the enemy overcame the saints in that they were driven from the county. (See "Zion shall Escape If . . ." —D&C 97:22-28).

Notwithstanding the experience of 1833-34 when the saints were driven from Zion, Latter-day Saints may confidently look forward to the time when there will be a temple built in that place. As the prophecy under consideration states, this generation will not all pass away until that temple is reared. Some have been concerned about the meaning of a generation, believing that a generation is the 100 years mentioned in the Book of Mormon, or the life-span of a man, say, about 70 years today, or even far less in Joseph Smith's day.[17] The meaning of the word is determined by its context, because the word is defined in varying lengths. For example: Jesus said an evil and adulterous generation sought after signs.[18] The world is still receiving the words of Joseph Smith through the revelations in the Doctrine and Covenants, the Pearl of

---

[14]Orson F. Whitney, *Life of Heber C. Kimball,* p. 397.
[15]D&C 101:43-62.
[16]*Ibid.,* vs. 46-50.
[17]Helaman 13:8-10.
[18]Matthew 12:39.

Great Price, the Book of Mormon, and his other writings.[19] The generation here used undoubtedly means the dispensation of the fulness of times. President Charles W. Penrose quoted Elder Orson Pratt as writing that the generation as used in Section 84 did not mean an hundred years as some had supposed.[20] President Wilford Woodruff understood this generation to be the time when the gospel is available to men; therefore, the dispensation of the fulness of times.[21]

Will the saints return to Missouri to build the temple and rear a city to the Most High? Elder Orson Pratt said: "Here then we see a prediction, and we believe it. Yes! The Latter-day Saints have as firm faith and rely upon this promise as much as they rely upon the promise of forgiveness of sins when they comply with the first principles of the Gospel. We just as much expect that a city will be built, called Zion, in the place and on the land which has been appointed by the Lord our God, and that a temple will be reared on the spot that has been selected, and the cornerstone of which has been laid, in the generation when this revelation was given; we just as much expect this as we expect the sun to rise in the morning and set in the evening; or as much as we expect to see the fulfillment of any of the purposes of the Lord our God, pertaining to the works of his hands."[22]

Application of the prophecies

Knowledgeable and faithful Latter-day Saints have no concerns about whether or not the temple will be built in Missouri, their only question is, when? They have learned to wait in patience for the revelation commanding the return to that area. They know that the saints were driven from the area because of transgressions and the malignity of the Missourians in Jackson County and later

---

[19]D&C 5:10.
[20]*Conference Report*, April 1924, pp. 13-14.
[21]*Journal of Discourses*, 21:195.
[22]*Ibid.*, 14:275.

from the entire state.[23] They also understand that when they were prevented from accomplishing the building of the city and temple, the Lord released those members of the Church from the responsibility at that time.[24] They believe with all their hearts that though their forebears were scattered they would eventually be gathered and the commandments given concerning Zion would be fulfilled.[25] Latter-day Saints know that in the due time of the Lord the word will come to fulfill the commandments pertaining to that land. In truth, they say with President Brigham Young:

"This people will surely go back to Jackson County. How soon that may be, or when it may be, I do not care; but that is not now the gathering place for the saints."[26]

They know that today they are living in the period known by Nephi almost 600 years before Christ when the saints would be scattered among the nations of the earth.[27] They also know that there will yet be a gathering of the saints to the New Jerusalem when world conditions are very troubleous. (See ". . . They Shall Be Gathered in Unto One Place . . ." —D&C 29:7-8; 45:65-71).

The Prophet Joseph Smith sent to the brethren in Zion a plat of the city and also of the temple.[28] Elder Orson Pratt said that the Temple will consist of twenty-four compartments. Of it, he said:

"Perhaps you may ask for what purpose these 24 compartments are to be built. I answer not to assemble the outside world in, nor to assemble the Saints all in one place, but these buildings will be built with a special view to the different orders, or in other words the different quorums or councils of the two Priesthoods that God has ordained on the earth. . . . but the Temple will be dedi-

---

[23]D&C 101:1-8; 103:1-4.
[24]*Ibid.*, 124:49-51.
[25]*Ibid.*, 101:17-22; 105:34-45.
[26]*Journal of Discourses*, 3:278.
[27]1 Nephi 14:14.
[28]*DHC* 1:359-362.

cated to the Priesthood of the Most High God, and for most sacred and holy purposes."[29]

As promised, the Lord Jesus Christ will come to his Temples, including the one in Zion. President Brigham Young said:

"When Jesus makes his next appearance upon the earth, but few of this Church will be prepared to receive him and see him face to face and converse with him; but he will come to his temple."[30] To some in that day the promise will be fulfilled that they shall see his face.[31] The Lord's presence has been manifest in the Salt Lake Temple according to the testimony of President Lorenzo Snow:

"Emerging from the room, the Apostle received a personal visitation from the Lord Jesus Christ, from whom he received instructions relative to the reorganization of the First Presidency when the mantle should fall upon him to lead the Church."[32]

The Lord's glory will rest upon his temples, provided no unclean thing enters therein. This promise is comparable to the prophecy in Section 84 in which it is said that a cloud shall rest upon it. We learn the following about this manifestation:

"The Lord manifested Himself in ancient Israel in a cloud, shaped as a pillar, which became luminous at night. It guided the people on the journey to Canaan. It stood at the entrance to the Sanctuary, and in it God spoke to Moses. It rested on the Sanctuary and filled it, when that sacred tent was set up. It was the visible sign of God's guiding and protecting care over His people. This glory of the Lord is known as the Shekinah. When the first temple was dedicated, it filled the house (II Chron. 7:1-3), and the people bowed down and worshiped. The Shekinah departed when the Temple was profaned (Ez. 10:19; 11:22), but Ezekiel, in his vision of the Temple in the latter days,

---

[29]Roy W. Doxey, *Zion In The Last Days*, pp. 61-66.

[30]*Discourses of Brigham Young*, p. 176.

[31]D&C 67:10; 93:1.

[32]Thomas C. Romney, *The Life of Lorenzo Snow*, p. 445.

saw the glory of the Lord returning. (Ezek. 43:2-3). The presence of the Lord will be manifested in this Temple of the Latter-day Zion."[33]

If Zion will follow the commandments, she shall prosper in becoming very great and glorious. Upon this truth, President John Taylor had this to say:

"We believe that we shall rear splendid edifices, magnificent temples and beautiful cities that shall become the pride, praise and glory of the whole earth. We believe that this people will excel in literature, in science and the arts and in manufactures. In fact, there will be a concentration of wisdom of the world as it now exists, but men will be inspired in regard to all these matters in a manner and to an extent that they never have been before. . . . Zion will become the praise of the whole earth."[34] (See "Zion Shall Escape If . . ." —D&C 97:22-28).

The following counsel from President Brigham Young is as good today as when it was given:

"When are we going back to Jackson County? Not until the Lord commands his people; and it is just as much as you and I can do to get ready to go when he does command us."[35] (See "This is the Blessing Which I Have Promised" —D&C 103:12-14).

---

[33]Hyrum M. Smith and Janne M. Sjodahl, *Doctrine and Covenants Commentary*, p. 497.

[34]*Journal of Discourses*, 10:147.

[35]*Ibid.*, 6:269.

Chapter 34

"Zion Shall Escape If . . ."
(D&C 97:22-28)

For behold, and lo, vengeance cometh speedily upon the ungodly as the whirlwind; and who shall escape it?

The Lord's scourge shall pass over by night and by day, and the report thereof shall vex all people; yea, it shall not be stayed until the Lord come;

For the indignation of the Lord is kindled against their abominations and all their wicked works.

Nevertheless, Zion shall escape if she observe to do all things whatsoever I have commanded her.

But if she observe not to do whatsoever I have commanded her, I will visit her according to all her works, with sore affliction, with pestilence, with plague, with sword, with vengeance, with devouring fire.

Nevertheless, let it be read this once to her ears, that I, the Lord, have accepted of her offering; and if she sin no more none of these things shall come upon her;

And I will bless her with blessings, and multiply a multiplicity of blessings upon her, and upon her generations forever and ever, saith the Lord your God. Amen.[1]

Background of the revelation

In the month of July 1833, a mob gathered in Independence, Jackson County, Missouri, to determine what should be done about the Mormons in their community. They began by destroying the Church printing plant, tarring and feathering two of the brethren and intimidating others. Section 97 was received before Oliver Cowdery arrived in Kirtland to report to the brethren what had happened in Missouri.

Background of the prophecy

A temple is commanded to be built in the center place of Zion (Jackson County, Missouri).[2] The promise is given

---
[1]D&C 97:22-28.
[2]*Ibid.* vs. 10-17.

that if the saints would keep the commandments and rear the temple, Zion would prosper.[3] Prosperity would come as the saints were imbued with the spirit of Zion—the pure in heart.[4]

Contents of the prophecy

(1) Judgments would come upon the wicked. (2) The Lord's scourge would visit the ungodly and would continue until the second coming of Christ. (3) Zion, however, would escape, provided she would do all things commanded of her. (4) If not, she will be chastened with plague, pestilence, sword, and fire. (5) Repentance (sin no more) is the remedy against calamity. (6) If faithful to the Lord's words, Zion's blessings will be innumerable.

Application to the saints of 1833

Elder Parley P. Pratt recorded the following observation concerning this prophecy:

"This revelation was not complied with by the leaders and Church in Missouri, as a whole; notwithstanding many were humble and faithful. Therefore, the threatened judgment was poured out to the uttermost, as the history of the five following years will show."[5]

In a subsequent revelation the Lord explains that the saints were driven from Jackson County "in consequence of their transgressions."[6] This same revelation contains a parable in which Zion is compared with a choice vineyard overseen by watchmen. The watchtower represented the temple which would have been the source of strength for the members of the Church, but the attitude of the people was: "What need hath my Lord of this tower, seeing this is a time of peace?"[7]

---

[3]*Ibid.* vs. 18-20.
[4]*Ibid.* vs. 10-21.
[5]Parley P. Pratt, *Autobiography of Parley P. Pratt*, 4 ed., p. 96.
[6]D&C 101:1-2.
[7]*Ibid.* vs. 43-54.

Fulfillment of the prophecy

It is true that the saints of Missouri felt the weight of calamity due to their transgressions and neglect in performing the Lord's word, as already indicated. But, again, the fulfillment of this prophecy must be completed when the Lord comes again.[8] In quoting this prophecy, President George Albert Smith emphasized that peace in this world will come when the Savior comes, that members of the Church will need to repent and keep in tune with the Spirit of the Lord else judgments will come upon them.[9] Elder Melvin J. Ballard also counseled the saints in the same manner.[10]

Application of the prophecy

President Joseph Fielding Smith wrote the following about this prophecy:

"The term Zion has several meanings. . . . The strict and definite meaning of the word is 'the pure in heart.' The pure in heart have been promised protection in the days of wickedness, when the judgments of the Almighty are passing over the nations. Nevertheless Zion, as that term has reference to the members of the Church collectively, shall also be punished 'if she observe not to do whatsoever I have commanded her,' the Lord has said. He will 'visit her with sore affliction, with pestilence, with plague, with sword, with vengeance, with devouring fire.' All of these things will be withheld while the nations are being punished, if the members of the Church will keep faithfully their commandments. If they will not, then we have received the warning that we, like the rest of the world, shall suffer His wrath in justice."[11]

Some of the brethren have indicated a fractional or an approximate number who must remain faithful in order

---

[8]*Ibid.* 97:22-24.

[9]*Conference Report*, October 1917, pp. 44-45.

[10]*Ibid.* June 1919, pp. 88-89.

[11]Joseph Fielding Smith, *The Progress of Man*, p. 468.

for the saints as a people to be spared the judgments. Elder Orson Pratt felt that "if the majority of this people will be faithful, the Lord will preserve them from their enemies, from every weapon that is lifted against them."[12] Reference has been made to the parable of the ten virgins,[13] by some of the authorities, such as President Wilford Woodruff, who said: ". . . if he finds one-half of those professing to be members of his Church prepared for salvation, it will be as many as can be expected, judging by the course that many are pursuing."[14] President Brigham Young said:

". . . we read that war, pestilence, plagues, famine, etc., will be visited upon the inhabitants of the earth; but if distress through the judgments of God comes upon this people, it will be because the majority have turned away from the Lord. Let the majority of the people turn away from the Holy Commandments which the Lord has delivered to us, and cease to hold the balance of power in the Church, and we may expect the judgments of God to come upon us; but while six-tenths or three-fourths of this people will keep the commandments of God, the curse and judgments of the Almighty, will never come upon them, though we will have trials of various kinds, and the elements to contend with—natural and spiritual elements. While this people will strive to serve God according to the best of their abilities, they will fare better, have more to eat and to wear, have better houses to live in, better associations, and enjoy themselves better than the wicked ever do or ever will do."[15]

In applying the parable of the ten virgins to our day, Elder Harold B. Lee of the Council of the Twelve, said:

"We cannot borrow from our Church membership. We cannot borrow from an illustrious ancestry. Whether or not

---

[12]*Journal of Discourses,* 15:363.
[13]D&C 45:56-59; 63:53-54.
[14]*Journal of Discourses,* 18:110.
[15]*Ibid.* 10:335-336.

we have oil in our lamps, I repeat, depends solely upon each one of us; it is determined by our faithfulness in keeping the commandments of the Living God."[16]

---

[16]*Conference Report*, October 1951, p. 27.

Chapter 35

"Mighty In Testimony"
(D&C 100:10)

And I will give unto him power to be mighty in testimony.[1]

Background of the revelations

On October 12, 1833, while at Perrysburg, New York, enroute to Canada, the Prophet Joseph Smith received Section 100 of the Doctrine and Covenants. Sidney Rigdon and the Prophet were accompanying Brother and Sister Freeman Nickerson whose married children were in Canada.

Background of the prophecy

While on this missionary trip where the Prophet was to teach the gospel to the Nickerson family the Lord promised both Sidney and Joseph that they should speak the thoughts he would put into their hearts, but they should be spoken in meekness and solemnity of heart.[2] If this regimen were followed, the Holy Ghost would testify of their teachings.

Sidney Rigdon was appointed spokesman to the Prophet.[3] This calling was prophesied by Joseph, son of Jacob of biblical fame, and related by Lehi about 600 B. C. when he said: "And the Lord said unto me also: I will raise up unto the fruit of thy loins [Joseph Smith, the latter-day seer]; and I will make for him a spokesman. And I, behold, I will give unto him that he shall write the writing of the fruit of thy loins, unto the fruit of thy loins; and the spokesman of thy loins shall declare it."[4]

---

[1]D&C 100:10.
[2]*Ibid.* vs. 5-8.
[3]*Ibid.* v. 9.
[4]2 Nephi 3:18.

Contents of the prophecy

This one sentence prophecy in its context implies that a spokesman was necessary to assist Joseph Smith in the delivering of the message, as Aaron was appointed to be a spokesman to Moses, but the Prophet would be powerful in testimony. The means by which he would have power would be, according to the context, through the Holy Ghost.

Fulfillment of the Prophecy

Upon reaching their destination, Mount Pleasant, Canada, the Prophet's party was welcomed at the homes of the two wealthy Nickersons, sons of Brother and Sister Freeman Nickerson. The reception accorded the Prophet and Brother Rigdon was out of respect for their parents, since they had read some newspaper accounts which were very unfavorable to their visitors. In fact, one of the sons when the party had gathered for a discussion, said to his wife about the Prophet: "Oh, just let him talk; I'll silence him if he undertakes to talk about the Bible. I guess I know as much about the scriptures as he does." The father of the family invited the Prophet and his missionary companion to explain their religious beliefs. Whereupon, the oldest son turned to his wife and whispered: "Now you'll see how I shall shut him up." The Prophet began by telling the story of the restoration of the gospel and Church through the instrumentality of angelic beings. From the history of Lydia Bailey Knight, the account continues as follows:

"As the speaker continued his wonderful narrative, Lydia, who was listening and watching him intently, saw his face become white and a shining glow seemed to beam from every feature.

"As his story progressed he would often allude to passages of scripture. Then Mr. Nickerson would speak up and endeavor to confound him. But the attempt was soon acknowledged even by himself to be futile.

"The Prophet bore a faithful testimony that the Priesthood was again restored to the earth, and that God and His Son had conferred upon him the keys of the Aaronic and Melchizedek Priesthoods. He states that the last dispensation had come, and the words of Jesus were now in force—'Go ye into all the world and preach the gospel to every creature. He that believeth and is baptized shall be saved; but he that believeth not shall be damned.' "[5]

Within a few days, Mr. Nickerson and his family were baptized. The testimony of the Prophet was convincing and powerful!

A classic example of the fulfillment of this prophecy was related by Elder Parley P. Pratt, an eyewitness to the following event which occurred in Richmond, Missouri, jail in November 1838:

"In one of those tedious nights, we had lain as if in sleep till the hour of midnight had passed, and our ears and hearts had been pained, while we had listened for hours to the obscene jests, the horrid oaths, the dreadful blasphemies and filthy language of our guards, Colonel Price at their head, as they recounted to each other their deeds of rapine, murder, robbery, etc., which they had committed among the 'Mormons' while at Far West and vicinity. They even boasted of defiling by force wives, daughters and virgins, and of shooting or dashing out the brains of men.

"I had listened till I became so disgusted, shocked, horrified, and so filled with the spirit of indignant justice that I could scarcely refrain from rising upon my feet and rebuking the guards; but had said nothing to Joseph, or any one else, although I lay next to him and knew he was awake. On a sudden he arose to his feet, and spoke in a voice of thunder, or as the roaring lion, uttering, as near as I can recollect, the following words:

" 'SILENCE, *ye fiends of the infernal pit. In the name of Jesus Christ I rebuke you, and command you to be still;*

---

[5]Gates, Susan (Young) *Lydia Knight's History*, pp. 17-18.

*I will not live another minute and hear such language.
Cease such talk, or you or I die THIS INSTANT!'*

"He ceased to speak. He stood erect in terrible majesty. Chained, and without a weapon; calm, unruffled and
dignified as an angel, he looked upon the quailing guards,
whose weapons were lowered or dropped to the ground;
whose knees smote together, and who, shrinking into a
corner, or crouching at his feet begged his pardon, and
remained quiet till a change of guards.

"I have seen the ministers of justice, clothed in magis-
terial robes, and criminals arraigned before them, while
life was suspended on a breath, in the Courts of England;
I have witnessed a Congress in solemn session to give laws
to nations; I have tried to conceive of kings, of royal
courts, of thrones and crowns; but dignity and majesty
have I seen but *once*, as it stood in chains, at midnight,
in a dungeon in an obscure village of Missouri."[6]

Application of the prophecy

The promise that the Prophet would be mighty in
testimony was literally fulfilled as he bore witness to the
truth that the gospel had been restored. The convincing
manner in which he wrote his testimony is also well presented in his story of the First Vision in which he beheld
the Father and the Son. The truth of this testimony is
evident to one who has the Spirit of the Lord with him.

"However, it was nevertheless a fact that I had beheld a vision. I have thought since, that I felt much like
Paul, when he made his defense before King Agrippa, and
related the account of the vision he had when he saw a
light, and heard a voice; but still there were but few who
believed him; some said he was dishonest, others said he
was mad; and he was ridiculed and reviled. But all this
did not destroy the reality of his vision. He had seen a
vision, he knew he had, and all the persecution under
heaven could not make it otherwise; and though they

---

[6]Parley P. Pratt, *Autobiography of Parley P. Pratt*, pp. 210-211.

should persecute him unto death, yet he knew, and would know to his latest breath, that he had both seen a light and heard a voice speaking unto him, and all the world could not make him think or believe otherwise.

"So it was with me. I had actually seen a light, and in the midst of that light I saw two Personages, and they did in reality speak to me; and though I was hated and persecuted for saying that I had seen a vision, yet it was true, and while they were persecuting me, reviling me, and speaking all manner of evil against me falsely for so saying, I was led to say in my heart: Why persecute me for telling the truth? I have actually seen a vision; and who am I that I can withstand God, or why does the world think to make me deny what I have actually seen? For I had seen a vision; I knew it, and I knew that God knew it, and I could not deny it, neither dared I do it; at least I knew that by so doing I would offend God, and come under condemnation."[7]

Not only the Prophet and the apostles may have the testimony of the Spirit to convince them but other faithful Latter-day Saints may enjoy this same blessing. Each member of the Church should have this witness that he might also convince others of the truth.[8]

---

[7]Joseph Smith 2:24-25.

[8]D&C 42:12-15; 43:15; 50:21-24.

Chapter 36

"I Will Raise Up Unto Myself A Pure People . . ."
(D&C 100:15-17)

Therefore, let your hearts be comforted; for all things shall work together for good to them that walk uprightly, and to the sanctification of the church.

For I will raise up unto myself a pure people, that will serve me in righteousness;

And all that call upon the name of the Lord, and keep his commandments, shall be saved. Even so. Amen.[1]

Background of the revelation

While accompanying the Nickerson family to the home of their children, the Prophet Joseph Smith and Sidney Rigdon stopped at Perrysburg, New York, enroute to Canada. Persecution was inflicted upon the saints in Jackson County, Missouri, at this time.

Background of the prophecy

After giving instructions concerning their missionary trip into Canada, the Lord gave counsel regarding the Zion of Missouri. "Zion shall be redeemed, although she is chastened for a little season."[2]

Contents of the prophecy

(1) Though Zion was being chastened in Missouri, the Prophet's heart should be comforted. (2) All things work for good for those who walk uprightly. (3) Good will result to those who labor for the sanctification of the church. (4) The Lord will raise up a pure people who will serve him in righteousness. (5) All who call upon the Lord in keeping his commandments will be saved.

---

[1]D&C 100:15-17.
[2]*Ibid.* v. 13.

Analysis of the prophecy

All things shall work for good for those who serve the Lord in righteousness. "Good" as indicated in the revelations may not agree with the ideas of men. Blessings pronounced "good" may arise out of persecution rather than luxurious living. Pain, suffering, and disappointments, if understood in terms of the purpose of life as found in the Gospel of Jesus Christ, may be good, ultimately. The determination of what is "good" is known to the Latter-day Saints by their understanding of the purpose of life. This knowledge is found only in the scriptures, and not in the theories of men.[3] When the Latter-day Saints realize that they are children of the Eternal Father with a godlike potential, that they were placed upon this earth by design and not by chance to prove themselves "to see if they will do all things whatsoever the Lord their God shall command them."[4] In other words, "good" is determined by what the Lord has revealed, to act upon or to be acted upon.

Blessings will come to those who work for the sanctification of the church. The individual goal for which all saints should strive is sanctification. This blessing is the ultimate in gospel understanding and practice, and, therefore, the purpose for which the Gospel and Church exist. When the Savior commanded that we should become perfect as his Father and he are perfect, he was saying that if one strives for that moral perfection he will become sanctified. Sanctification comes through the Holy Ghost bestowed upon each person who has worthily received the atonement of Jesus Christ through water and spirit baptism by an authorized servant of God.[5] The Spirit will not strive with the unworthy member of Christ's Church.[6] Sanctification comes to him who yields his heart to God and who thus serves him with all his might, mind, and strength.[7] To

---

[3] *Ibid.* 52:9, 36.
[4] Abraham 3:25.
[5] 3 Nephi 11:32-39.
[6] 1 Corinthians 3:16-17; D&C 1:31-33.
[7] D&C 20:31-34; Helaman 3:35.

become purified by the Holy Ghost by dedicated consecration of time, effort, and means, to the building of the Kingdom of God will bring the sanctifying influence of the Spirit in producing a new creature in Christ Jesus.[8]

A "pure people" are those who have received the atonement of Jesus Christ for their individual salvation, and who serve the Lord diligently to the end. They have come out of the bondage of sin (spiritual death) into spiritual life.[9]

It is insufficient for salvation for one to call on the Lord for forgiveness of sins without accepting his atonement through the appointed gospel means. Confession of Christ as one's Savior involves acceptance of the fulness of the gospel with all of its requirements.[10]

Fulfillment of the prophecy

The faithful, devout, Latter-day Saint is comforted in the knowledge that what the Lord has promised will be fulfilled.[11] In fact, those members of the Church who have sought with all their hearts to know by the Spirit that Joseph Smith is a prophet and that the scriptures are true have received a divine testimony by the Holy Ghost that the Lord's prophecies and promises are true.[12]

By the same means, the Spirit, one may know that even though death may have overtaken faithful saints as they have sought to keep the commandments, as the pure in heart in Missouri, their salvation is secure.[13]

The strength and power of the personal witness borne of the Holy Ghost is a convincer of truth. The following testimonies affirm the prophecy probably better than any other means of the past and of its certain fulfillment in the future:

---

[8]*Ibid.*, 88:66-68.
[9]*Ibid.* 29:41-45.
[10]Acts 2:21, 37-39.
[11]D&C 1:37-38.
[12]*Ibid.* v. 39.
[13]*Ibid.* 124:54.

President Brigham Young:

"My testimony is positive. . . . I know that Joseph Smith was a Prophet of God, and that he had many revelations. Who can disprove this testimony? Any one may dispute it, but there is no one in the world who can disprove it. I have had many revelations; I have seen and heard for myself, and know these things are true, and nobody on earth can disprove them. The eye, the ear, the hand, all the senses may be deceived, but the Spirit of God cannot be deceived; and when inspired with that Spirit, the whole man is filled with knowledge, he can see with a spiritual eye, and he knows that which is beyond the power of man to controvert."[14]

On a blessing that follows a faithful life, President Heber J. Grant testified:

"I never think of my wives and my dear mother and my two boys, my daughter, and my departed friends, and beloved associates being in the graveyard. I think only of the joy and the happiness and the peace and satisfaction that my mother is having in meeting with the Prophet and the Patriarch and Brigham Young and my father and the beloved friends that she knew from the days of Nauvoo to the day that she died. I think only of the joy they have in meeting with father and mother and loved ones who have been true and faithful to the gospel of the Lord Jesus Christ. My mind reaches out to the wonderful joy and satisfaction and happiness that they are having, and it robs the grave of its sting."[15]

The Lord declared that he will raise up unto himself a pure people. This prophecy is a continuing one. Men and women of strong faith in Christ and in the restoration of the Church in these last days, have graced the earth since 1830. These individuals have suffered and lived valiantly. Purity of life is an earmark of the saint, for he has received

[14]*Journal of Discourses* 16:46.

[15]G. Homer Durham (comp.), *Gospel Standards*, p. 366.

the power and strength to overcome the frailties of the flesh by adherence to the commandments.

Application of the prophecy

Alma, the Book of Mormon prophet known as the Younger, said: "And the Lord said unto me: Marvel not that all mankind, yea, men and women, all nations, kindreds, tongues and people, must be born again; yea, born of God, changed from their carnal and fallen state, to a state of righteousness, being redeemed of God, becoming his sons and daughters;

"And thus they become new creatures; and unless they do this, they can in nowise inherit the kingdom of God."[16]

To become a new creature through keeping the commandments is to become sanctified. In this condition, the saint commits his life, everything, to the Church and to the building of Zion upon the earth. His time and interests are centered in the well being of others. By his rebirth, he is a more effective servant of the Kingdom; he becomes witness of the truth, imbued with the Spirit. As an exemplar of righteousness his influence is felt among his associates, and thereby, he assists in the sanctification of the Church— the members thereof. His total contribution goes beyond himself and his family, and it spreads out far and everlastingly into the lives of others.

The Lord's words to his saints of today bring this message of fulfillment:

"Behold, that which you hear is as the voice of one crying in the wilderness—in the wilderness, because you cannot see him—my voice, because my voice is Spirit; my Spirit is truth; truth abideth and hath no end; and if it be in you it shall abound.

"And if your eye be single to my glory, your whole bodies shall be filled with light, and there shall be no darkness in you; and that body which is filled with light comprehendeth all things.

---

[16]Mosiah 27:25-26.

"Therefore, sanctify yourselves that your minds become single to God, and the days will come that you shall see him; for he will unveil his face unto you, and it shall be in his own time, and in his own way, and according to his own will."[17] (See ". . . You Shall See Me And Know That I Am. . . ."—D&C 67:10-14; 88:66-68; ". . . From Him Shall Be Taken Even The Light Which He Has Received"— D&C 1:31-33; 50:23-24; 88:67.)

---

[17]D&C 88:66-68.

Chapter 37

". . . When The Cup Of Their Iniquity Is Full . . ."

(D&C 101:10-12; 29:17)

(A) I have sworn, and the decree hath gone forth by a former commandment which I have given unto you, that I would let fall the sword of mine indignation in behalf of my people; and even as I have said, it shall come to pass.

Mine indignation is soon to be poured out without measure upon all nations; and this will I do when the cup of their iniquity is full.

And in that day all who are found upon the watch-tower, or in other words, all mine Israel, shall be saved.[1]

(B) And it shall come to pass, because of the wickedness of the world, that I will take vengeance upon the wicked, for they will not repent; for the cup of mine indignation is full; for behold, my blood shall not cleanse them if they hear me not.[2]

Background of the revelations

(A) By December 16, 1833, when Section 101 was received, the saints in Jackson County, Missouri, had been afflicted, persecuted, and driven from their homes by force of arms. The scattered saints sought refuge in neighboring counties.

(B) Section 29 was received that missionaries might be prepared with some fundamental doctrines relative to the times.

Background of the prophecies

(A) The Lord took cognizance of the afflicted, and persecuted saints and indicated that they had been driven from the land of their inheritance because of their transgressions.[3] They were reminded that chastening is neces-

---

[1] D&C 101:10-12.
[2] *Ibid.*, 29:17.
[3] *Ibid.*, vs. 1-2.

sary as a trial of their faith in order that they might one day make up the Lord's jewels. The desecration of their inheritances was due to their jarrings, strifes, covetous desires, and contentions. It is common to forget the Lord in the days of plenty, but in the time of trouble, he is sought after.[4] Despite their transgressions, the saints were not to be completely cast away.[5]

(B) Those who are to serve as missionaries are to gather the humble by being faithful in the discharge of their duties. The humble do not harden their hearts against the message of salvation. There will be a gathering place on this continent as protection against tribulation. (See ". . . They Shall be Gathered In Unto One Place . . ."—D&C 29:7-8; 45:65-71). The Lord says that he will dwell on the earth with the righteous for a thousand years, but the wicked will not enjoy this blessing. There shall be a resurrection preceded by many signs and wonders.

Contents of the prophecies

(1) The Lord has sworn that his indignation (righteous anger) is kindled in behalf of his people. (2) Not only this time but also on other occasions he has prophesied this fact. (3) His anger will be poured out upon all nations when their cup of iniquity is full. (4) Only those of Israel who are his servants will be saved. (5) Wickedness will increase until the Lord will take vengeance upon the world because they will not repent. (6) The cup of the Lord's wrath is kindled against the wicked. "When the cup of their iniquity is full:" The Lord has promised that his judgments will fall upon the wicked when they are fully ripe in iniquity.[6] The promise made to the Jaredites, ancient inhabitants of the land of America, and also to the Nephites is that only by righteousness could they be preserved.[7] The destruction of these two ancient civilizations is an example of the results of iniquity.[8]

---

[4] *Ibid.*, vs. 3-8.
[5] *Ibid.*, v. 9.
[6] *Ibid.*, 29:7-8; 45:65-71.
[7] 2 Nephi 28:16.
[8] Ether 2:8-12; 9:20.

A purpose of the revealing of the Book of Mormon in our times is that we might profit from the experiences of the Nephites and Jaredites. During the period of material prosperity, they sought for luxuries and pleasures rather than for spiritual benefits. Following the period of peace and prosperity begun with the visit of the resurrected Lord, their hearts became hardened against the commandments. Costly apparel and the fine things of the world, with a disregard for the poor and the righteous became a part of their lives. Class divisions arose and secret combinations among the wicked led to the persecution of the followers of Christ. These combinations fostered robberies and murders and the seeking of gain.[9] In time, the Nephites became so wicked that the Lamanites destroyed them. Mormon reports that he knew ". . . the judgments of the Lord which should come upon them; for they repented not of their iniquities, but did struggle for their lives without calling upon that Being who created them."[10]

The rejection of the Lord's servants sent to teach the everlasting gospel is a sure sign that a people's cup of iniquity is full. The killing of the prophet, the Lord's anointed, compounds the judgments to pour out upon a wicked people. President George Q. Cannon, a counselor in the First Presidency to President Lorenzo Snow, once wrote:

"There is no sin that nation can commit which the Lord avenges so speedily and fearfully as He does the shedding of innocent blood or, in other words, the killing of His anointed and authorized servants. No nation which has been guilty of this dreadful crime has ever escaped His vengeance . . . It is a rank offense against the majesty of Heaven and the authority of the Creator which He never suffers to pass unrebuked, for such men act in His stead and are His representatives on the earth . . ."[11]

---

[9]Mormon 6; Ether 15.

[10]4 Nephi

[11]Mormon 5:2.

The people of the city of Ammonihah were stiffnecked and hard-hearted in that they would not repent of their sins; consequently, they cast the Prophets Alma and Amulek from their midst.[12] The destruction of the Ammonihahites was swift ". . . even every living soul . . . and also their great city, which they said God could not destroy, because of its greatness."[13]

Fulfillment of the prophecy

This prophecy has been fulfilled in part only. Five months before, in August, a revelation was received in which similar judgments were prophesied upon the wicked and also upon the saints if they failed to keep the commandments of the Lord. It, also, has had only partial fulfillment. (See "Zion Shall Escape If . . ."—D&C 97:22-28.)

The Lord blesses the faithful, and he also punishes the wicked because of disobedience to his laws.[14] The Lord permits men to use their free agency and oftentimes they bring upon themselves wars, pestilence and strife. However, men should understand that sometimes wars and convulsions of nature, as earthquakes, tempests, and tidal waves, are directed by God to serve his own purposes.[15] Elder Orson F. Whitney, an apostle of this dispensation, gave the following comments upon this subject:

"And who, after reading what follows, can doubt divine participation in these troubles: 'For I the Almighty have laid my hand upon the nations to scourge them for their wickedness; and plagues shall go forth, and they shall not be taken from the earth until I have completed my work, which shall be cut short in righteousness. Until all shall know me, who remain, even from the least unto the greatest, and shall be filled with the knowledge of the Lord and shall see eye to eye'. . . .[16]

---

[12]*Millennial Star* 26:361-363.
[13]Alma 15:1, 15.
[14]*Ibid.*, 16:9.
[15]D&C 97:22-28.
[16]*Ibid.*, 84:96-98.

"Who will cause these terrible calamities? Not man—that is certain; though his conduct may justify them. Man can stir up strife and precipitate war. They can even bring pestilence and famine. But they cannot stir up tempests and earthquakes, cause whirlwinds and tidal-waves, or govern the action of sun, moon and stars. These, with other convulsions of nature, no less than war, famine and pestilence, are among God's judgments upon the workers of iniquity. Satan, 'prince of the powers of the air,' may be immediately responsible for these fearful disturbances; but he can do only what he is permitted to do by the All-just and All-merciful, who looses him or holds him in check.[17]

"And what is the purpose—the ultimate purpose of it all? Destruction? No, a thousand times no, except in so far as destruction must at times precede reconstruction, and is necessary to preserve what is worth preserving. The world's welfare is the object in view. God's wrath, however fiercely it burns, is not comparable to petty human anger. His work and his glory is 'to bring to pass the immortality and eternal life of man,' and if, in the process, He uses the powers of destruction, as well as the powers of construction—for 'all power' is his, 'in heaven and in earth'—it is because such a course has become necessary and is for the best. However severe his chastisements, we can rest assured of this: Hatred of humanity has no place in the heart of Him who 'so loved the world' that he 'gave his Only Begotten Son' to save it from eternal damnation.

"Calamities do not come on the world merely to scourge the wicked and avenge the wrongs of the righteous. The primal aim of Divine Punishment is to purify, and if possible save those upon whom the 'Great Avenger' lays a chastening hand. The object is to bring sinners to repentance to throw down the barriers that prevent men from coming to Christ, and turn into the upward path those bent upon pursuing the downward road. The Gospel saves all who are willing to be saved, and who show their willing-

---

[17]3 Nephi 9; D&C 63:32-35.

ness by their obedience, their faith by their works. It also aims to save the unwilling and disobedient—here if possible, and if not here, then hereafter. Wars and other woes are sent to put a stop to men's evil practices, lest they add sin to sin and pile up guilt to their greater condemnation. To be swept off the earth and ministered to in the spirit world, is not the worst fate that can befall the wicked. Omnipotence wields the powers of destruction in such a way as to make of them instruments of salvation. It may seem cruel, but in reality it is kind."[18]

Application of the prophecies

As early as 1830, the Lord promised his servants that the wicked in modern Babylon would receive desolation. His servants would be blessed in their preaching the Gospel ". . . and their enemies shall be under their feet; and I will let fall the sword in their behalf, and by the fire of mine indignation will I preserve them."[19] Despite the destructions upon the wicked, the Lord will preserve his people by fire, if necessary.[20]

If the Lord's people, who have made covenants with him in baptism and in holy places, seek the protection promised in the prophecies, it must be done by keeping God's commandments. Humility, the virtue of the faithful Latter-day Saint, when replaced by pride, arrogance, and a disregard for the teachings of the Gospel of Jesus Christ because of wicked practices, or intellectualism, brings unhappiness and a loss of the guarantee of safety. Pride was the besetting sin of the Nephites and the Jaredites before them. The Nephites boasted of their strength in battle, sought costly things at the expense of others, and indulged in immoral practices.[21]

To us of this generation the Lord has given the following counsel:

[18]Orson F. Whitney, *Saturday Night Thoughts*, pp. 200-203.
[19]D&C 35:14.
[20]2 Nephi 30:10.
[21]Mormon 2:8; 3:9; 4:8; Moroni 9:9-10.

"And if ye seek the riches which it is the will of the Father to give unto you, ye shall be the richest of all people, for ye shall have the riches of eternity; and it must needs be that the riches of the earth are mine to give; but beware of pride, lest ye become as the Nephites of old."[22]

---

[22]D&C 38:39.

Chapter 38

"Triumph of the Kingdom of God"
(D&C 103:5-8)

But verily I say unto you, that I have decreed a decree which my people shall realize, inasmuch as they hearken from this very hour unto the counsel which I, the Lord their God, shall give unto them.

Behold they shall, for I have decreed it, begin to prevail against mine enemies from this very hour.

And by hearkening to observe all the words which I, the Lord their God, shall speak unto them, they shall never cease to prevail until the kingdoms of the world are subdued under my feet, and the earth is given unto the saints, to possess it forever and ever.

But inasmuch as they keep not my commandments, and hearken not to observe all my words, the kingdoms of this world shall prevail against them.[1]

Background of the revelation

Beginning in the summer of 1833 and continuing into the winter of 1834, the saints in Jackson County, Missouri, were driven from their homes, and at the time this revelation was received, February, 1834, were locating in other counties of Missouri. They were in poverty, subsisting in huts and dugouts and depending upon the charity of the people of Clay County. The inclemency of the weather added to their woes. Elder Parley P. Pratt and Lyman Wright traveled to place before the Prophet Joseph Smith and the brethren the plight of the saints and to receive instruction.

Background of the scripture

The Lord speaks of a vengeance to come upon those who have smitten his people; yet, the saints were being chastened because they did not hearken altogether to his commandments.[2]

---

[1]D&C 103:5-8.
[2]Ibid., 103:1-5.

Contents of the prophecy

The prophecy stated in three verses may be summarized as follows: (1) The saints will prevail against God's enemies, provided, they observe his words. (2) By their obedience they shall continue to prevail against the kingdoms of this world. (3) Their inheritance will eventually be the earth, to possess it forever.

Fulfillment of the prophecy

The number of members of the Church in 1834 is not known, but six years later in 1840, there were an estimated 30,000, but during those six years the Church had considerable growth. At the close of 1968 there were almost 2,700,000 members of the Church found in many nations. The annual increase in convert baptism is from 60,000 to 80,000. Needless to say, the Church has grown materially also. With almost 500 stakes and about 4,400 wards and independent branches, and 13 temples with three others to be constructed soon, the increase continues. The five auxilliary organizations, each with its hundreds of thousands of members, were not in existence in 1834. Whereas, there were only a very few missionaries in the mission field at that time, there are now about 12,000 preaching the gospel annually.

By the testimony of the Holy Ghost Latter-day Saints are empowered to affirm that this prophecy will continue to be fulfilled. President Joseph F. Smith gave the following testimony in this regard:

"Is there a person within the sound of my voice, or anywhere else upon the face of the wide earth, who can say that this promise [D&C 103:5-7] has failed, that this prediction is not founded in truth, that so far it has not been fulfilled? I stand before this vast congregation, and am at the defiance of any human being to say, that this was not pronounced by the spirit of truth, by the inspiration of the Almighty, for it has been fulfilled, and is being fulfilled, and that, too, in the face of opposition of the most deadly character: and what remains will be fulfilled literally and completely."[3]

Application of the prophecy

"By hearkening to observe all the words which I, the Lord their God, shall speak . . ." concerns (1) the individual member of the Church and (2) the Church as a whole. The Church has seen many of its members fall away and even some in high places, as in 1837, but the strength of the Church has moved forward despite persecution and hardships.

The fulfillment of the prophecy attests to the fact that, by and large, the individual members constituting the Church have lived well enough for the Lord to recognize their efforts. It is still no doubt true, as it was in 1831, that the following is the Lord's evaluation of the Church:

". . . the only true and living Church upon the face of the whole earth, with which I, the Lord, am well pleased, speaking unto the church collectively and not individually—

"For I the Lord cannot look upon sin with the least degree of allowance;

"Nevertheless, he that repents and does the commandments of the Lord shall be forgiven;

"And he that repents not, from him shall be taken even the light which he has received; for my Spirit shall not always strive with man, saith the Lord of Hosts."[4]

The Church will continue to flourish, because there will be a sufficient number of its members who will be striving to "observe all the words" which the Lord has given. (See "I Will Raise Up Unto Myself a Pure People . . ." —D&C 100:15-17) The question, always must be: Am I living so that I shall be numbered among those who are seeking for the individual salvation to which I am entitled by my faithfulness?

---

[3]*Journal of Discourses* 25:98.
[4]D&C 1:30-33.

Chapter 39

". . . This Is The Blessing Which I Have Promised . . ."
(D&C 103:11-14)

But verily I say unto you, I have decreed that your brethren which have been scattered shall return to the lands of their inheritances, and shall build up the waste places of Zion.

For after much tribulation, as I have said unto you in a former commandment, cometh the blessing.

Behold, this is the blessing which I have promised after your tribulations, and the tribulations of your brethren—your redemption, and the redemption of your brethren, even their restoration to the land of Zion, to be established, no more to be thrown down.

Nevertheless, if they pollute their inheritances, they shall be thrown down; for I will not spare them if they pollute their inheritances.[1]

Background of the revelation

With the driving of the saints from Jackson County into other countries of Missouri, the Lord revealed that men would never stop his work, but if the saints were to be participants in the building of Zion, they would have to keep his commandments. (See "Triumph of the Kingdom of God," —D&C 103:5-8).

Contents of the prophecy

If the saints, "who were set to be a light unto the world, and to be the saviors of men" and who had been scattered from Jackson County, Missouri, would faithfully keep the commandments, the goal of building Zion would be realized. This would not occur until "after much tribulation." The promised blessing of faithfulness would be (1) their own redemption (salvation) and (2) the restoration of Zion to be established forever.

---

[1]D&C 103:11-14.

Fulfillment of the prophecy

Those faithful saints who helped lay the foundations of the Zion of Missouri have gone on to their reward—to their redemption as promised. In the midst of the Jackson County persecutions the Lord said to his saints:

"And all they who suffer persecution for my name, and endure in faith, though they are called to lay down their lives for my sake yet shall they partake of all this glory.

"Wherefore, fear not even unto death; for in this world your joy is not full, but in me your joy is full.

"Therefore, care not for the body, neither the life of the body; but care for the soul, and for the life of the soul.

"And seek the face of the Lord always, that in patience ye may possess your souls, and ye shall have eternal life."[2]

Two thoughts emerge from these two revelations—Sections 101 and 103—the redemption of the loyal participants in the redeeming of Zion who might live or die; the "redemption of your brethren"[3] and "their children".[4] Implicit in gospel understanding is the truth that though one may not realize all of his promised blessings in this life, he may yet on the other side of the veil participate in the activities of this life. President Joseph F. Smith said:

"... our fathers and mothers, brothers, sisters and friends who have passed away from this earth, having been faithful, and worthy to enjoy these rights and privileges, may have a mission given them to visit their relatives and friends upon the earth again, bringing from the divine Presence messages of love, of warning, or reproof and instruction, to those whom they had learned to love in the flesh."[5]

---

[2]*Ibid.* 101:35-38.
[3]*Ibid.* 103:13.
[4]*Ibid.* 101:18.
[5]Joseph F. Smith, *Gospel Doctrine*, p. 436.

As in patriarchal blessings, so in these two revelations where apparently promises were made to the scattered saints to return to build Zion,[6] promises are made to eternal beings who at every moment are living in eternity; therefore, they may be fulfilled in the present or in the future beyond this earth-life. So implies the Lord in these verses:

"For those that live shall inherit the earth, and those that die shall rest from all their labors, and their works shall follow them; and they shall receive a crown in the mansions of my Father, which I have prepared for them.

"Yea, blessed are they whose feet stand upon the land of Zion, who have obeyed my gospel; for they shall receive for their reward the good things of the earth, and it shall bring forth its strength."[7]

Application of the prophecy

The Lord has said that Zion's redemption will come only by the obedience of the people. President George Q. Cannon gave this testimony:

"I have not an earthly doubt that this revelation given in 1834 [Section 103] would have been fulfilled to the very letter, had our people obeyed the Lord as he desired; neither do I believe now that the redemption of Zion will be long deferred if the people will obey the Lord and keep His commandments. But the difficulty is, our hearts are hard and almost impenetrable, in many instances."[8]

Elder Orson Pratt, one among many of the authorities, expressed his conviction about returning to the center place of Zion:

"We want to tell you where our eyes are fixed. . . . they are fixed upon a land—not in the distant islands of the Indian Ocean, nor in the Pacific Ocean, nor in South America, but our eyes are fixed upon a land on the western boundaries of the State of Missouri and boundaries of the

---

[6]D&C 101:17-19; 103:11-13.
[7]*Ibid.* 59:2-3.
[8]*Conference Report,* October 1899, p. 50.

State of Kansas. We expect to go there just as much as we expect the sun will rise and set. We have no other expectation. We expect to return there just as much as Jews expect to return to old Jerusalem in the latter days. Perhaps you may inquire if we expect to return as a majority. Yes. Do we expect to return in a peaceful manner? Of course, have you ever seen any other feeling on the part of the Latter-day Saints, only to promote peace wherever they settle? What has been our object from commencement? Peace and good will to all men."[9]

---

[9]*Journal of Discourses* 24:23.

Chapter 40

". . . I Will Fight Your Battles . . ."
(D&C 105:14-15)

For behold, I do not require at their hands to fight the battles of Zion; for, as I said in a former commandment, even so will I fulfil—I will fight your battles.

Behold, the destroyer I have sent forth to destroy and lay waste mine enemies; and not many years hence they shall not be left to pollute mine heritage, and to blaspheme my name upon the lands which I have consecrated for the gathering together of my saints.[1]

Background of the revelation

Section 105 of the Doctrine and Covenants is sometimes referred to as the Fishing River revelation, the place in Missouri where it was received by the Prophet Joseph Smith on June 22, 1834. The revelation disbands Zion's Camp composed of 205 men who left Ohio to assist the saints who had been evicted from Jackson County. Fourteen of this number died of cholera, as the Prophet said, because of punishment of wrongdoing. It is in this revelation that the redemption of Zion is placed in abeyance until the saints are in possession of the area.[2]

Background of the prophecy

Reasons are given for the failure to redeem Zion at that time. The elders were instructed to wait for a little season for that redemption.

Contents of the prophecy

(1) The Church did not have the responsibility to fight to redeem Zion. (2) The Lord declared that he would fight Zion's battles. (3) The destroyer would lay waste the Lord's enemies. (4) Not many years would pass away until those who blasphemed and polluted the land of Zion would waste away.

[1]D&C 105:14-15.
[2]Ibid., v. 34.

Fulfillment of the prophecy

In the modern revelations the word destroyer is found three times.

In Section 61, verse 19, it probably means Satan because William W. Phelps saw the destroyer riding on the face of the waters and became frightened; consequently, the Prophet inquired of the Lord and received the revelation. The Lord says that he permits the destroyer to so act. The second time the destroyer is mentioned is in Section 101, verse 54, having reference to those who destroyed the Lord's vineyard (Jackson County) in the parable of the Watchmen and the Vineyard. The last time is in the prophecy under consideration. It appears that the works of Satan, to destroy, despoil, disrupt, and thwart the work of the Lord may be the meaning of the word. Such manifestations as wars, sicknesses, earthquakes, desolations, and plagues are some of the ways in which the destroyer works. In connection with this prophecy, the *Doctrine and Covenants Commentary* mentions cholera, which was present in many places at the time, as the destroyer.[3]

President Joseph Fielding Smith wrote that the Lord brings upon wicked generations his destructions as they become ripened in iniquity:

"This promise made in June 1834, was literally fulfilled by plague, bloodshed in the Civil War and punishment of those who so wickedly fought the Church. The Lord does send forth the destroyer in the shape of plague and famine, and also his angels to execute his authority from time to time upon those who blaspheme his name."[5]

Elder B. H. Roberts quotes a prophecy made by Joseph Smith concerning Jackson County, Mo. in addressing General A. W. Doniphan, lawyer:

---

[3]Hyrum M. Smith and Janne M. Sjodahl, *Doctrine and Covenants Commentary*, pp. 682-683.

[4]Helaman 12:3; 3 Nephi 9; D&C 63:33.

[5]Joseph Fielding Smith, *Church History and Modern Revelation*, Vol. 3, p. 38.

"Doniphan, I advise you not to take that Jackson county land in payment of the debt. God's wrath hangs over Jackson county. God's people have been ruthlessly driven from it, and you will live to see the day when it will be visited by fire and sword. The Lord of Hosts will sweep it with the besom of destruction. The fields and farms and houses will be destroyed, and only the chimneys will be left to mark the desolation."[6]

An eyewitness testifies that this prophecy was literally fulfilled in regard to the destruction of the area during the Civil War.[7]

In a longer discussion of the punishment which came to Missouri because of its treatment of the saints, and especially in Jackson County, Elder Roberts describes the havoc and destruction of that area during the Civil War. Among many other statements, Elder Roberts says:

"In other states the war lasted at most but four years; but counting her western border warfare in the struggle for Kansas, the war was waged in western Missouri from 1855 to 1865, ten years; and for many years after the close of the Civil War, a guerilla warfare was intermittently carried on by bands of outlaws harbored in western Missouri —especially in Jackson, Ray, Caldwell and Clay counties —that terrorized the community and shocked the world by the daring and atrocity of their crimes—including bank robberies in open day, express train wrecking and robberies, and murders. Not until 1881 was this effectually stopped by the betrayal and murder of the outlaw chief of these bands."[8]

Application of the prophecy

Peace is the objective of gospel teachings. If mobs despoil and ravage the Lord's people, they will come to judgment, for he will not permit his work to be destroyed.

---

[6]B. H. Roberts, *New Witnesses for God*, Vol. 1:298-299.
[7]*Ibid.*
[8]B. H. Roberts, *A Comprehensive History of the Church*, Vol. 1, p. 556.

He allows his people to suffer afflictions and tribulations for the sake of righteousness. (See "My People Must Be Tried In All Things . . ." —D&C 136:31; 121:7-8; 122:5-7). The saints anciently were commanded to raise the standard of peace before smiting their enemies.[9] The saints were told that the land of their inheritance, Jackson County, Missouri, should be obtained by purchase, not by blood.[10] The Lord will, however, recompense each person for the deeds done in the body. (See ". . . When The Cup of Their Iniquity Is Full . . ." —D&C 101:10-12; 29:17).

---

[9]D&C 98:23-48.
[10]Ibid., 63:26-31.

Chapter 41

". . . The Children of Judah . . ."
(D&C 109:61-64)

But thou knowest that thou hast a great love for the children of Jacob, who have been scattered upon the mountains for a long time, in a cloudy and dark day.

We therefore ask thee to have mercy upon the children of Jacob, that Jerusalem, from this hour, may begin to be redeemed;

And the yoke of bondage may begin to be broken off from the house of David;

And the children of Judah may begin to return to the lands which thou didst give to Abraham, their father.[1]

Background of the revelation

This revelation is the dedicatory prayer of the Kirtland Temple at Kirtland, Ohio, March 27, 1836. This temple was the first in this dispensation.

Background of the scripture

The plea is made just before verses 61-64 that the heads of nations may have their hearts softened that the missionaries might teach their people the fulness of the gospel.[2] The Lord's people are to gather in the stakes of the Church other than the one at Kirtland.[3] Reference is made to the saints as "sons of Jacob", who are "identified with the gentiles."[4] Being identified with the gentiles refers to the fact that a part of Israel became members of the gentile nations.

Contents of the prophecy

(1) Acknowledgement is made of the fact that God has a great love for the children of Jacob (Israel), who

---

[1]D&C 109:61-64.
[2]*Ibid.* vs. 55-58.
[3]*Ibid.* v. 59.
[4]*Ibid.* v. 60.

have been scattered. (2) Israel is to be redeemed and Jerusalem also and thus their yoke of bondage would be removed. (3) The desire is expressed that the children of Judah (Jews) will begin to return to their lands which were given to Abraham.

Other prophecies

There are prophecies in the Old Testament and the Book of Mormon regarding the scattering and eventual gathering of the Jewish people in the last days.[5]

Fulfillment of the prophecy

An important reason for the restoration of the gospel is that the various branches of scattered Israel might be gathered. In fact, on April 3, 1836, in the Kirtland Temple the resurrected Moses appeared to the Prophet Joseph Smith and Oliver Cowdery and conferred the keys of the gathering of Israel from the four parts of the earth.[6]

One of the miracles of the ages is the perpetuity of the Jewish people, one branch of Israel. They have been scattered among the nations, persecuted, and in many instances slaughtered. The 6,000,000 Jews who perished during the Hitler regime in World War II are a witness of this fact. Yet, as the ancient prophets foretold and the modern prophets have predicted, the Jewish people have been returning to their homeland.

By divine direction, Elder Orson Hyde, a member of the Quorum of the Twelve Apostles, journeyed to Palestine and on October 24, 1841, on the summit of the Mount of Olives, he dedicated the land for the return of the Jewish people. After expressing his gratitude for blessings received he prayed:

"O thou, who didst covenant with Abraham, thy friend, and who didst renew that covenant with Isaac, and confirm the same with Jacob with an oath, that thou

---

[5]Deuteronomy 28:25-64; Amos 9:9; 1 Nephi 22:1-4; Jeremiah 16:12-16; 37:7-8, 10-12; 2 Nephi 25:9-17; Jacob 5.

[6]D&C 110:11.

wouldst not only give them this land for an everlasting inheritance, but that thou wouldst remember their seed forever. Abraham, Isaac, and Jacob have long since closed their eyes in death, and made the grave their mansion. Their children are scattered and dispersed abroad among the nations of the Gentiles like sheep that have no shepherd, and are still looking forward for the fulfillment of those promises which thou didst make concerning them; and even this land, which once poured forth nature's richest bounty, and flowed, as it were, with milk and honey, has, to a certain extent, been smitten with barrenness and sterility since it drank from murderous hands the blood of him who never sinned.

"Grant, therefore, O Lord, in the name of thy well-beloved Son, Jesus Christ, to remove the barrenness and sterility of this land, and let springs of living water break forth to water the thirsty soil. Let the vine and olive produce in their strength, and fig-tree bloom and flourish. Let the land become abundantly fruitful when possessed by its rightful heirs; let it again flow with plenty to feed the returning prodigals who come home with a spirit of grace and supplication; upon it let the clouds distil virtue and richness, and let the fields smile with plenty. Let the flocks and the herds greatly increase and multiply upon the mountains and the hills; let thy great kindness conquer and subdue the unbelief of thy people. . . . Incline them to gather in upon this land according to thy word. Let them come like clouds and like doves to their windows. Let the large ships of the nations bring them from the distant isles; and let kings become their nursing fathers and queens with motherly fondness wipe the tear of sorrow from their eye.

"Thou, O Lord, did once move upon the heart of Cyrus to show favor unto Jerusalem and her children. Do thou also be pleased to inspire the hearts of kings and the powers of the earth to look with a friendly eye toward this place, and with a desire to see thy righteous purposes executed in relation thereto. Let them know that it is thy good pleasure to restore the kingdom unto Israel—raise up Jerusalem as its capital, and constitute her people a distinct nation and government, with David thy servant, even a descendant from the loins of ancient David to be their king.

"Let that nation or that people who shall take an active part in the behalf of Abraham's children, and in the raising up of Jerusalem, find favor in thy sight. Let not their enemies prevail against them, neither let pestilence or famine overcome them, but let thy glory of Israel over-shadow them, and the power of the highest protect them; while that nation or kingdom that will not serve thee in this glorious work must perish, according to thy word: 'Yea, those nations shall be utterly wasted.' "[7] (Following the part quoted above is a plea for blessings upon those who assisted Elder Hyde to the Holy Land, for Zion and her stakes, for the members of the Church who have been persecuted, and upon the First Presidency, the Twelve, and upon every faithful member in the Church.)

In March 1842, a letter from Elder Orson Hyde to the editor of the *Millennial Star* in Liverpool, England, carried the following belief concerning Great Britain:

". . . I will here hazard the opinion, that by political power and influence they will be gathered and built up; and further, that England is destined in the wisdom and economy of heaven to stretch forth the arm of political power, and advance in the front ranks of this glorious enterprize."[8]

On December 11, 1917, General Edmund Allenby at the head of British Troops took Jerusalem from the Turks, thus opening the door for the Jews to return to the Holy Land. Great Britain with the approval of France, Italy and the United States, adopted the policy to establish Palestine as a national home for the Jewish people.

---

[7] *Millennial Star*, Vol. 19, 1856, pp.
[8] *Ibid.* 2:169.

The return of the Jews to Palestine has demonstrated the validity of the prophecies relative to their eventual return and also the prayer on the Mount of Olives by an apostle of the Lord Jesus Christ. In 1841, when dedicated, the land was the home of fewer than 5,000 Jews. In 1872, another dedication of Palestine was made by President George A. Smith, accompanied by Elder Lorenzo Snow, of the Council of the Twelve. This second dedication was presumably that there might be witnesses to the dedication. By 1876 there were from 15-20,000 Jews in that land. The following table from the *Statistical Abstract of Israel,* 1965,[9] indicates at various intervals the Jewish population of Palestine:

1882—24,000	1925—122,000	1945—563,800
1900—50,000	1935—355,200	1947—630,000
1914—85,000	1940—467,500	

Although there has been a steady increase of Jewish immigration over those years with the help of Great Britain and other powers, Great Britain attempted to prohibit further immigration because of Arab demands. However, the mandate which Great Britain exercised over Palestine ended on May 14, 1948, when the Jewish people received their own government, known as Israel. With the opening of this new Jewish state to citizenship of all having Jewish blood, the following table indicates the rapid rise of Jewish population since that time:

1948—649,600	1954—1,526,000	1962—2,068,900
1951—1,404,400	1957—1,762,700	1963—2,115,600

It is believed that the present (1969) Jewish population is upwards of 2,500,000.

The victorious six-day war in June 1967 between Arab nations and Israel greatly enlarged her borders, including all of Jerusalem which was prophecied to be built up as a holy city of the Lord in the last days.[10]

---

[9]*Statistical Abstract of Israel,* 1965.
[10]Ether 13:5, 11.

Application of the prophecy

Not only ancient prophets foresaw the gathering of the Jews in the last days, but also the Lord inspired the Prophet Joseph Smith to know that in the dispensation of the fulness of times they would return to the Holy Land. Book of Mormon prophets foretold this gathering. (2 Nephi 25:16-17; 3 Nephi 20:29-31; 21:24-29) Inasmuch as Joseph Smith was the Lord's instrument in bringing forth the Book of Mormon and the Doctrine and Covenants, members of the Church are strengthened in their faith in the divine mission of the Prophet and the work he established. They look upon the fulfillment of this prophecy as evidence that the Lord fulfills his word.

Other prophecies concerning the gathering of Israel given in Section 109 of the Doctrine and Covenants are considered in the following: ". . . The Lamanites Shall Blossom As The Rose . . ." —D&C 29:24; 109:65-66; ". . . The Scattered Remnants of Israel . . ." —D&C 109:67).

Chapter 42

". . . The Scattered Remnants of Israel . . ."
(D&C 109:67)

And may all the scattered remnants of Israel, who have been driven to the ends of the earth, come to a knowledge of the truth, believe in the Messiah, and be redeemed from oppression, and rejoice before thee.[1]

Background of the revelation

The dedicatory prayer of the Kirtland Temple was received by revelation and read by the Prophet Joseph Smith at the dedicatory services March 27, 1836. Some of the remnants of Israel, converted in the United States and Canada were present for this service. Many manifestations of the Holy Ghost were present during the dedicatory services.

Background of the prophecy

The gathering of the various branches of Israel are mentioned in the context of this prophecy. The Jewish people are to return to Jerusalem and the Lamanites are to flourish. ("See ". . . The Children of Judah . . ."—D&C 109:61-64 in this series, and ". . . The Lamanites Shall Blossom As The Rose . . ." —D&C 49:24; 109:65-66)

Contents of the prophecy

This prophecy does not include the Jewish people and the Lamanites, but (1) Israel, other than the ten tribes who will return from the land of the north, who was scattered among the nations after the Assyrian captivity. (2) They are to come to a knowledge of the Gospel, believe in Jesus Christ, and be redeemed from oppression.

---

[1]D&C 109:67.

The Scattering of Israel

The Patriarch Abraham received promises of having his seed bear God's authority and the Gospel of Jesus Christ through the stream of time.[2] These blessings were continued through his son Isaac and his grandson Jacob (Israel). Jacob (or Israel) had twelve sons, one of whom was Joseph, who had two sons—Manasseh and Ephraim. Ephraim received the birthright over all the sons of Israel. For almost 400 years the descendants of Israel were in Egyptian bondage, being delivered by the power of God through Moses.[3] Following their sojourn in the wilderness and their occupying the land of Canaan, judges ruled, and then a United Kingdom was divided into the Northern Kingdom (Israel) and the Southern Kingdom of Judah. The Kingdom of Israel was led by the descendants of Ephraim, consisting of most of the tribes of Israel.

In or about the year 721 B. C., the Kingdom of Israel was overthrown and the people taken captive into Assyria. That they would eventually come from the north countries as the ten lost tribes is known in the modern revelations.[4] The ten tribes of Israel, except Judah, were to return from the north where they are lost, having been scattered as they journeyed north. The Kingdom of Judah was overcome and scattered about 588 B.C. After seventy years they were allowed to return. They came under Roman rule and in A.D. 71, because of rebellion, they were scattered again.

Fulfillment of the prophecy

The scattered shall be gathered in the due time of the Lord. The resurrected Savior said that the other tribes of Israel, other than some of Joseph who were in America, would be gathered in the last days that the covenant made

---

[2]Abraham 2:9-11.
[3]Exodus 13 and 14.
[4]D&C 133:23-34.

with all the house of Israel might be fulfilled.[5] Biblical prophets have predicted that gathering.[6]

Latter-day Saints Are of Israel

The Tenth Article of Faith of the Church reads: "We believe in the literal gathering of Israel. . . ." In fact, the Lord said that the restored gospel is here to recover his people who are of the House of Israel.[7] Latter-day Saints are a part of that literal gathering.[8] Their bishops are "judges in Israel."[9] The saints have received the Priesthood as literal descendants of Israel; consequently, in these latter-days they shall be a light unto the gentiles and "a savior unto my people Israel."[10] The salvation of scattered Israel is a common theme in the modern revelations. In a context of persecution of the saints in being driven from Jackson County, Missouri, the Lord said that the faithful, "all mine Israel, shall be saved."[11] The redemption of Zion (Missouri) was placed in abeyance, until among other conditions, "the army of Israel becomes very great."[12] The Doctrine and Covenants closes with a revelation concerning the trek across the plains by pioneer companies in which they are assured that the Lord's "arm is stretched out in the last days, to save my people Israel."[13]

Fulfillment of the prophecy

The literal gathering of the tribe of Joseph (Ephraim and Manasseh) from the nations of the earth has continued since the Church was organized in 1831. The unique missionary system whereby the missionary supports himself to "save Israel" has been an important reason for the

---

[5]3 Nephi 16:4-5.
[6]Isaiah 11:12-16; Jeremiah 3:14; 16:14-16; 31:8-10.
[7]D&C 39:11.
[8]*Ibid.* 103:17.
[9]*Ibid.* 58:17; 107:72, 76.
[10]*Ibid.* 86:8-11.
[11]*Ibid.* 101:12.
[12]*Ibid.* 105:26.
[13]*Ibid.* 136:21-22.

steady increase in membership until today its membership is almost 2,700,000.

The history of the Church of Jesus Christ of Latter-day Saints abounds in examples of its converts being brought out of thraldom, oppression, and misery. One man born in Europe wished that he had been born a horse, for the animal was cared for, while he was not considered of the same value. As expressed in the words of President George Q. Cannon:

"This man's statement concerning his feelings was very strongly put; but his condition was that of thousands when this Gospel reached them. What has it done for them? It has lifted them up; it has made them feel that they are the children of God—peers of everyone else on the earth, no matter how rich, no matter how learned, no matter how many advantages others may possess, they are equal before the Lord with all of them. 'Mormonism' has done this for the world. . . . Every man that has embraced this Gospel is raised to this dignity and to this power."[14]

Above all else the Gospel has brought not only escape from sordid economic conditions, but it has brought relief to men's hearts and souls in giving them a concept of God, heaven, and earth-life which gives them dignity and freedom from error and a reason for existence. Converts from out of the world have rejoiced in their new life of knowing the purpose of this existence, the divine destiny of the obedient, and deep, sincere, faith in God as their Father. [15] As Elder John A. Widtsoe said:

"Do you know of a happier people? I find happiness wherever I go, for Latter-day Saints understand the truth. They have seen the beginning and they know the end of the designs of God with respect to his children. They do not grope in darkness."[16]

---

[14]*Conference Report,* April 1899, pp. 18-19.
[15]*Ibid.*
[16]*Ibid.* October 1921, p. 109.

Who are these Israelites who are being gathered into the Gospel net? Charles Dickens, English author, though not a Latter-day Saint, bears the following testimony about those whom he observed on a "Mormon" emigrant ship, 1863:

"Now I have been in emigrant ships before this day in June. And these people are so strikingly different from all other people in like circumstances whom I have seen, that I wonder aloud, 'what would a stranger suppose these emigrants to be!' "

"I should have said they were in their degree the pick and flower of England . . .

"I afterwards learned that a Dispatch was sent home by the captain before he struck out into the wide Atlantic, highly extolling the behavior of these Emigrants, and the perfect order and propriety of all their social arrangements . . . . I went on board their ship to bear testimony against them if they deserved it, as I fully believed they would; to my great astonishment they did not deserve it; and my predispositions and tendencies must not affect me as an honest witness. I went over the *Amazon's* side, feeling it impossible to deny that, so far, some remarkable influence had produced a remarkable result, which better known influences have often missed."[17]

Application of the prophecy

To one of the house of Israel gathered out of the world, as a convert or by birth in the Church, this prophesy brings grave responsibilities and great blessings. The Priesthood of God was to be held by Abraham's descendants in the last days through Jacob or Israel. This promise is again given to modern Israel in the following words:

"Therefore, thus saith the Lord unto you, with whom the priesthood hath continued through the lineage of your fathers—

"For ye are lawful heirs, according to the flesh, and have been hid from the world with Christ in God—

---

[17]Charles Dickens, *The Uncommercial Traveller*, pp. 200-201.

"Therefore your life and the priesthood have remained, and must needs remain through you and your lineage until the restoration of all things spoken by the mouths of all the holy prophets since the world began.

"Therefore, blessed are ye if ye continue in my goodness, a light unto the Gentiles, and through this priesthood, a savior unto my people Israel. The Lord has said it. Amen.[18] (See ". . . Ye Are Lawful Heirs . . . Blessed Are Ye If Ye Continue In My Goodness . . .")

What is the over-all objective of the restoration of the Church and the Priesthood? It is to prepare a people for the second coming of Christ, and ultimately that they may receive the blessings of Abraham to be exalted in the celestial kingdom of God. Latter-day Saints have received their mission, as stated by President Wilford Woodruff:

"You are literally and lawfully heirs of the Priesthood through the lineage of your fathers, and that Priesthood will continue throughout eternity; therefore, you have received your appointment, and the Lord looks to you to build up his Zion and kingdom upon the earth."[19]

To build Zion that the kingdom of God will come when the Savior reigns is the grand objective of Latter-day Saints!

---

[18]D&C 86:8-11.
[19]*Journal of Discourses,* 18:120.

Chapter 43

"Yea The Hearts Of Tens of Thousands Shall . . . Rejoice . . . And The Fame Of This House Shall Spread . . ."
(D&C 110:7-10; 88:119-120).

(A) For behold, I have accepted this house, and my name shall be here; and I will manifest myself to my people in mercy in this house.

Yea, I will appear unto my servants, and speak unto them with mine own voice, if my people will keep my commandments, and do not pollute this holy house.

Yea the hearts of thousands and tens of thousands shall greatly rejoice in consequence of the blessings which shall be poured out, and the endowment with which my servants have been endowed in this house.

And the fame of this house shall spread to foreign lands; and this is the beginning of the blessing which shall be poured out upon the heads of my people. Even so. Amen.[1]

(B) Organize yourselves; prepare every needful thing; and establish a house, even a house of prayer, a house of fasting, a house of faith, a house of learning, a house of glory, a house of order, a house of God;

That your incomings may be in the name of the Lord; that your outgoings may be in the name of the Lord; that all your salutations may be in the name of the Lord, with uplifted hands unto the Most High.[2]

Background of the revelations

(A) Section 110 is the historical account of the appearance of four personages—Jesus Christ, Moses, Elias, and Elijah—to Joseph Smith and Oliver Cowdery.

(B) Section 88, known as the Olive Leaf, is one of the longest and most informative revelations in the Doctrine and Covenants. It was named the Olive Leaf by the Prophet because it is a message of peace to the saints.

---

[1]D&C 110:7-10.
[2]*Ibid.* 88:119-120.

Background of the prophetic promises

(A) Joseph Smith and Oliver Cowdery on April 3, 1836, in the Kirtland (Ohio) Temple "saw the Lord standing upon the breastwork of the pulpit, before us; and under his feet was a paved work of pure gold, in color like amber."[3]

(B) The Lord revealed events before and after Jesus' second coming and the Millennium, even to the time when everything is done for the salvation of men belonging to this earth. There follows in the revelation a series of great truths, with the command to call a solemn assembly.

Contents of the prophetic promises

(1) The Lord Jesus Christ accepted the Kirtland Temple. (2) He will appear to his servants and manifest mercy to his people. (3) These blessings will follow if the people keep the commandments and thereby not pollute the Temple. (4) Thousands will rejoice because of the blessings to be poured out. (5) The fame of the temple will be known in foreign lands. (6) The temple is to be a house of prayer, fasting, faith, learning, glory, order, of God. (7) Those who enter therein should be prayerful people.

Fulfillment of the prophetic promises

The Kirtland Temple was used as a house of learning, prayer, fasting, and faith to the glory of God.

"There were two schools conducted in Kirtland. One was a school of the Elders where they carried out some of the provisions of this revelation (Sec. 88) in seeking knowledge of countries and kingdoms and languages, all such information as may be gained in the regular daily school. . .

"The other was the 'School of the Prophets,' and a very good description of this school and its purpose is given in this section of the Doctrine and Covenants, (Sec. 88:117 to the end of the section). . . . This School of the

[3]D&C 110:2.

Prophets and the schools where the ordinary branches were taught continued in Kirtland until the exodus from that place. It was for this school that the lectures on faith were prepared and which were delivered to the Elders."[4]

A function of the Kirtland Temple was the holding of public meetings which set this temple apart from the other temples erected by the Church. The endowment administered in that Temple was only partial.[5] Meetings, such as fast meetings, solemn assemblies, and sacrament meetings were held there. There was every opportunity to exercise and to build faith, receive learning, pray, fast, and contemplate the glory of God in that holy house. In fact, glorious days were enjoyed by faithful saints as they were participants in marvelous spiritual manifestations. The endowment mentioned in the prophetic promise probably refers not only to the partial endowment administered but also to the spiritual occurences which came into the lives of God's servants during the period March-April 1836. Some of the brethren saw angels, others spoke in tongues with the interpretation being given. The Prophet called upon the congregation to encourage the Spirit that prophecy and other manifestations might be enjoyed. Elder George A. Smith prophesied, and in the words of the Prophet:

". . .a noise was heard like the sound of a rushing mighty wind, which filled the Temple, and all the congregation simultaneously arose, being moved upon by an invisible power; many began to speak in tongues and prophesy; others saw glorious visions; and I beheld the Temple was filled with angels, which fact I declared to the congregation. The people of the neighborhood came running together (hearing an unusual sound within, and seeing a bright light like a pillar of fire resting upon the Temple), and were astonished at what was taking place.

---

[4]Joseph Fielding Smith, *Church History and Modern Revelation*, Series 2, pp. 136-137.

[5]*Journal of Discourses*, 19:24.

This continued until the meeting closed at eleven p.m."[6]

Elder Heber C. Kimball in referring to the meeting of April 6th, 1836, said:

"The meeting continued on through the night; the spirit of prophecy was poured out upon the assembly, and cloven tongues of fire sat upon them; for they were seen by many of the congregation. Also angels administered to many, for they were also seen by many.

"This continued several days and was attended by a marvelous spirit of prophecy. Every man's mouth was full of prophesying, and for a number of days or weeks our time was spent in visiting from house to house, administering bread and wine, and pronouncing blessings upon each other to that degree, that from the external appearances one would have supposed that the last days had truly come, in which the Spirit of the Lord was poured out upon all flesh, as far as the Church was concerned, for the sons and daughters of Zion were full of prophesying."[7]

Did the saints in Kirtland continue to keep the commandments that the Temple might not be polluted? Lucy Mack Smith, mother of the Prophet, refers to the time shortly after the completion of the Temple when "Joseph had a vision, which lasted until he besought the Lord to take it from him; for it manifested to him things which were painful to contemplate. It was taken from before his eyes for a short time, but soon returned again, and remained until the whole scene was portrayed before him."[8] The following day, he preached a sermon in which he prophetically said:

"We have accomplished more than we had any reason to expect when we began. Our beautiful house is finished, and the Lord has acknowledged it, by pouring out his Spirit upon us here, and revealing to us much of his will in regard to the work which he is about to perform. . . .

---

[6] *DHC* 2:428.

[7] Orson F. Whitney, *Life of Heber C. Kimball*, p. 93.

[8] Lucy Mack Smith, *History of Joseph Smith By His Mother*, p. 239.

"But, brethren, beware; for I tell you in the name of the Lord, that there is an evil in this very congregation, which, if not repented of, will result in setting many of you, who are here this day, so much at enmity against me, that you will have a desire to take my life; and you even *would do it,* if God should permit the deed. But, brethren, I now call upon you to repent, and cease all your hardness of heart, and turn from those principles of death and dishonesty which you are harboring in your bosoms, before it is eternally too late, for there is yet room for repentance."[9]

In the spring of 1837, Elder Parley P. Pratt returned to Kirtland from Canada and found ". . .there were jarrings and discords in the Church at Kirtland, and many fell away and became enemies and apostates. There were also envyings, lyings, strifes and divisions, which caused much trouble and sorrow. By such spirits I was also accused, misrepresented and abused. And at one time, I also was overcome by the same spirit in a great measure, and it seemed as if the very powers of darkness which war against the Saints were let loose upon me. But the Lord knew my faith, my zeal, my integrity of purpose, and he gave me the victory."[10]

This spirit of apostasy which had taken hold of the saints in Kirtland was manifest in the Temple. In her history of her son the Prophet's mother wrote of the time that a fight occurred and a sword was drawn by one of the apostles against the person of William Smith.[11] Wilford Woodruff mentioned the occasion when this same spirit of bitterness was demonstrated against the Prophet by another apostle when he cursed him while the sacrament was being passed during a Temple meeting:

"He turned as black in the face almost as an African with rage and with the power of the devil. What did he

---

[9]*Ibid.* pp. 239-240.
[10]Parley P. Pratt, *Autobiography of Parley P. Pratt,* p. 168.
[11]*Ibid.* pp. 240-241.

do? He ate and drank damnation to himself. He did not go and hang himself, but he did go and drown himself, and the river went over his body while his spirit was cast into the pit where he ceased to have the power to curse either God or His Prophet in time or eternity."[12]

By the end of 1837 and the beginning of 1838, Brigham Young and Sidney Rigdon, and the Prophet fled Kirtland in order to save their lives. In a relatively short time the Kirtland Temple was lost to the Church. It was further desecrated, until on January 19, 1841, the Lord revealed that there was no place upon the earth to which he could come and give the fulness of the Priesthood to the members of the Church. A new Temple was to be erected in Nauvoo (Illinois) where the full priesthood endowment might be administered to faithful saints.[13]

A summary of the history of the saints in Kirtland, Ohio, and the present status of the Kirtland Temple is given by Elder James E. Talmage, as follows:

"Within two years following the dedication, a general exodus of the Saints had taken place, and the Temple soon fell into the hands of the persecutors. The building is yet standing, and serves the purposes of an ordinary meeting-house for an obscure sect that manifests no visible activity in temple building, nor apparent belief in the sacred ordinances for which temples are erected. The people whose sacrifice and suffering reared the structure no longer assert claims of ownership. What was once a Temple of God, in which the Lord Jesus appeared in person, has become but a house—a building whose sole claim to distinction among the innumerable structures built by man, lies in its wondrous past."[14]

"Its wondrous past" is the foundation for the fulfillment of the prophetic promise: "And the fame of this

---

[12]*Millennial Star* 57:339-340.
[13]D. & C. 124:25-34; 40-43.
[14]James E. Talmage, *The House of the Lord*, p. 123.

house shall spread to foreign lands; and this is the beginning of the blessing which shall be poured out upon the
heads of my people."[15] On April 3, 1836, the Savior appeared in the Kirtland Temple; Moses restored the keys
of the gathering of Israel; Elias restored the Gospel of
Abraham, which blessings are received in the House of
the Lord; and the blessings of the sealing powers of the
Priesthood, with the genealogical powers of research and
temple activity were restored. The power and influence
of these keys of authority have publicized the name and
fame of this Temple wherever the gospel has been preached. In the hearts of the "tens of thousands" of people
who become members of The Church of Jesus Christ of
Latter-day Saints annually, the fame of the Temple and
the blessings which originated in that House of the Lord
not only bring them into the Church, but inspires them
to receive the ordinances of exaltation in temples accepted
by the Lord Jesus Christ as his House. They walk in the
Lord's paths by having been taught in the House of the
Lord.[16]

Application of the prophetic promises

Two lessons may be derived from the fulfillment of
these prophetic promises: (1) that even faithful members
of the Church may fall into apostasy, and (2) they who
have not yet received the blessings of the House of the
Lord should work to that end.

Though a person may have reached the heights of
great knowledge and become sanctified by the Holy Ghost,
he may fall from the faith.[17] (See "Pray Always Lest You
. . .Lose Your Reward"—D&C 31:12; 61:39; 10:5; 93:49;
". . .From Him Shall Be Taken Even The Light Which
He Has Received"—D&C 1:31-33).

The Lord has decreed that the fulness of blessings
available to his children comes only by obedience to the

[15]D&C 110:10.
[16]Isaiah 2:2-3; Micah 4:1-2.
[17]D&C 20:30-34.

fulness of the Gospel of Jesus Christ. The capstone of salvation ordinances are the temple endowment and marriage for eternity.[18]

---

[18]*Ibid.* 76:51-62; 124:28, 36-42; 131:1-4; 132:15-25.

Chapter 44

". . . Upon My House Shall It Begin . . ."
(D&C 112:23-26)

Verily, verily, I say unto you, darkness covereth the earth, and gross darkness the minds of the people, and all flesh has become corrupt before my face.

Behold, vengeance cometh speedily upon the inhabitants of the earth, a day of wrath, a day of burning, a day of desolation, of weeping, of mourning, and of lamentation; and as a whirlwind it shall come upon all the face of the earth, saith the Lord.

And upon my house shall it begin and from my house shall it go forth, saith the Lord;

First among those among you, saith the Lord, who have professed to know my name and have not known me, and have blasphemed against me in the midst of my house, saith the Lord.[1]

Background of the revelation

The year 1837 was a critical time for the Church. The Prophet Joseph Smith refers to this period as one of speculation in lands and property of all kinds which took hold of many members of the Church. The failure of the "Kirtland Safety Society," a church-owned institution, due to the dishonesty of some of its officers, brought some disaffection among some Church members. "No quorum in the Church was entirely exempt from the influence of those false spirits who were striving against me for the mastery. . ." said the Prophet. Amidst these conditions, Section 112 was received. It was addressed to Elder Thomas B. Marsh, President of the Twelve Apostles, for his benefit and also that of the Quorum.[2]

Contents of the prophecy

(1) A state of apostasy from the truth engulfs the world. (2) This condition will bring judgments upon the

---

[1]D&C 112:23-26.
[2]DHC 2:487-489, 499.

inhabitants of the earth. It will be a time of burning, probably referring to the destruction at the time of the second coming of Christ, which will bring mourning and lamentation. (3) The "vengeance" prophesied will begin with the Lord's Church[3] and from thence it shall go forth. (4) Those members of the Church who have blasphemed the Lord's name will receive his vengeance.

Fulfillment of the prophecy

In the context given above, this prophecy was fulfilled in part when, as the *Doctrine and Covenants Commentary* states: "The day of wrath came, and the Church was first sifted. Those who professed to be Saints and were not, were separated from the Church, through persecution, and the Church itself was then brought to a place of safety, in the mountain chambers."[4]

This prophecy, however, has been interpreted by some authorities as yet to be fulfilled. In 1873, Elder Orson Pratt said these words when speaking of the failure of members of the Church to teach their children to keep the commandments:

"What will be the consequences? There is a day of reckoning and judgment coming, and it shall begin at the Lord's house, and from there it shall go forth among all the nations of the earth. Let parents awake and see to it, lest the same destruction that will overtake the children because of their apostasy, come upon them also."[5]

President Wilford Woodruff in 1880 said:

"Judgments are going to begin at the house of God. They will go forth and will not be taken from the earth until all has been fulfilled."[6]

In recalling that the Lord brought the saints out west

---

[3]Hebrews 10:21.

[4]Hyrum M. Smith and Janne M. Sjodahl, *Doctrine and Covenants Commentary*, p. 736.

[5]*Journal of Discourses*, 15:330.

[6]*Conference Report*, April 1880, p. 10.

where they might have refuge from the storm, Elder Melvin J. Ballard in 1922 expressed deep concern for the world because of a lack of repentance, and then, he said:

"Therefore we stand in peril, many of us! for do you think that the Lord who has given us greater light and greater knowledge than the world, will pass us by in our sins and our transgressions? I say to you that if we do not live better than the world, if our standard of morality is not in excess of theirs, if we do not observe the law and maintain it better than any other people, we ought to be ashamed of ourselves, and we shall stand under great condemnation before the Lord, because we know more than anybody else. The light and knowledge that the Lord has given to us place us in a very peculiar position, and if we are not careful the judgment of the Lord shall begin at the house of the Lord."[7]

Application of the prophecy

It is apparent from the foregoing prophets, seers and revelators, that members of the Church who are indifferent, careless toward their covenant obligations, and corrupt in their lives will receive judgments in this life as well as punishment in the eternal worlds. Everyone of them may not receive the predicted judgments indicated in verses 23 through 26 of Section 112, in this life, but the judgment in the future life is certain. The punishment in the spirit world will awaken one "to a lively sense of his own guilt . . . and pain, and anguish, which is like an unquenchable fire, whose flame ascendeth up forever and ever."[8]

As time moves closer and closer to the predicted calamities which will spread throughout the earth as a whirlwind, all saints should be mindful of their covenant relationship to the Lord. The sacramental prayers furnish an excellent review of obligations made in baptism: (1) to

---

[7]*Ibid.* October 1922, p. 59.
[8]Mosiah 2:36-38.

take upon oneself the name of Christ (2) to always remember him and, (3) to keep his commandments.[9]

A prophecy closely associated with the one discussed here is Section 97:22-28. (See "Zion Shall Escape If . . .")

---

[9]D&C 20:77-79.

Chapter 45

A Prophecy With A Date
(D&C 118:4-6)

And next spring let them depart to go over the great waters, and there promulgate my gospel, the fulness thereof, and bear record of my name.

Let them take leave of my saints in the city of Far West, on the twenty-sixth day of April next, on the building-spot of my house, saith the Lord.

Let my servant John Taylor, and also my servant John E. Page, and also my servant Wilford Woodruff, and also my servant Willard Richards, be appointed to fill the places of those who have fallen, and be officially notified of their appointment.[1]

Background of the revelation

The spirit of apostasy was rampant in the Church. Some of the leading brethren planned the destruction of the Church, but their efforts failed. Numbered among the apostates who were excommunicated were the following members of the Council of the Twelve Apostles: John G. Boynton, Lyman E. Johnson, Luke S. Johnson, who later returned to the Church, and William E. McLellin. Several high councilors and other priesthood members also fell at this time. Mobocracy prevailed in Missouri during the fall of 1838, including the issuance of the exterminating order by Governor William Boggs, driving the saints from Missouri.

Contents of the prophecy

The Twelve were commanded to leave for missions across the waters to Europe in the spring of 1839. They were to leave from the site of the temple lot at Far West, Missouri, on April 26, 1839. The business of the meeting at the temple lot was to appoint brethren to fill the vacancies created by apostasy.

---

[1]D&C 118:4-6.

Fulfillment of the prophecy

With the saints expelled from the state of Missouri by its citizenry, including the governor of the state, there was serious concern on the part of some members of the Church as to whether or not the meeting should be held. Several members of the Twelve, some being absent, met with other members of the Church at the building site of the temple on April 26, 1839, as commanded, and transacted the business appointed. The minutes of that meeting are as follows:

"At a conference held at Far West by the Twelve, High Priests, Elders, and Priests, on the 26th day of April, 1839, the following resolution was adopted:

"Resolved: That the following persons be no more fellowshiped in The Church of Jesus Christ of Latter-day Saints, but excommunicated from the same viz.: [the names of the excommunicants follow]

"The council then proceeded to the building spot of the Lord's House; when the following business was transacted: Part of a hymn was sung, on the misson of the Twelve.

"Elder Alpheus Cutler, the master workman of the house, then recommenced laying the foundation of the Lord's House, agreeable to revelation, by rolling up a large stone near the southeast corner."

The following of the Twelve were present: Brigham Young, Heber C. Kimball, Orson Pratt, John E. Page, and John Taylor, who proceeded to ordain Wilford Woodruff, and George A. Smith, ". . . who had been previously nominated by the First Presidency, accepted by the Twelve, and acknowledged by the Church, to the office of Apostles and members of the quorum of the Twelve, to fill the places of those who were fallen. Darwin Chase and Norman Shearer (who had just been liberated from the Richmond prison, where they had been confined for the cause of Jesus Christ) were then ordained to the office of the Seventies.

"The Twelve then offered up vocal prayer in the following order: Brigham Young, Heber C. Kimball, Orson Pratt, John E. Page, John Taylor, Wilford Woodruff, and George A. Smith. After which we sang Adam-ondi-Ahman, and then the Twelve took their leave of the following Saints, agreeable to the revelation, viz.: [Names of these individuals follow].

"Elder Alpheus Cutler then placed the stone before alluded to in its regular position, after which, in consequence of the peculiar situation of the Saints, he thought it wisdom to adjourn until some future time, when the Lord shall open the way; expressing his determination then to proceed with the building; whereupon the conference adjourned.

Brigham Young, President.

John Taylor, Clerk."[2]

Elder John E. Page, mentioned in verse 6 of the prophecy, was ordained an apostle December 19, 1838, and Elder Willard Richards was in Europe and was ordained April 14, 1840.

The following account was related by Elder Wilford Woodruff with reference to his call to the apostleship:

"In the time of the great apostasy in Kirtland the Spirit of the Lord said to me. 'Get you a partner and go to Fox Islands.' I knew no more what was in Fox Islands than what was in Kolob. I went there, however, baptized a hundred and brought them up to Zion with me. It was upon that island where I received a letter from Joseph Smith, telling me that I was called by revelation to fill the place of one of the Twelve who had fallen. You will see it in the Doctrine and Covenants. That thing was revealed to me before I received the letter from Joseph Smith, but I did not feel disposed to tell it to any mortal man, for I knew it was my duty to keep such things to myself."[3]

---

[2]*DHC* 3:336-339.
[3]*Conference Report*, April 1898, pp. 30-31.

Following the reporting of the minutes of the meeting, the Prophet Joseph Smith wrote the following:

"Thus was fulfilled a revelation of July 8, 1838, which our enemies had said could not be fulfilled, as no 'Mormon' would be permitted to be in the state.

"As the Saints were passing away from the meeting, Brother Turley said to Elders Page and Woodruff, 'Stop a bit, while I bid Isaac Russell goodbye;' and knocking at the door, called Brother Russell. [He and his wife had just been excommunicated because of apostasy]. His wife answered, 'Come in, it is Brother Turley.' Russell replied, 'It is not; he left here two weeks ago;' and appeared quite alarmed; but on finding it was Brother Turley, asked him to sit down; but the latter replied, 'I cannot, I shall lose my company.' 'Who is your company?' inquired Russell. 'The Twelve.' 'The Twelve!' 'Yes, don't you know that this is the twenty-sixth, and the day the Twelve were to take leave of their friends on the foundation of the Lord's House, to go to the islands of the sea? The revelation is now fulfilled, and I am going with them.' Russell was speechless, and Turley bid him farewell."[4]

Application

Although this prophecy is not as momentous as the one on the wars of the latter days, which began with the American Civil War, it nonetheless is outstanding in the execution of its fulfillment due to the circumstances which developed subsequently. (See ". . . The Wars That Will Shortly Come To Pass. . ." Part I—The American Civil War—D&C 87:1-3.) In any case, as a prophecy, it adds one more to the numerous prophecies given by the Prophet Joseph Smith to attest to his calling as a prophet.

The circumstances under which the prophecy was fulfilled provide Latter-day Saints with increased assurance that the Lord will assist his servants to accomplish the mission to which they are called. The words of Nephi

---

[4]*DHC* 3:339-340.

are remembered by members of the Church as significant
in this regard: ". . .I will go and do the things which the
Lord hath commanded, for I know that the Lord giveth
no commandments unto the children of men, save he shall
prepare a way for them that they may accomplish the
thing which he commandeth them."[5]

---

[5]1 Nephi 3:7.

Chapter 46

"God Shall Give You Knowledge By His Holy Spirit . . ."

(D&C 121:26-29; 42:61; 76:5-10; 101:32-34)

(A) God shall give unto you knowledge by his Holy Spirit, yea, by the unspeakable gift of the Holy Ghost, that has not been revealed since the world was until now;

Which our forefathers have awaited with anxious expectation to be revealed in the last times, which their minds were pointed to by the angels, as held in reserve for the fulness of their glory;

A time to come in which nothing shall be withheld, whether there be one God or many gods, they shall be manifest.

All thrones and dominions, principalities and powers, shall be revealed and set forth upon all who have endured valiantly for the gospel of Jesus Christ.[1]

(B) If thou shalt ask, thou shalt receive revelation upon revelation, knowledge upon knowledge, that thou mayest know the mysteries and peaceable things—that which bringeth joy, that which bringeth life eternal.[2]

(C) For thus saith the Lord—I, the Lord, am merciful and gracious unto those who fear me, and delight to honor those who serve me in righteousness and in truth unto the end.

Great shall be their reward and eternal shall be their glory.

And to them will I reveal all mysteries, yea, all the hidden mysteries of my kingdom from days of old, and for ages to come, will I make known unto them the good pleasure of my will concerning all things pertaining to my kingdom.

Yea, even the wonders of eternity shall they know, and things to come will I show them, even the things of many generations.

And their wisdom shall be great, and their understanding reach to heaven; and before them the wisdom of the wise shall perish, and the understanding of the prudent shall come to naught.

For by my Spirit will I enlighten them, and by my power will I make known unto them the secrets of my will—yea, even those things which eye has not seen, nor ear heard, nor yet entered into the heart of man.[3]

---

[1]D&C 121:26-29.
[2]Ibid. 42:61.
[3]Ibid. 76:5-10.

(D) Yea, verily I say unto you, in that day when the Lord shall come, he shall reveal all things—

Things which have passed, and hidden things which no man knew, things of the earth, by which it was made, and the purpose and the end thereof—

Things most precious, things that are above, and things that are beneath, things that are in the earth, and upon the earth, and in heaven.[4]

Background of the revelations

(A) This revelation is captioned "Prayer and Prophecies," written by the Prophet while in jail at Liberty, Missouri, on March 20, 1839.

(B) Section 42 is known as the "Law to the Church," consisting of several laws for the guidance of members, missionaries, and administrators.

(C) Section 76 is the revelation about the kingdoms which will exist following the resurrection of man. The degrees of glory for the host of mankind, and perdition, a kingdom of no glory, are revealed.

(D) This revelation constitutes a message of hope for the members of the Church, some of whom were undergoing persecution in Missouri.

Background of the prophecies and promises

(A) The first part of Section 121 is a prayer of the Prophet relative to the sufferings of the saints and the Lord's answer. The condemnations which await the apostates and enemies of the Church preceed the promise.

(B) The following laws precede the prophecy: the law of preaching the gospel, of moral conduct, of consecration, of administration to the sick, and the law of sundry duties.

(C) The prophetic promises in Section 76 are a part of the introduction to the revelation. The greatness of God's power and wisdom are indicated.

(D) Information is given concerning the saints who were persecuted in Jackson County, Missouri; the Lord's

[4]*Ibid.* 101:32-34.

indignation upon the nations; the scattered saints will eventually return to Missouri to build the city of Zion; and conditions on the earth during the Millennium.

Contents of the prophecies and promises

(1) By the Holy Ghost, God will give knowledge to saints. (2) Our forefathers have anxiously awaited this day. (3) One must ask to receive the mysteries of God's Will. (4) All wisdom will eventually be given to the faithful. (5) When the Savior comes, he will reveal all things.

Analysis of the prophecies and promises

It is evident that the greatness of the Dispensation of the Fulness of Times consists of its being the period when all things revealed to the prophets in other dispensations will become a part of the fulness of times.[5] The prophecies and promises under consideration indicate this same thing—revelations held in reserve, all knowledge, and the further fact that the fulness of times *includes the Millennium*. Furthermore, it is apparent that some of the blessings will come following the resurrection.

In addition, since the promises made in Section 76 received by Joseph Smith and Sidney Rigdon by vision, are introductory to a view of the eternal worlds after the resurrection, what was revealed to them constituted some of the "things which eye has not seen, nor ear heard, nor yet entered into the heart of man."[6]

It is also clear that neither man's researches about himself and the earth are presently known nor revealed in the revelations in full.

Fulfillment of the prophecies and promises

Latter-day Saints testify that insofar as these prophecies and promises pertain to this earth life the following have been and are in the process of fulfillment: "God shall give unto you knowledge by his Holy Spirit, and "if thou

---

[5] Acts 3:19-21; Ephesians 1:9-10.
[6] D&C 76:10, c.f. vs. 114-119.

shalt ask, thou shalt receive revelation upon revelation, knowledge upon knowledge, that thou mayest know the mysteries and peaceable things."

There are at least two categories of knowledge mentioned in these prophecies: (1) testimonies of the truth and (2) revelation in religious and temporal matters.

(1) Thousands of Latter-day Saints can testify that by the Holy Ghost they have received the knowledge that God lives and Jesus is the Son of God; the scriptures are true; that Joseph Smith was the initiator, under divine guidance, to establish God's only true Church and thus usher in the Dispensation of the fulness of times; and that those who have succeeded the Prophet as President of the Church of Jesus Christ of Latter-day Saints hold the keys of the Priesthood by which salvation may come to the obedient. For the centennial year of the Church, 1930, there was published a book containing over 100 testimonies of general authorities, beginning with the Prophet Joseph Smith and a few active mission presidents, under the title: *Testimonies of the Divinity of the Church of Jesus Christ of Latter-day Saints by Its Leaders* (Zion's Printing and Publishing Co.). In the Preface written by Joseph E. Cardon and Samuel O. Bennion, the following appears: "The testimonies contained in this book are but a few of the hundreds of thousands of similar ones that have been borne in this latter dispensation. . .

"The publications of the Church are so filled with beautiful testimony that it is impossible to compile in one volume the smallest fraction of those that have been given. . ."[7]

The following testimony from President Charles W. Penrose, counselor in the First Presidency from 1911 to 1925, is typical of those which are found in this volume:

"I bear my testimony that I know this work is God's work. I know that he lives, that He is our Father, the

---

[7] *Testimonies of the Divinity of the Church of Jesus Christ of Latter-day Saints by Its Leaders*, p. 3.

Father of our spirits; I bear testimony that Jesus of Nazareth was the Christ and is the Christ, the Son of the living God, in body and in spirit; that He is our Redeemer, and that by obedience to His laws and commandments we shall go on through all eternity increasing in light, and knowledge, and bliss, and power, and dominion. I bear testimony that we are led today by the living oracles. The man who stands at the head succeeds to all the keys and powers and authorities revealed from God, through men who lived on the earth in the past, who restored their keys to the prophet Joseph Smith."[8]

Revelation in religious and temporal matters is as common as the type of testimony just discussed: (a) Revelation regarding doctrines, principles, and religious duties and practices constitute a very large body of material. President Wilford Woodruff mentioned the time when an angelic personage gave him instruction by vision regarding the two general resurrections;[9] and of the time when he was prompted to move his carriage from a tree, and in a few moments his animals, for within minutes the tree was blown down and would have probably killed him, his wife, and children and animals.[10] The *Life of Wilford Woodruff* contains numerous instances of divine guidance in his life.

President Heber J. Grant told of the time when he called by revelation to the apostleship Elder Melvin J. Ballard rather than a close friend, whom he had intended to call.[11]

(b) An important part of the Gospel of Jesus Christ is the truth that all things, including temporal matters, are spiritual.[12] This doctrine means that there "is a spiritual meaning of all human acts and earthly events."[13] Many

[8]*Ibid.* p. 97.
[9]*Journal of Discourses* 22:332-333.
[10]*Millennial Star* 53:642-643.
[11]G. Homer Durham, (comp) *Gospel Standards*, pp. 196-197.
[12]D&C 29:34-35.
[13]*Conference Report*, April 1922, pp. 96-97.

times in modern revelations, the Lord gave instructions pertaining to temporal matters, as the building of houses,[14] the selling or not selling of a farm,[15] building lots,[16] and many other similar instructions. In these and other cases, instructions and guidance have been received throughout the dispensation. President Brigham Young, for example, received a vision of the completed Salt Lake Temple.[17]

President George Albert Smith related the experience of the saints in the Bear River area of Utah, when, for ten years the frost had taken their crops. At the conclusion of a stake conference the President of the Church observed their faithfulness and said: "The Lord knows what you need, and I can say to you that from this time forth you shall raise your crop." Then President Smith said to the general conference: "Imagine after ten years, but they have raised a crop in that valley ever since."[18]

The remainder of these prophecies and promises apparently pertain to the future when man will live in the Millennium or receive his reward after his resurrection. Definite promises are given regarding the revelation of certain knowledge after the Savior comes to reign upon the earth. The Prophets looked forward to the time when they and their people might reap the blessings promised through their faithfulness to God's commandments; in fact, the time when nothing would be withheld, even the bestowing of thrones, principalities and powers. The wonders of heaven and all mysteries concerning the earth and its people will be revealed. The sealed portion of the gold plates contains some of this information to be revealed during this time of righteousness.[19]

The prophecy from Section 101 provided us with sufficient information that should put at rest the ideas of

---

[14]D&C 94:15-16.
[15]*Ibid.* 64:20-21.
[16]*Ibid.* 104:20; 96:2-3.
[17]*Journal of Discourses* 1:133.
[18]*Conference Report*, October 1948, p. 185.
[19]2 Nephi 27:6-8, 10.

men relative to the creation of the earth, animal and plant life, as well as that of man. When the Master comes he will reveal the manner of creation of ". . .things that are above, and things that are beneath, things that are in the earth, and upon the earth, and in heaven."[20] In other words, man does not now know the process by which these things were made.

Application of the prophecies and promises

The following words from President Daniel H. Wells, counselor to President Brigham Young for twenty years, describes the place of the individual testimony in the life of the Latter-day Saint:

"The Lord will reveal to any faithful individual all that is necessary to convince him that this work is true. None need depend for that testimony upon others; all can have it for themselves, and that will be like a well of water within them, springing up to everlasting life, revealing to them the things of God, and all that is needful to make them wise unto salvation. They need not depend upon my testimony, or upon that of President Young or President Smith, nor upon any but God. He will direct the course of all who try to serve Him with full purpose of heart. He will show them whether we are placed here properly, or whether any mistake has been made concerning the calling of Joseph Smith. The testimony of the Lord will tell whether we teach things of ourselves or of the Lord; that testimony will tell its possessors whether the servants of God who stand here tell the truth about this work or not."[21]

Elder Harold B. Lee of the Council of the Twelve, explains another purpose of personal revelation to the members of the Church:

"If there should come a problem as to what kind of business a man should be engaged in, whether he should

---

[20]D&C 101:32-34.

[21]*Testimonies of the Divinity of the Church of Jesus Christ of Latter-day Saints by Its Leaders*, pp. 83-84.

invest in this matter or that, whether he should marry this girl or marry that girl, where he should marry, and how he should marry, when it comes to the prosecuting of the work to which we are assigned, how much more certainly would those decisions be made, if always we recalled that all we do, and the decisions we make, should be made with that eternal goal in mind, with an eye single to the ultimate glory of man in the celestial world.

"If all our selfish motives, then and all our personal desires, and expediency, would be subordinated to a desire to know the will of the Lord, one could have the companionship of heavenly vision. If your problems be too great for human intelligence or too much for human strength, you too, if you are faithful and appeal rightly unto the source of divine power, might have standing by you in your hour of peril or great need an angel of God. . ."[22]

The following prophetic promises from modern revelation confirm in different language the thoughts expressed above:

"And I give unto you a commandment, that ye shall forsake all evil and cleave unto all good, that ye shall live by every word which proceedeth forth out of the mouth of God.

"For he will give unto the faithful line upon line, precept upon precept; and I will try you and prove you herewith."[23]

"Yea, blessed are they whose feet stand upon the land of Zion, who have obeyed my gospel; for they shall receive for their reward the good things of the earth, and it shall bring forth in its strength.

"And they shall also be crowned with blessings from above, yea, and with commandments not a few, and with revelations in their time—they that are faithful and diligent before me."[24]

---

[22]*Conference Report*, October 1946, p. 146.
[23]D&C 98:11-12.
[24]*Ibid.* 59:3-4.

Chapter 47

"And Thy People Shall Never Be Turned Against Thee . . ."
(D&C 122:1-3)

The ends of the earth shall inquire after thy name, and fools shall have thee in derision, and hell shall rage against thee;

While the pure in heart, and the wise, and the noble, and the virtuous, shall seek counsel, and authority, and blessings constantly from under thy hand.

And thy people shall never be turned against thee by the testimony of traitors.[1]

Background of the revelation

While a prisoner in the jail at Liberty, Missouri, in March, 1829, the Prophet received this comforting revelation. It, more than any other source, provides the answer to adversities in life.[2]

Background of the prophecy

The three verses constituting the prophecy under consideration begin the revelation.

Contents of the prophecy

(1) People in all parts of the earth are to inquire after the Prophet. (2) Fools shall rage against him, but the pure in heart shall seek his counsel. (3) The people who loved the Prophet would not turn against him.

Analysis of the prophecy

The expression, "the ends of the earth" suggests that the day will come when the name of Joseph Smith will be known throughout the world. A "fool" is one of little judgment, common sense, or wisdom. In this sense the prophets, knowing the truth, have inveighed against those

---

[1]D&C 122:1-3.
[2]*Ibid.* vs. 5-7.

who have rejected or fought against it. Nephi was declared to be a fool by his brothers because he thought
that he could build a ship.³ Solomon said: "Fools make
a mock at sin . . ."⁴

"The pure in heart" are those who have accepted
the fulness of the Gospel and seek to keep the command-
ments.⁵ They shall see God.⁶

Fulfillment of the prophecy

The first part of this prophecy—the Prophet's name
would be known widely, and fools would deride him, while
the virtuous would seek wisdom from him—was stated
in different words by the Angel Moroni on September
21-22, 1823: "He called me by name, and said unto me
that he was a messenger sent from the presence of God
to me, and that his name was Moroni; that God had a
work for me to do; and that my name should be had
for good and evil among all nations, kindreds, and tongues,
or that it should be both good and evil spoken of among
all people."⁷

Elder John A. Widstoe, an apostle of this dispensation,
wrote the following about some of the character charges
made against Joseph Smith:

"Nearly all the serious character charges against him
refer to the period between the visit of the ancient American Prophet, Moroni, three years after the First Vision,
and the obtaining of the golden plates four years later;
that is, from his eighteenth to his twenty-second year. . . ."

"A new church had been organized by Joseph Smith,
claiming to be the restored Church of Jesus Christ, therefore, a threat to existing churches! Every effort even to
exaggeration must be made to destroy the newcomer—so,
many people thought. Many believed, of course, that

---

³1 Nephi 17:17.
⁴Proverbs 14:9.
⁵D&C 97:21.
⁶Matthew 5:8; D&C 97:16.
⁷Joseph Smith 2:33.

Joseph Smith had had no vision or plates but that his story was a colossal lie. To fortify this new conception of his character, unfounded charges against the Prophet were bandied about.

"He was said to be a crystal or peepstone gazer, a digger for lost treasure, and a devotee of the black arts. He came of a low ancestry, they said, and was reared in a superstitious, untruthful family. . . ."

"He had to meet men who charged him with some breach of the law in the courts of the day but he was never convicted. Significantly, no charges of immorality were hurled against him until polygamy was introduced. Liars themselves to save their own skins dare not go too far. . . ."

"In fairness it should be said that while he was hounded and persecuted by enemies, usually inspired by ministers, many friends not members of the Church stood by, and helped him. The attorneys whom he employed to defend him became his lifelong friends. They became convinced of his high character. . . ."

". . . one of the attorneys, made a public address in Nauvoo, on the 17th of May, 1844, in which he corroborated the unfounded persecutions of Joseph Smith."[8] Elder Widstoe proceeds to discuss various books written by men who sought to blacken the Prophet's character by the use of questionable sources:

"The muckrakers past and present have made desperate, dishonest, but unsuccessful attempts to destroy Joseph Smith and his work. There is grim humor in the failure of their splashing in garbage pails to prove Joseph a false prophet. The test of Joseph Smith's veracity is in his work and teachings. They are convincing to all who will apply the test of truth sincerely.

"After the Church was organized and had won hosts of converts, the fury of enemies grew. In New York, Ohio and Missouri unbridled talk lead to persecution often with

---

[8]Joseph Smith, pp. 72-73.

terrible consequences. At length in Illinois, the hatred of truth, because it differed from tradition, became so ugly that Joseph Smith was murdered."[9]

There are those today who will villify his name because they do not agree with the teachings of The Church of Jesus Christ of Latter-day Saints. In many respects the reason is the same—the Church founded by Joseph Smith challenges all churches regarding their authority to represent God and the truth of their teachings!

The "pure in heart" during the Prophet's lifetime sought wisdom, counsel, and blessings from his hand, and today, members of the Church are continuing to derive wisdom from the work begun by him.[10] Wherever Latter-day Saints reside they are the beneficiaries of the Scriptures, the writings, and the works of the Prophet. Almost 75,000 converts per year join the growing Church in receiving Gospel truth.

"Thy people shall never be turned against thee by the testimony of traitors" was said while the Prophet was in jail. The knowledge of his faithful followers that he was God's anointed was captured in the following verses from the inspired pen of William W. Phelps:

> Praise to the man who communed with Jehovah!
>   Jesus anointed "that Prophet and Seer"—
> Blessed to open the last dispensation;
>   Kings shall extol Him, and nations revere.
>
> Praise to His memory, He died as a martyr,
>   Honored and blest be His ever great name!
> Long shall His blood, which was shed by assassins,
>   Plead unto heav'n while the earth lauds His fame.
>
> Great is His glory, and endless His Priesthood,
>   Ever and ever the keys He will hold;
> Faithful and true, He will enter His kingdom,
>   Crown'd in the midst of the Prophets of old.

---

[9]*Ibid.* pp. 80-81.
[10]D&C 5:10.

Sacrifice brings forth the blessings of heaven;
Earth must atone for the blood of that man;
Wake up the world for the conflict of justice;
Millions shall know "brother Joseph" again.

Hail to the Prophet, ascended to heaven!
Traitors and tyrants now fight Him in vain;
Mingling with Gods, He can plan for his brethren;
Death cannot conquer the Hero again.[11]

With the martyrdom of Joseph Smith and his brother Hyrum at Carthage, Illinois, those who followed him in life accepted the leadership of the Church appointed by revelation through the Prophet, and followed him though dead.[12] Their destiny and place had been given by the Prophet in 1842 when he prophesied that they would be driven to the Rocky Mountains and become a great people.[13] They and their progenitors, joined by thousands and thousands since, rejoice in the knowledge that "traitors and tyrants now fight him in vain."

Application of the prophecy

Latter-day Saints do not claim that Joseph Smith was perfect, for there was only one who was perfect—the Savior Jesus Christ. Elder B. H. Roberts expressed these ideas regarding the Prophet:

"Joseph Smith was a man of like passions with other men; struggling with the same weaknesses; subjected to the same temptations; under the same moral law, and humiliated at times, like others, by occasionally, in word and conduct, falling below the high ideals presented in the perfect life and faultless character of the Man of Nazareth.

"But though a man of like passions with other men, yet to Joseph Smith was given access to the mind of

---

[11]*Latter-Day Saint Hymns*, 1927, p. 167.
[12]D&C 90:1-5.
[13]*DHC* 5:85.

Deity, through the revelations of God to him; and likewise to him was given a divine authority to declare that mind of God to the world."[14]

Again, "fools shall have thee in derision." As a commentary says regarding this prophecy:

"Never was a truer word spoken. It is the fool who says in his heart that there is no God, and who holds 'Mormonism' in derision. A man may have university education but, as a scoffer he is a fool, no matter how many doctor degrees he may have.

"It is also true that the wise, noble and virtuous embrace 'Mormonism,' when they understand it. It appeals to them and to none else."[15]

From the Prophet Nephi we learn:

"O that cunning plan of the evil one! O the vainness, and the frailties, and the foolishness of men! When they are learned they think they are wise, and they hearken not unto the counsel of God, for they set it aside, supposing they know of themselves, wherefore, their wisdom is foolishness and it profiteth them not. And they shall perish.

"But to be learned is good if they hearken unto the counsels of God."[16]

And finally: "Fools mock, but they shall mourn; and my grace is sufficient for the meek, that they shall take no advantage of your weakness;

"And if men come unto me I will show unto them their weakness. I give unto men weakness that they may be humble; and my grace is sufficient for all men that humble themselves before me; for if they humble themselves before me, and have faith in me, then will I make weak things become strong unto them."[17]

---

[14]B. H. Roberts, *A Comprehensive History of the Church*, Vol. 2, pp. 360-361.

[15]Hyrum M. Smith and Janne M. Sjodahl, *Doctrine and Covenants Commentary*, p. 761.

[17]Ether 12:26-27.

Chapter 48

". . . The Tribe Of Judah, After Their Pain Shall Be Sanctified . . ."

(D&C 133:35; 45:48-53; 133:20; 77:15)

(A) And they also of the tribe of Judah, after their pain shall be sanctified in holiness before the Lord, to dwell in his presence day and night, forever and ever.[1]

(B) And then shall the Lord set his foot upon this mount, and it shall cleave in twain, and the earth shall tremble, and reel to and fro, and the heavens also shall shake.

And the Lord shall utter his voice, and all the ends of the earth shall hear it; and nations of the earth shall mourn, and they that have laughed shall see their folly.

And calamity shall cover the mocker, and the scorner shall be consumed; and they that have watched for iniquity shall be hewn down and cast into the fire.

And then shall the Jews look upon me and say: What are these wounds in thine hands and in thy feet?

Then shall they know that I am the Lord; for I will say unto them: These wounds are the wounds with which I was wounded in the house of my friends. I am he who was lifted up. I am Jesus that was crucified. I am the Son of God.

And then shall they weep because of their iniquities; then shall they lament because they persecuted their king.[2]

(C) For behold, he shall stand upon the mount of Olivet, and upon the mighty ocean, even the great deep, and upon the islands of the sea, and upon the land of Zion.[3]

(D) Q. What is to be understood by the two witnesses, in the eleventh chapter of Revelation?

A. They are two prophets that are to be raised up to the Jewish nation in the last days, at the time of the restoration, and to prophesy to the Jews after they are gathered and have built the city of Jerusalem in the land of their fathers.[4]

---

[1] D&C 133:35.

[2] *Ibid.* 45:48-53.

[3] *Ibid.* 133:20.

[4] *Ibid.* 77:15.

Background of the revelations

(A, C) Section 133 is known as the "Appendix." This revelation was received on November 3, 1831, immediately after the conference where the "Preface" to the Doctrine and Covenants Section 1 was received. Some elders were desirous to learn about preaching the Gospel, and the doctrine of the gathering.

(B) Section 45 was received to combat some false ideas which were being circulated about the Church. Its contents are largely prophetic concerning the last days.

(D) Section 77 is an explanation of certain verses in the Book of Revelation, the last book of the New Testament.

Background of the prophecies

(A, C) Preparation should be made for the second coming of Christ. No one knows the day nor the hour when he shall come; consequently, the elders should be sent forth to proclaim the gospel. Great physical changes will come upon the earth. The ten lost tribes will return from the land of the north to receive their blessings at the hands of Ephraim.

(B) Following the reasons why Latter-day Saints should be obedient to the commandments, the Lord relates his conversation with his ancient disciples concerning the signs of the times in the Dispensations of the Meridian of Times and of the Fulness of Times. Included in the events of the last days is the fulfillment of this prophecy.

(D) Verse 15 of Section 77 is the last verse in the revelation. The revelation provides a key for the interpretation of the Book of Revelation. Immediately preceding the prophecy is an explanation of a mission given to the author of Revelation, John the Apostle, who has a mission to gather the tribes of Israel, a part of which is Judah.

Contents of the prophecies

(1) Before the Jewish people are sanctified, they will suffer pain. (2) The Lord will stand upon Mount Olivet

in Jerusalem and nations will mourn. (3) The Jewish people will ask when he received the wounds in his hands and feet, and he shall reply: "In the house of my friends." (4) Jesus will then identify himself as the crucified Son of God. (5) The Jews will mourn because of their rejection of him. (6) Two prophets will be raised up to the Jewish nation after the restoration of the Jews to their land and the building of Jerusalem.

Analysis of the prophecies

The Mount of Olivet, or Olives, is a hill east of the Jerusalem city wall. On the western side is the Garden of Gethsemane.

Beginning with the 16th verse of Section 45, the Lord relates his conversation with his former day disciples regarding the signs of his coming. In the first unit of this material[5], the circumstances of the Jewish people in the meridian dispensation are told. The temple in Jerusalem will be thrown down, and the people scattered among all nations. The scattering of the Jews was preceded by a Roman seige of Jerusalem which left about one and one-half million dead and many sold into slavery. "But they shall be gathered again; but they shall remain until the times of the Gentiles be fulfilled.

"And in that day shall be heard of wars and rumors of wars, and the whole earth shall be in commotion, and men's hearts shall fail them, and they shall say that Christ delayeth his coming until the end of the earth."[6] For information about the gathering of Judah to her homeland, see "The Children of Judah" —D&C 109:61-64. (Information which is complementary to Section 45 can be found in the revision of Matthew chapter 24, which is found in Joseph Smith 1:1-21).

Fulfillment of the prophecies

With the return of the Jewish people to the state of Israel, the stage is set for the predicted events in these

---

[5]*Ibid.* 45:16-24.
[6]*Ibid.* vs. 25-26.

prophecies. (A, B, C). Elder Parley P. Pratt has given an account of the fulfillment of these prophecies. It is as follows:

"Zechariah, in his 14th chapter, has told us much concerning the great battle and overthrow of the nations who fight against Jerusalem, and he has said, in plain words, that the Lord shall come at the very time of the overthrow of that army, yes, in fact, even while they are in the act of taking Jerusalem, and have already succeeded in taking one-half the city, and spoiling their houses, and ravishing their women. Then, behold their long-expected Messiah, suddenly appearing, shall stand upon the Mount of Olives, a little east of Jerusalem, to fight against those nations and deliver the Jews. Zechariah says the Mount of Olives shall cleave in twain, from east to west, and one-half of the mountain shall remove to the north, while the other half falls off to the south, suddenly forming a very great valley, into which the Jews shall flee for protection from their enemies as they fled from the earthquake in the days of Uzziah, king of Judah, while the Lord cometh and all the saints with him. Then will the Jews behold that long, long-expected Messiah, coming in power to their deliverance, as they always looked for Him. He will destroy their enemies, and deliver them from trouble at the very time they are in the utmost consternation, and about to be swallowed up by their enemies. But what will be their astonishment when they are about to fall at the feet of their Deliverer, and acknowledge Him their Messiah! They discover the wounds which were once made in His hands, feet, and sides; and, on inquiry, at once recognize Jesus of Nazareth the King of the Jews, the man so long rejected. Well did the Prophet say, they shall mourn and weep, every family apart, and their wives apart. But, thank heaven, there will be an end to their mourning; for He will forgive their iniquities and cleanse them from uncleanness. Jerusalem shall be a holy city from that time forth, and all the land shall be turned as a plain from Geba to Rimmon, and she shall be lifted up and inhabited in her place, and men shall dwell there, and there shall be no more utter destruction of Jerusalem; 'And in that day there shall be one Lord, and his name one, and He shall be king over all the earth.' (Zech. 14:9).

"John, in his 11th chapter of Revelation, gives us many more particulars concerning this same event. He informs us that, after the city and temple are rebuilt by the Jews, the Gentiles will tread it under foot forty and two months, during which time there will be two Prophets continually prophesying and working mighty miracles. And it seems that the Gentile army shall be hindered from utterly destroying and overthrowing the city, while these two Prophets continue. But, after a struggle of three years and a half, they at length succeed in destroying these two Prophets, and then overrunning much of the city; they send gifts to each other because of the death of the two Prophets, and in the meantime will not allow their dead bodies to be put in graves, but suffer them to lie in the streets of Jerusalem three days and a half; during which the armies of the Gentiles, consisting of many kindreds, tongues and nations, passing through the city, plundering the Jews, see their dead bodies lying in the street. But, after three days and a half, on a sudden, the spirit of life from God enters them, and they will arise and stand upon their feet, and great fear will fall upon them that see them. And then they shall hear a voice from heaven saying, 'Come up hither,' and they will ascend up to heaven in a cloud, and their enemies beholding them. And having described all these things, then comes the shaking, spoken of by Ezekiel, and the rending of the Mount of Olives, spoken of by Zechariah. John says, 'The same hour was there a great earthquake, and the tenth part of the city fell, and in the earthquake were slain of men seven thousand.' And then one of the next scenes that follow is the sound of voices, saying, 'The kingdoms of this world are become the kingdom of our Lord, and of his Christ; and he shall reign forever and ever.'

"Now, having summed up the description of these great events spoken of by these Prophets, I would just remark, there is no difficulty in understanding them all to be perfectly plain and literal in their fulfillment.

"Suffice it to say, the Jews gather home, and rebuild Jerusalem. The nations gather against them in battle. Their armies encompass the city, and have more or less power over it for three years and a half. A couple of Jewish Prophets, by their mighty miracles, keep them from utterly overcoming the Jews; until at length they are slain, and the city is left in a great measure to the mercy of their enemies for three days and a half; the two Prophets rise from the dead and ascend up into heaven. The Messiah comes, convulses the earth, overthrows the army of the Gentiles, delivers the Jews, cleanses Jerusalem, cuts off all wickedness from the earth, raises the Saints from the dead, brings them with Him, and commences His reign of a thousand years; during which time His Spirit will be poured out upon flesh; men and beasts, birds and serpents, will be perfectly harmless, and peace and the knowledge and glory of God shall cover the earth as the waters cover the sea; and the kingdom and the greatness of the kingdom under the whole heaven, shall be given to the Saints of the Most High."[7]

Soon after the nation of Israel was organized in 1947, the Arabs attempted to overcome this little nation, but as told by Arthur U. Michelson, it appears that God intervened in their behalf and thwarted this attempt. According to this account in at least two battles though the Arabs were the stronger of the two armies, they stopped fighting and gave up their arms. When asked the reason, it was said they believed they saw three men with long beards, who warned them not to fight any longer. Becoming frightened they gave up. On another occasion during the war, the Jews were surrounded by the Egyptians, when the Arabs surrendered. The Jews were told that the

---

[7]Parley P. Pratt, *A Voice of Warning*, pp. 40-42.

Egyptians saw an old man, dressed in a long robe, who warned them not to fight, else they would perish. Elder LeGrand Richards of the Council of the Twelve, who published Mr. Michelson's account, suggests the possibility that these persons might have been the Three Nephites.[8] These ancient American prophets were promised by the Savior that they would not die until his second coming, and as Mormon said:

"And behold they will be among the Gentiles, and the Gentiles shall know them not.

"They will also be among the Jews, and the Jews shall know them not."[9]

Enmity between the Jews and the Arabs has continued through the years. In June 1967, Israel defeated the Arab armies in a six-day war. Since that time there have been almost daily, if not daily, border skirmishes between the Arab nations of Lebanon, Syria, Jordan and Egypt. These clashes are continuing unabated despite United Nations efforts to bring quiet to the area. The Soviet Union which supplied the Arab nations with fighting equipment before their defeat in 1967 is rebuilding the Arab arsenal for a future confrontation with Israel. The Soviets are also building up their Mediterranean fleet far beyond any earlier period with the avowed purpose of assisting the Arabs.

Application of the prophecies

The prophecies, ancient and modern, indicate that the seige of the Jewish people in their homeland is a major sign of the imminence of the second coming of Christ to the world. The second coming of the Savior will consist of three appearances rather than one to the world at large. His first appearance will be to the saints, in their temples, and at Adam-ondi-Ahman. (Malachi 3:3; D&C 84:21-34; *Teachings of the Prophet Joseph Smith*, pp. 171-

---

[8]LeGrand Richards, *Israel! Do You Know?*, pp. 229-233.
[9]3 Nephi 28:27-28.

173). The second appearance will be to the Jews, as indicated, and the third, to the world in power and glory to destroy the wicked.[10]

The sanctification of the Jewish people will be in the same manner as that of any individual. Salvation comes individually when they accept the Gospel of Jesus Christ by faith in Christ, repentence of sin, baptism, and the receiving of the Holy Ghost by an authorized servant of the Lord. That Judah will receive the benefits of the atonement was prophesied by Nephi in these words:

"And now my beloved brethren, I have read these things that ye might know concerning the covenants of the Lord that he has covenanted with all the house of Israel—

"That he has spoken unto the Jews, by the mouth of his holy prophets, even from the beginning down, from generation to generation, until the time comes that they shall be restored to the true church and fold of God; when they shall be gathered home to the lands of their inheritance, and shall be established in all their lands of promise."[11]

Before this time, however, they will "begin to believe in Christ."[12]

When the Jewish nation will undergo the grave calamity mentioned in these prophecies is not known, but what is known is that it will surely come to pass. Only revelation holds the answer to the future.

---

[10]Roy W. Doxey, *The Doctrine and Covenants and the Future* pp. 53-56.

[11]2 Nephi 9:1-2.

[12]*Ibid.* 30:7.

Chapter 49

"My People Must Be Tried In All Things . . ."
(D&C 136:31; 121:7-8; 122:5-7).

(A) My people must be tried in all things, that they may be prepared to receive the glory that I have for them, even the glory of Zion; and he that will not bear chastisement is not worthy of my kingdom.[1]

(B) My son, peace be unto thy soul; thine adversity and thine afflictions shall be but a small moment;

And then, if thou endure it well, God shall exalt thee on high; thou shalt triumph over all thy foes.[2]

(C) If thou art called to pass through tribulation; if thou art in perils among false brethren; if thou art in perils among robbers; if thou art in perils by land or by sea;

If thou art accused with all manner of false accusations; if thine enemies fall upon thee; if they tear thee from the society of thy father and mother and brethren and sisters; and if with a drawn sword thine enemies tear thee from the bosom of thy wife, and of thine offspring, and thine elder son, although but six years of age, shall cling to thy garments, and shall say, My father, my father, why can't you stay with us? O, my father, what are the men going to do with you? And if then he shall be thrust from thee by the sword, and thou be dragged to prison, and thine enemies prowl around thee like wolves for the blood of the lamb;

And if thou shouldst be cast into the pit, or into the hands of murderers, and the sentence of death passed upon thee; if thou be cast into the deep; if the billowing surge conspire against thee; if fierce winds become thine enemy; if the heavens gather blackness, and all the elements combine to dredge up the way; and above all, if the very jaws of hell shall gape open the mouth wide after thee, know thou, my son, that all these things shall give thee experience, and shall be for thy good.[3]

Background of the revelations

(A) Section 136, the last revelation in the Doctrine and Covenants is "The Word and Will of the Lord" given to

---
[1]D&C 136:31.
[2]*Ibid.* 121:7-8.
[3]*Ibid.* 122:5-7.

President Brigham Young in preparation for the pioneer treks across the plains.

(B) (C) Sections 121 and 122 are excerpts from an important communication to the Church at large, written between the 20th and 25th of March 1839, while the Prophet Joseph Smith and others were in jail at Liberty, Missouri.[4]

Background of the prophetic promises

(A) The Lord instructed Brigham Young to organize the pioneer companies with captains of hundreds, fifties, and tens, with a president and his two counselors at their head, under the direction of the Twelve Apostles. A number of instructions dealing with the manner in which the pioneers should govern their lives were given.

(B) The Prophet prays concerning the saints who had been driven from their homes in Missouri and of the time when they would be avenged.

(C) A prophecy about the Prophet's name being known throughout the world begins Section 122. (See "And Thy People Shall Never Be Turned Against Thee . . ."—D&C 122:1-3). Traitors have brought trouble and imprisonment to him.

Contents of the prophetic promises

(1) The Lord's people must be tried in all things to receive the glory prepared for them. (2) Those who do not bear chastisement are not worthy to receive the Lord's glory. (3) Joseph Smith is told that if he bears his afflictions well, God shall exalt him. (4) A series of tribulations through which Joseph Smith had passed or which might come to him are mentioned. (5) All of these afflictions will give him experience and shall be for his good.

Analysis of the prophetic promises

Those who accept Christ's atonement by becoming members of his Church become his children; therefore, he

---

[4]*DHC* 3:289-301.

calls them "my people."[5] Inasmuch as covenants are made with the Lord in baptism, the manner in which they keep their covenants determines their ultimate status in the eternal worlds.[6] To continue to be known as his people, belief in him as the Savior and to keep the commandments are necessary.[7]

The expression "the glory of Zion" has several meanings in the revelations. If reference is made to the center place of Zion—Jackson County, Missouri—then its glory is the magnificence of its buildings, including the temple, and also the wisdom which will be there.[8] These conditions will exist in such abundance that Zion will become the praise of the world. The fact that Zion will house the throne of the Savior and his glory will be there will make it a magnificent place.[9] (See "Inasmuch As My People Build A House Unto Me . . ."—D&C 97:15-20; 84:4-5).

The emphasis in these prophetic promises is the need to bear tribulation, even chastisement, to be worthy of the glory of Zion. The key to understanding the place of afflictions in this life is that the experience gained shall be ultimately for the person's good. We are to endure these adversities well; that is, to recognize their purpose, that they are a part of the plan of salvation. If a person knows the reason for tribulation, it is often then possible to endure it better. It is true that no one is immune to discouragement, sorrow, pain, suffering, and trials. The following counsel was given by Lehi to his son Jacob:

"And now, Jacob, I speak unto you: Thou art my firstborn in the days of my tribulation in the wilderness. And behold, in thy childhood thou hast suffered afflictions and much sorrow, because of the rudeness of thy brethren.

"Nevertheless, Jacob, my firstborn in the wilderness,

---

[5]D&C 25:1; 34:2.
[6]*Ibid.* 41:1.
[7]*Ibid.* 42:1.
[8]*Journal of Discourses*, 6:169.
[9]*Ibid.* 15:338; D&C 64:41-43.

thou knowest the greatness of God; and he shall consecrate thine afflictions for thy gain."[10]

The following ideas about adversity in life are, in the main, the product of the revelations and the modern prophets: (1) The answer to the subject of adversities must come from revelation. Man's experiences have proved the scriptures to be true.[11] (2) Premortally we made a covenant that we would come to earth to work out our salvation amid adversities.[12] (3) Since the temporalities of life have their spiritual influences, then adversities have a spiritual meaning for us, either positively or negatively.[13] (4) Since the earth life is designed to prove the children of God, it was planned that the tribulations of mortal life should be the method of testing faith.[14] (5) There is no assurance that the faithful will be free of adversities; in fact, it appears that sometimes their trials are even greater than others.[15] (6) The real purpose for adversities is that experience might be gained to develop sympathy, understanding, and purification of soul, that progression might be possible.[16] (7) Calamities become blessings for nations and for individuals provided they are accepted as good.[17] (Lesson 92, "Adversity," *The Relief Society Magazine*, October 1968, pp. 778-783).

Fulfillment of the prophetic promises

Two of these promises were made to the Prophet Joseph Smith while he was in jail, under false charges. (B, C). Before this, as indicated in Section 122, verses 5 through 7, he had been harassed by mobs and mob-militia. On November 1, 1838, a mob-militia court martial was held and the Prophet and other prisoners were condemned

---

[10]Jacob 2:1-2.

[11]2 Nephi 4:34-35; 9:28-29; D&C 42:61.

[12]Moses 4:1-4; D&C 29:36-38.

[13]D&C 29:34-35; *Journal of Discourses*, 8:150; 9:292.

[14]D&C 29:39; 93:30; Moses 6:55-56.

[15]Ether 12:6; D&C 58:2-5.

[16]*Improvement Era*, 22:5.

[17]Joseph F. Smith, *Gospel Doctrine*, pp. 54-55.

to be shot to death the next day. General Alexander W. Doniphan, who was commanded by General Samuel D. Lucas to carry out the order, refused and threatened to hold General Lucas responsible for he said, "it is cold blooded murder."[18]

In a summary of Joseph Smith's life, George Q. Cannon gives the following:

"One cannot fail to be struck with the unceasing opposition with which he had to contend. From the day that he received the first communication from heaven up to the day of his martyrdom his pathway was beset with difficulties, his liberty and life were constantly menaced. Had he been an ordinary man he would have been crushed in spirit and sunk in despair under the relentless attacks which were made upon him. To find a parallel to his case we must go back to the days of our Savior and His Apostles and the prophets who preceded them. Joseph's life was sought for with satanic hate. The thirst for his blood was unappeasable. Had there not been a special providence exercised in his behalf to preserve him until his mission should be fulfilled, he would have been slain by murderous hands long before the dreadful day at Carthage."[19]

In order that no one may claim immunity from afflictions, the Lord gave this truth: "The Son of Man hath descended below them all. Art thou greater than he?"[20]

Then, to assure the Prophet that his calling was secure and the bounds of the enemies to destroy him were set, these comforting words were spoken to him: "Therefore, hold on thy way, and the priesthood shall remain with thee; for their bounds are set, they cannot pass. Thy days are known, and thy years shall not be numbered less; therefore fear not what man can do; for God shall be with you forever and ever."[21]

---

[18]Joseph Fielding Smith, *Essentials in Church History*, p. 241.
[19]George Q. Cannon, *Life of Joseph Smith*, p. 519.
[20]D&C 122:8.
[21]*Ibid.* v. 9.

Members of The Church of Jesus Christ of Latter-day Saints shared with their Prophet and other leaders the enmity of Satan and his followers in that they suffered persecutions for their religious beliefs. Slander in the press and from the pulpit heaped upon them the disdain of their fellowmen. The expulsion from Jackson County, Missouri, in the summer and fall of 1833 was the first of the great persecutions. Having found a home in other counties of Missouri, their resting place was not without its persecutions. In the early fall of 1838, mobs began their rampage against the saints. By the spring of 1839, efforts were made by Brigham Young, president of the Twelve, to locate another residence for the body of the Church, while the Prophet was in a Missouri jail. In the interim, however, the work of destruction took place. Under orders of Governor Lilburn W. Boggs, the state militia operated ofttimes as mobs against the saints with the presumed purpose of maintaining the peace. The first apostolic martyr, David W. Patten, with Patrick O'Banion gave their lives in the Crooked River battle. Names that will live in the history of this period are the Latter-day Saint communities of: De Witt, Far West, and Haun's Mill, and other places in Caldwell and Davies counties. When the Governor's exterminating order was issued the militia commander near Haun's Mill broke the peace treaty with the saints there, and slew in a brutal manner men, women, and children. The saints in Far West gave up their arms, and then the bloody work began, as told by George Q. Cannon:

"It was a joy to the sectarian ministers of the neighborhood to see this work of ruin; and many of them visited Far West to exult over the prisoners and their suffering families.

"Many privations and tortures were endured. The captives were kept without food until they were on the verge of starvation. The mob continued their work of ruin, hunting and shooting human beings like wild beasts; and ravishing and mudering women."[22]

---

[22]George Q. Cannon, *Life of Joseph Smith*, pp. 265-266.

The Illinois era is another chapter of persecution. Two years after the martyrdom of Joseph and Hyrum at Carthage, Illinois, on July 27, 1844, the saints were driven from that state, leaving their beautiful city of Nauvoo.

The trek over the plains to their resting place in the western mountains was fraught with many privations and tribulations. The severity of the weather, the hardness of the journey, the malignity of the Indians, and the lack of medical care, all tried the faith of the pioneers. It is estimated that about 6,000 laid down their lives from 1846 to the coming of the railroad to Utah Territory in 1869.

But these difficult times were not the end of hard times for the saints. The hard pioneer life and the persecution of families because of plural marriage, tried the faith of many. They had come to realize the truth of what the Lord said many years before.

"For verily I say unto you, blessed is he that keepeth my commandments, whether in life or in death; and he that is faithful in tribulation, the reward of the same is greater in the kingdom of heaven.

"Ye cannot behold with your natural eyes, for the present time, the design of your God concerning those things which shall come hereafter, and the glory which shall follow after much tribulation.

"For after much tribulation come the blessings. Wherefore the day cometh that ye shall be crowned with much glory; the hour is not yet, but is nigh at hand.

"Remember this, which I tell you before, that you may lay it to heart, and receive that which is to follow."[23] (See "After Much Tribulation"—D&C 58:3-5).

From two revelations the saints had learned that they who endure in faith, even in the laying down of their lives, will yet receive eternal glory. They must be proved in all things as a test of faith, while those who do not abide in this covenant are not worthy of the Lord.[24]

---

[23]D&C 58:2-5.
[24]*Ibid.* 98:12-15; 101:35-38.

Application of the prophetic promises

The glory which awaits the faithful is the attainment of exaltation in the celestial kingdom. The glory is that of becoming equal with the Eternal Father, and a joint heir with Jesus Christ.[25]

To attain this great blessing, one must "bear chastisement," endure to the end, and make every necessary sacrifice for the advancement of the kingdom of God. As President George Q. Cannon said: "I, therefore, do not expect that any man will ever enter in the Celestial Kingdom of our God until he is tested and proved in all things."[26] In 1880 he said:

"God will have a tried and peculiar people. We have been tried to some extent but not the extent which we probably will be; there are many things in which we will be greatly tried before we get through. Every Latter-day Saint who gains a celestial glory will be tried to the very uttermost. If there is a point in our character that is weak and tender, you may depend upon it that the Lord will reach after that, and we will be tried at that spot for the Lord will test us to the utmost before we can get through and receive that glory and exaltation which He has in store for us as a people.[27]

---

[25] *Ibid.* 84:38; 132:19-21.
[26] George Q. Cannon, *Gospel Truth,* p. 104.
[27] *Ibid.* p. 103.

Chapter 50

"Be Diligent In Keeping All My Commandments . . ."
(D&C 136:42; 3:10-11; 19:20, 63:23; 93:20)

(A) Be diligent in keeping all my commandments, lest judgments come upon you, and your faith fail you, and your enemies triumph over you. So no more at present. Amen and Amen.[1]

(B) But remember, God is merciful; therefore, repent of that which thou has done which is contrary to the commandment which I gave you, and thou art still chosen, and art again called to the work;

Except thou do this, thou shalt be delivered up and become as other men, and have no more gift.[2]

(C) Wherefore, I command you again to repent, lest I humble you with my almighty power; and that you confess your sins, lest you suffer these punishments of which I have spoken, of which in the smallest, yea, even in the least degree you have tasted at the time I withdrew my Spirit.[3]

(D) But unto him that keepeth my commandments I will give the mysteries of my kingdom, and the same shall be in him a well of living water, springing up unto everlasting life.[4]

(E) For if you keep my commandments you shall receive of his fulness, and be glorified in me as I am in the Father; therefore, I say unto you, you shall receive grace for grace.[5]

Background of the revelations

(A) The last revelation printed in the Doctrine and Covenants, known as "The Word and Will of the Lord," was received on January 14, 1847, by Brigham Young, President of the Quorum of the Twelve. The instructions given therein are about the trek of the pioneer companies which journey westward.

---

[1]D&C 136:42.
[2]*Ibid.* 3:10-11.
[3]*Ibid.* 19:20.
[4]*Ibid.* 63:23.
[5]*Ibid.* 93:20.

(B) Section 3 was received by the Prophet July 1828, and relates to the loss of the 116 pages of manuscript, the contents of which came from the Book of Mormon plates.

(C) Section 19 was received for the benefit of Martin Harris though its contents apply to all. It is an important doctrinal revelation.

(D) Section 63 was received at Kirtland, Ohio, in August 1831. It contains information about the land of Zion, particularly the gathering of the saints, the purchase of land, and other matters.

(E) Section 93, received on May 6, 1833, is considered one of the great doctrinal revelations in the Doctrine and Covenants. Its contents are about Jesus Christ and man.

Background of the prophetic promises

(A) After giving some details about the organization of the camps of Israel and how members should comport themselves while traveling, reference is made to the martyrdom of the Prophet Joseph Smith.

(B) Because Joseph Smith had implored of the Lord to permit him to allow Martin Harris to take some of the translated material from the Book of Mormon to show to some of his relatives, it was lost, and the Prophet came under censure. The prophetic promise is preceded by the warning that if the Prophet transgresses he may fall from his appointed place.

(C) The doctrines of everlasting punishment, and the atonement of Jesus Christ, especially the great suffering he underwent to redeem man from his sins, precede the prophetic promise.

(D) A warning is issued to the wicked that the day of wrath approaches in which they will be punished. The sign seeker is condemned. Among the saints there were adulterers and adulteresses, all of whom will one day be made known. The punishment of hell awaits these unrepentent people.

(E) The doctrine in Section 93 preceding the prophetic promise is John's testimony of Christ as the Son of God.

Contents of the prophetic promises

(1) Keep the Lord's commandments. (2) Judgments follow disobedience to the commandments. (3) Repentance of sin is commanded, which includes confession of them. (4) The rewards of repentance (keeping the commandments) are: (a) a continuation of the gift received; (b) surcease from punishment; (c) receive the mysteries of the kingdom; (d) receive the fulness of glory.

Analysis of the prophetic promises

Diligence means constancy of performance. If one does not keep the commandments, judgments follow; that is, punishment by withdrawal of the spirit. The judgments may be mental punishment in the prison of the spirit world, and eventually loss of the highest kingdom following the resurrection.[6]

Man's enemies are not always those who come to do him physical harm, but sins which prevent him from accepting and living the way of salvation. The Prophet Joseph Smith said: "Salvation means a man's being placed beyond the power of all his enemies."[7] That the enemies here mentioned includes knowledge and the ability to apply that knowledge for salvation is apparent in the following from the Prophet: "Salvation is nothing more nor less than to triumph over all our enemies and put them under our feet. And when we have power to put all enemies under our feet in this world, and a knowledge to triumph over all evil spirits in the world to come, then we are saved, as in the case of Jesus, who was to reign until He had put all enemies under His feet, and the last enemy was death."[8]

Repentance in its fullest sense means to keep the commandments, not only to desist from a specific sin but to be diligent in keeping other commandments. Repentance

---

[6]*Ibid.* 76:73-76; 84:88.
[7]*DHC* 5:392.
[8]*Ibid.* 5:387-388.

includes confession to the bishop. The loss of the Spirit
brings darkness of mind and reduces the ability to repent.
(See ". . . From Him Shall Be Taken Even The Light
Which He Has Received." —D&C 1:31-33).

All people sin to a certain degree, some more griev-
ously than others. Sexual sin is one of the most heinous,
and, if not repented of, brings loss of faith and eternal
damnation.[9]

All members of the Church are entitled to one or
more gifts of the Holy Ghost, but they must seek them.[10]

The "mysteries of the kingdom" include at least two
kinds of information: (1) an understanding of the principles of salvation that may be received by everyone, such
as the fundamental principles and ordinances of the gospel,
the doctrines of resurrection, eternal judgment, future
kingdoms, and so forth; (2) the principles and ordinances
of exaltation which are received only in the temple.

The "fulness of glory" is exaltation, or eternal life,
the highest measure of salvation available. (See "They Are
They . . . Who Have Received Of His Fulness, And Of
His Glory . . ." —D&C 76:50-60; 132:4-5; 131:1-4; 132:
15-22).

Fulfillment of the prophetic promises

In the early days of the Church Ezra Booth and
Isaac Morley were chastized by the Lord for sins which
they had committed. Although specific information is
lacking regarding the precise sins committed, there were
many at this time who were charging the Prophet as being
false. The revelation says of these two brethren: "They
condemned for evil that thing in which there was no evil."
The following is found in the revelation:

"Behold, I, the Lord, was angry with him who was
my servant, Ezra Booth, and also my servant Isaac Morley,
for they kept not the law, neither the commandment.

---

[9]D&C 42:22-26.
[10]*Ibid.* 46:10-12.

"They sought evil in their hearts, and I, the Lord, withheld my Spirit. They condemned for evil that thing in which there was no evil; nevertheless I have forgiven my servant Isaac Morley."[11]

The prophetic promises say that diligence in keeping the commandments is required of all, but if one repents, he shall be forgiven. However, there are times when the sin committed is so serious, or the individual lacks sufficient faith to seek for the spirit of repentance that apostasy results. The two brethren—Booth and Morley—are examples of the unrepentant and the repentant. The Lord forgave Brother Morley because he repented, and thus he remained "my servant." On the other hand, Ezra Booth did not repent, and as a consequence he lost the Spirit and became an apostate.

Although complete information is not available on Brother Booth's life after his apostasy, the following is given concerning him:

"About this time Ezra Booth came out as an apostate. He came into the Church upon seeing a person healed of an infirmity of many years standing. He had been a Methodist priest for some time previous to his embracing the fulness of the Gospel, as developed in the Book of Mormon; and upon his admission into the Church he was ordained an Elder. As will be seen by the foregoing revelation [Sec. 64:15-16], he went up to Missouri as a companion of Elder Morley; but when he actually learned that faith, humility, patience, and tribulation go before blessing, and that God brings low before He exalts; that instead of the 'Savior's granting him power to smite men and make them believe,' (as he said he wanted God to do in his own case)—when he found he must become all things to all men that he might peradventure save some; and that, too, by all diligence, by perils by sea and land; as was the case in the days of Jesus—then he was disappointed. In the 6th chapter of St. John's Gospel, 26th verse, it is

---

[11]D&C 64:15-16.

written: 'Verily, verily I say unto you, Ye seek me, not because ye saw the miracles, but because ye did eat of the loaves, and were filled.' So it was with Booth; and when he was disappointed by his own evil heart, he turned away, and as said before, became an apostate, and wrote a series of letters, which by their coloring, falsity, and vain calculations to overthrow the work of the Lord, exposed his weakness, wickedness, and folly, and left him a monument of his own shame, for the world to wonder at."[12]

The letters to which reference is made by the Prophet, were printed in the Ohio Star, a paper printed in Ravenna. These nine letters were republished several times, according to Elder George A. Smith, in opposition to the Church. His apostasy also culminated in forming a mob which tarred and feathered the Prophet, and caused an adopted infant to die.[13]

Ezra Booth did not completely eliminate the enemies of his soul, and he became as other natural men, without the gift of the Holy Ghost, and he was left to his own devices.

Isaac Morley, on the other hand, is an example of one who repented, retained the gift, and remained faithful to the end. In a revelation not included in the Doctrine and Covenants, Isaac Morley is commended for the integrity of his heart in laboring in the vineyard, and his sins were forgiven him.[14] He was a counselor in the bishopric to Bishop Edward Partridge, and he underwent the persecutions in Missouri. The last ten years of his life in Utah, where he settled in Sanpete County, were spent as patriarch, a calling to which he was ordained by the Prophet Joseph Smith. In this exalted office one can believe that the mysteries of the kingdom were in him "a well of living water, springing up unto everlasting life."

---

[12]*DHC* 1:215-217.
[13]*Journal of Discourses*, 11:4-5.
[14]*DHC* 2:302-303.

Numerous examples of the faithful and the unfaithful whose lives demonstrated the provisions of these prophetic promises might be given. The unrepentant, who have fought against the kingdom are remembered only in infamy, but honest, devoted Latter-day Saints have left a posterity and a people who revere their names, and the eternities await their coming in glory.

Application of the prophetic promises

When one has accepted the atonement of Christ for his individual salvation in the waters of baptism, he covenants to keep all of the commandments. "And again, every person who belongeth to his church of Christ, shall observe to keep all the commandmnts and covenants of the church."[15]

When covenants are broken by disobedience, the loss of the Spirit removes the protection which helped and assisted the person to overcome his enemies. No longer is the covenant of force, and blessings formerly pronounced upon him are not available. (See "The Covenant . . . They Made Unto Me Has Been Broken . . . It Has Become Void." —D&C 54:4-6; 82:21; 84:41; 104:4-9).

---

[15]D&C 42:78.

Bibliography

Newspapers and Periodicals

Conference Report (Annual and Semi-annual) of The Church of Jesus Christ of Latter-day Saints. Salt Lake City, Utah.

Deseret News. Salt Lake City, Utah, 1892, 1968.

Deseret News. Salt Lake City, Utah (Church section) 1931.

The Improvement Era. Salt Lake City, Utah, 1926, 1942, 1956.

The Juvenile Instructor. Salt Lake City, Utah, 1928.

The Literary Digest. New York, 1934. Vol. 117, p. 13.

The Millennial Star. Liverpool, England, 1895.

The New York Times. 1937.

The Relief Society Magazine. Salt Lake City, Utah, 1968.

Times and Seasons. Nauvoo, Illinois, 1844.

The Utah Genealogical and Historical Magazine. Salt Lake City, Utah, 1931.

The Young Women's Journal. Salt Lake City, Utah. Vol. 5.

Articles and Books

Advisory Committee to the Surgeon General of the United States Public Health Service. *Smoking and Health,* 1964.

Bennett, Archibald F. *Saviors on Mount Zion.* Salt Lake City, Utah: Deseret Sunday School Union Board. The Deseret News Press, 1950.

Bible. Authorized King James Version.

Bloch, I. S. *The Future of War.* New York: Doubleday & McClure Co., 1899.

Book of Mormon. Translated by Joseph Smith Jr. Salt Lake City, Utah: The Church of Jesus Christ of Latter-day Saints. (Designated in the footnotes as individual scriptures)

Bordon, Neil H. and Marshall, Martin L. *Advertising Management.* Homewood, Ill.: Richard D. Irwin Inc., 1959.

Brown, Hugh B. *Eternal Quest.* Salt Lake City, Utah: Bookcraft Inc., Publishers, 1956.

Cannon, George Q. *Gospel Truth.* Salt Lake City, Utah: Zion's Book Store, 1957.

————————. *Life of Joseph Smith.* (2nd edition). Salt Lake City, Utah: The Deseret News, 1907.

Chambers, F.P., Harns, C.P., Bagley, C.C. *This Age of Conflict.* Harcourt, Brace, and Co. Inc., 1943.

Corbett, Pearson H. *Hyrum Smith Patriarch.* Salt Lake City, Utah: Deseret Book Company, 1963.

Dickens, Charles. *The Uncommercial Traveller.* New York: F.M. Lupton, 1889.

Doctrine and Covenants. The Church of Jesus Christ of Latter-day Saints, containing revelations given to Joseph Smith, the Prophet. Salt Lake City, Utah: The Church of Jesus Christ of Latter-day Saints. (Designated in footnotes as D&C.)

Doxey, Roy W. *The Doctrine and Covenants and the Future.* Deseret Book Company, 1964.

——————. *The Doctrine and Covenants Speaks.* Vol. 1. Salt Lake City, Utah: Deseret Book Company, 1964.

——————. *Zion in the Last Days.* Salt Lake City, Utah: Bookcraft Inc., 1968.

——————. *The Latter-day Prophets and the Doctrine and Covenants.* Vol. 1, 3. Salt Lake City, Utah: Deseret Book Company, 1963, 1964.

Durham, Dr. G. Homer (comp.). *Gospel Standards.* Salt Lake City, Utah: The Deseret News Press, 1941.

Fuller, J.F.C. *A Military History of the Western World.* Vol. 3. Funk & Waggnalls Co., 1956.

Gates, Susan (Young). *Lydia Knight's History.* by "Homespun." Salt Lake City, Utah. Juvenile Instructor office, 1883.

Hesseltine, William B. and Smiley, David L. *The South in American History.* (2nd edition) Englewood Cliffs: New Jersey Prentice-Hall, 1960.

Hinkley, Bryant S. *Sermons and Missionary Services of Melvin Joseph Ballard.* Salt Lake City, Utah: Deseret Book Company, 1949.

Jenson, Andrew (ed.). *The Historical Record.* Vol. 5-8. Salt Lake City, Utah, 1889.

——————. *LDS Biographical Encyclopedia.* Vol. 1. Salt Lake City, Utah: Andrew Jenson History Company. The Deseret News, 1901.

Journal of Discourses. 26 Vol. The Church of Jesus Christ of Latter-day Saints. 15 Wilton Street, London, England: F.D. and S.W. Richards.

Lee, Harold B. "Faith." *BYU Speeches of the Year,* 1955.

Lundwall, N.B. (comp. and pub.). *Temples of the Most High.* Salt Lake City, Utah, 1941.

McKay, David O. *Gospel Ideals.* An Improvement Era Publication. Salt Lake City, Utah: The Deseret News Press, 1953.

Montross, Lynn. *War Through the Ages.* New York and London: Harper and Brothers Publishers, 1944.

Newquist, Jarreld L. (comp.) *Gospel Truth.* Vol. 1. Salt Lake City, Utah: Zion's Book Store, 1957.

Nibley, Preston. *Missionary Experiences.* Salt Lake City, Utah: The Deseret News Press, 1842.

Oaks, L. Weston. *The Word of Wisdom and You*. Salt Lake City, Utah: Bookcraft Inc., 1958.

Pearl of Great Price. A selection from the revelations, translations, and narrations of Joseph Smith. Salt Lake City, Utah: The Church of Jesus Christ of Latter-day Saints. (Designated as individual scriptures in the footnotes.)

Petersen, Mark E. *Your Faith and You*. Salt Lake City, Utah: Bookcraft Publishers, 1953.

Pratt, Orson. *Orson Pratt's Works*. Salt Lake City, Utah: Juvenile Instructor Office, 1884.

Pratt, Parley P. (ed.). *Autobiography of Parley Parker Pratt*. (4 ed.). Salt Lake City, Utah: Deseret Book Company, 1950.

——————————. *A Voice of Warning*. Independence, Jackson County, Missouri: Zion's Printing and Publishing Company, 1846.

Richards, LeGrand. *Israel! Do You Know?* Salt Lake City, Utah: Deseret Book Company, 1967.

Roberts, B.H. *A Comprehensive History of the Church*. Vol. 1, 2. Salt Lake City, Utah: Deseret News Press, 1930.

——————————. *New Witnesses for God*. Salt Lake City, Utah: The Deseret News, 1911.

Romney, Thomas C. *The Gospel In Action*. Salt Lake City, Utah: Deseret Sunday School Union Board [c1949.]

——————————. *The Life of Lorenzo Snow*. Salt Lake City, Utah: Sugarhouse Press, 1955.

Rozwenc, Edwin C. (ed.). *Slavery As A Cause of the Civil War*. Boston: D.C. Heath and Co. [c1949].

Sjodahl, Janne M. *An Introduction to the Study of the Book of Mormon*. Salt Lake City, Utah: The Deseret News Press, 1927.

Smith, Hyrum and Sjodahl, Janne M. *Doctrine and Covenants Commentary*. Salt Lake City, Utah: Deseret Book Company, 1957.

Smith, Joseph. *History of the Church*. Ed. B.H. Roberts. The Church of Jesus Christ of Latter-day Saints. Salt Lake City, Utah: Deseret News Press, 1902. (Designated as *DHC* in the footnotes.)

Smith, Joseph F. *Gospel Doctrine*. (6th Edition). Salt Lake City, Utah: Deseret Book Company, 1943.

Smith, Joseph Fielding. *Answers to Gospel Questions*. Vol. 1. Salt Lake City, Utah: Deseret Book Company, 1966.

——————————. *Church History and Modern Revelation*. Series 2, 3. A Course of Study for the Melchizedek Priesthood Quorums. Salt Lake City, Utah: The Deseret Press, 1948, 1949.

——————————. *Doctrines of Salvation*. Vol. 2. Bruce R. McConkie (comp.). Salt Lake City, Utah: Bookcraft, Inc.

——————————. *Essentials in Church History*. (13th Edition). Salt Lake City, Utah: The Deseret Book Company, 1907.

_____. *Origin of the "Reorganized" Church.* Independence, Jackson County, Missouri: Zion's Printing and Publishing Company, 1929.

_____. *The Progress of Man.* Salt Lake City, Utah: Deseret Book Company, 1964.

_____. (comp.). *Teachings of the Prophet Joseph Smith.* (3d Edition). Salt Lake City, Utah: The Deseret News Press, 1942.

Smith, Lucy Mack. *History of Joseph Smith by His Mother.* Salt Lake City, Utah: Stevens and Wallis, Inc., 1945.

Statistical Abstract of Israel. No. 16. Published by the Central Bureau of Statistics, 1965.

Statistical Abstract of the United States. Published by the U.S. Bureau of the Census, 1968.

Talmage, James E. *The House of the Lord.* Salt Lake City, Utah: Deseret Book Company, 1968.

_____. *The Vitality of Mormonism.* Boston: The Goeham Press, 1919.

Testimonies of the Divinity of The Church of Jesus Christ of Latter-day Saints By Its Leaders. Salt Lake City, Utah: Zion's Printing and Publishing Co., 1930.

Tullridge, Edward Wheelock. *The Life of Brigham Young; or Utah and Her Founders.* New York [n. p.]. 1877.

Twentieth Report of the Committee on Government Operations. Washington, D.C.: United States Government Printing, 1958.

Whitney, Orson F. *History of Utah.* Salt Lake City, Utah: Cannon & Sons, 1892.

_____. *Life of Heber C. Kimball.* (2nd Edition). Salt Lake City, Utah: Stevens and Wallis, 1945.

_____. *Saturday Night Thoughts.* Salt Lake City, Utah: The Deseret News, 1921.

_____. *Through Memory's Halls, The Life Story of Orson F. Whitney As Told By Himself.* Independence, Missouri: Press of Zion's Printing and Publishing Company, 1930.

Widtsoe, John A. (comp.). *Discourses of Brigham Young.* Salt Lake City, Utah: Deseret Book Company, 1954.

_____. *Joseph Smith Seeker After Truth Prophet of God.* Salt Lake City, Utah: Bookcraft, 1957.

_____. and Widtsoe, Leah D. *The Word of Wisdom, A Modern Interpretation.* Salt Lake City, Utah: Deseret Book Company, 1937.

Williams, Neville. *Chronology of the Modern World.* New York: David McKay Company, Inc., 1966.

Index

charged with deceiving public, 203; advertising is deceptive, 203.

Cincinnati, Prophet and elders instructed to go to, 68.

Civil War begins fulfillment of prophecy, 19; beginning of modern war, 19; impact of, 20; heralded in Doctrine and Covenants in 1831, 190; commences in 1861, 191; American, was first of modern wars, 192; destruction of Jackson County during, 262.

Clark, J. Reuben, speaks of descendants of pioneers, 121.

Clawson, Rudger, quoted on family relationship beyond the veil, 172; imprisoned for polygamy, 224.

Coffee industry directs selling toward children, 204; and tea, condemned in Word of Wisdom, 206.

"Commandments, be diligent in keeping my," 323.

Common consent, the law of, 59.

Confession of sin, repentance includes, 325.

Confidence a blessing of prayer, 54.

Conflicts, terms used to report, 18.

Consecration instituted in 1831, law of, 125.

"Conspiring men in the last days," 200.

Converts rejoice in "new life" brought by gospel, 273.

Copley, Leman, converted from "Shaking Quakers," 109; breaks covenant, 127.

Corbett, Pearson H., writes biography of Hyrum Smith, 104.

Cornelius and the Holy Ghost, 15.

Cortez ravaged natives of South America, 111.

Council of Twelve, statement concerning original, 63; is second quorum in authority, 216.

"Covenant made unto me has been broken," 123; condemnations of those who break the, 125; breakers should be dealt with according to laws of Church, 129.

Covenants, blessings of those who keep the, 125; Lord's promises to those who keep, 126; taken in baptism, 126; may be voided by the Lord, 130; Brigham Young urges members consider their, 131.

Cowdery, Oliver, Elijah visits, 24; retains

testimony, 25; revelation given for, 29; one of Three Special Witnesses, 36; sees plates, 38; true to testimony, 39; Section 6 given for, 42; among three witnesses, 45; sustained as second elder by law of common consent, 59; given testimony of calling of Joseph Smith, 101; counseled to work for establishment of Zion, 101; told to exercise gifts, 101; sees heavenly visitors in Kirtland Temple, 103; learned many mysteries as a scribe, 103; appointed to Lamanite mission, 104; Christ, moses, Elias and Elijah appear to, 276, 277.

Cowley, Matthew, named to Lamanite Committee, 114.

Creation to be revealed by Master, processes of, 299.

Creeds an abomination in God's sight, 8.

"Cursing instead of a blessing, leaving a", 67; how, is accomplished, 68.

Cutler, Alpheus, lays foundation at Far West, 289.

Daniel's prophecy explained by Joseph Smith, 152.

Darkness is opposite of light, 14.

David anointed king of Israel, 94.

Dead, salvation for the, 2; interested in their salvation, 3; vision of the redemption of the, 3; salvation for the, 24; temple ordinances for the, 27; ordinances for the, essential, 27; Joseph Smith speaks on salvation for the, 27.

Death part of eternal plan, 98; is sweet unto faithful, 98; judgment after, 177; was Christ's last enemy, 325.

Declaration of Independence, Wilford Woodruff relates experience with signers of, 3.

Destroyer probably means Satan, 261.

Destroying Angel discussed by Marion G. Romney, 208.

Devil to have power, 18.

Dickens, Charles, writes of Mormon emigrant ship, 274.

Die unto the Lord, they shall, 94.

Discernment discussed, gift of, 108.

Disciples, Lord's warning to go forth by, 2.

Disobedience, regret for, 6.

Dispensation of the Fulness of Times, greatness of the, 295.

Law given, all kingdoms have a, 87; of
Consecration is a socio-economic order,
93; of Consecration instituted in 1831,
125; of Remuneration for services, 177.
Law, William, becomes an apostate, 144;
instructed to purchase stock in Nauvoo
House, 144.
Laying on of hands for healing of the sick,
93.
Lee, Harold B., relates witnessing healings,
98; relates experience of Don B. Colton,
211; applies parable of Ten Virgins to
our day, 233; explains purpose of
personal revelation, 299.
Liahona is described, 38.
Liberty Jail, prayer and prophecy revelation given in, 294; prophet receives
Section 122 in, 301.
Life, purpose of, 174.
"Light which he has received," 12.
Light reveals errors and iniquities, 4; that
which is of God is, 12; more, received by
obedience, 13; darkness is opposite of,
14; Gospel is the true, 14; diminished
by little acts, 16.
Liquor advertising is deceptive, 203.
Lord, every person to hear voice of, 2;
power of, to be revealed, 8; shall reign,
18; the, will spare his people, 22; is in
our midst, 87; meaning of receiving the,
178; will dwell on earth with righteous
for 1000 years, 247.
Lord's coming, preparation necessary for
the, 8; scourge to visit ungodly, 231;
Spirit is promised, 50.
Lost manuscript of Book of Mormon, Section 3 relates to, 324.
Love "suffereth long, etc," 44.
Lucas, Gen. Samuel D., orders shooting of
prophet, 319.

Malachi prophecy is about Elijah, 23.
Marriage is ordained of God, 118; in temple is a covenant ordinance, 126; new
and everlasting covenant of, necessary,
168; temple, is one of new and everlasting covenants, 169; in the resurrection discussed by Melvin J. Ballard, 171;
for eternity, 171.
"Marrow to the bones" is discussed, 208.
Marsh, Thomas B., Section 112 given for,
49; instructions given to, 79; apostatizes
over milk strippings incident, 82; revelation received for, 284.

"Marvelous work is about to come forth,"
29.
Marvelous, meaning of word, 30; work is
restoration of gospel, 33.
McKay, David O., calls "every member a
missionary," 48; relates blessings from
prayer, 54; relates experience attesting
to "gifts," 106.
McLellin, William E., excommunicated,
288.
Meat is good for man, 118.
Medo-Persian kingdom replaces Babylonia,
150.
"Meekness of my spirit" is explained, 138.
Melchizedek Priesthood restored, 30;
restored by Peter, James and John, 59;
members authorized to bless the sick,
94; powers are given, 124; penalty of
turning away from oath and covenant
of, 126; necessary to prepare to see
God, 159.
Men, gospel is for all, 2; will never stop
the Lord's work, 256.
Mentally retarded are without sin, 2.
Michelson, Arthur U., writes on wars of
Jews and Arabs, 312.
Millennial Star publishes accounts of
healings, 97.
Millennium, events before and after the,
277; to be included in fulness of times,
295.
Miracle, Newell Knight subject of first, 64.
Miracles, a part of marvelous work, 35;
performed by the priesthood, 176.
Missionaries counseled on purse and scrip,
68; should be directed by spirit, 69;
should seek for spirit, 72; commanded
to purify hearts, 87; Lord is mindful of
his, 176; 12,000, preaching in world
today, 254.
Missionary system of Church, unique, 3;
force described, 47; Section 75 is a,
revelation, 67; sent to prove the world,
176; promises to the faithful, 176;
system to "save Israel," 272.
Missouri, reasons for settling in, 132; Saints
in poverty, 253; mobocracy prevails in,
288.
Morley, Isaac, told to sell farm, 144; chastized for sins, 326; repents of sins,
commended for integrity, 328.
Moroni instructs Joseph Smith, 23; said
Elijah to reveal priesthood, 24; explains
curse of earth, 24; Angel, visits Joseph

Smith, 30; Angel, appears to Joseph Smith, 37; Angel, warns David Whitmer, 41; speaks of Joseph Smith's name, 302.

Moses anointed Aaron, 94; restores power to earth, 151; sees God in the flesh, 158; appears to Joseph Smith, 265; restores keys of gathering of Israel, 265; frees Children of Israel, 271.

Mount of Olives is located, 309.

Mount Olivet, Lord will stand upon, 308.

Murdock, John, given instructions, 68.

"My people must be tried in all things," 315.

Mysteries are simple principles of gospel, 102; of kingdom are explained, 326.

Nations, Lord's anger to be poured out on all, 247.

Nauvoo, Heber C. Kimball makes prophecy on, 133; instructions concerning, House, 144; Saints driven from, 321.

Nauvoo Temple, served divine purpose, 224; to be erected, 281.

Nebuchadnezzar, King, dream is interpreted, 150.

Nephi teaches of importance of prayer, 51; speaks of "wisdom" of the learned, 306; speaks of covenants of Lord with Israel, 314.

Nephite civilization is destroyed, 110; destruction of, an example, 247; pride a besetting sin of the, 251.

Netherlands, insurrections in the, 19.

New and everlasting covenant is fulness of the gospel, 126; revealed to prophet, 130; of marriage necessary for exaltation, 168.

New England Historical and Genealogical Society, 26.

New Jerusalem, a city of refuge, 73; Saints to purchase inheritance in, 75; is also known as Zion, 75; to be centerplace of gathering, 75; Lamanites to assist in building the, 111; is known as Zion, 119; Jackson County designated as, 132; the temple in the, 176; gathering of Saints to, 227.

New York Genealogical and Biographical Society, 26.

Nibley, Hugh, gives examples of customs unknown when Book of Mormon was published, 31.

Nickerson, Freeman, Joseph Smith teaches gospel to family of, 235.

Noble, Joseph, healed in Nauvoo, 96.

North and South America is Zion, 119.

Nullification, Proclamation of, 190.

Oaks, Dr. L. Weston, discusses use of alcohol, 204; discusses "health in the navel," 207.

Oath and covenant of the Higher Priesthood, 125.

Obedience, more light received by, 13; blessings come by, to God's laws, 52; to teachings of Christ makes a man spiritual, 158; to gospel brings fulness of blessings, 282.

Ohio Star printed in Ravenna, 328.

Oil, anointing the patient with, 94.

Old Jerusalem known as Zion, 118.

Olive Leaf, Section 88 known as, 12; is Section 88, 49; revelation speaks of peace, 157; a most informative revelation, 276.

Olive oil, use of, 94.

"Oracles be given, through you shall the," 214.

Oracles, meaning of, 216.

Order of Enoch matters revealed, 124; or United Order given in Sections 82 and 104, 128; Orson Pratt speaks of, 128.

Page, John E., fails to follow prophetic promise, 62; ordained an apostle, 290.

Palestine by the Israelites, three temples erected in, 223; dedicated for return of Jews, 265; established as national home of Jews, 267; table shows number of Jews in, 268; mandate of Great Britain ended in 1948, 268.

Parable of the Ten Virgins, 11; of the wheat and the tares, 43; explanation of, of wheat and tares, 182.

Paschal Feast observed in Jewish homes, 25.

Patience and humility should characterize LDS missionaries, 72.

Patten, David W., last words of, 66; gave life in Crooked River battle, 320.

"Peace shall be taken from the earth," 18.

"Peace in this world, even," 137.

Peace is explained, 18; no, since World War II, 21; assured Latter-day Saints despite turmoil, 22; in the world is reward for works of righteousness, 137;